IMPLEMENTING VALUE AT RISK

IMPLEMENTING VALUE AT RISK

Philip Best

John Wiley & Sons
Chichester • New York • Weinheim • Brisbane • Singapore • Toronto

Other Wiley Editorial Offices

John Wiley & Sons, Inc., 605 Third Avenue,
New York, NY 10158-0012, USA

WILEY-VCH Verlag GmbH, Pappelallee 3,
D-69469 Weinheim, Germany

Jacaranda Wiley Ltd, 33 Park Road, Milton,
Queensland 4064, Australia

John Wiley & Sons (Asia) Pte Ltd, 2 Clementi Loop #02-01,
Jin Xing Distripark, Singapore 129809

John Wiley & Sons (Canada) Ltd, 22 Worcester Road,
Rexdale, Ontario M9W 1L1, Canada

Library of Congress Cataloging-in-Publication Data

Best, Philip W.
      Implementing value at risk/Philip W. Best.
         p.   cm. – (Wiley series in financial engineering)
      Includes index.
      ISBN 0-471-97205-3 (alk. paper)
      1. Asset-liability management.   2. Bank investments.   I. Title.
      II. Series.
      HG1615.25.B49   1998   98-4098
      332.1′754′0681–dc21   CIP

British Library Cataloguing in Publication Data

A catalogue record for this book is available from the British Library

ISBN 0-471-97205-3

Typeset in 10/12pt Times by MHL Typesetting, Coventry.
Printed and bound in Great Britain by Biddles, Guildford and King's Lynn.
This book is printed on acid-free paper responsibly manufactured from sustainable forestry, in which at
least two trees are planted for each one used for paper production.

For my wife Gabriella and my children, Chiara, Isabella and Leonora, without whose forbearance and support this book would never have been completed.

Contents

Preface

This book came about through a series of speeches given at industry seminars on value at risk and stress testing. Participants and presenters often asked over coffee: Aren't these methods written down anywhere? The methods referred to are a framework for managing market risk using value at risk (VAR) and its companion stress testing. The objectives of this book are to explain:

- What VAR is – and isn't.
- How to calculate VAR – the three main methods.
- Why stress testing is needed alongside VAR.
- How to make stress testing effective.
- How to use VAR and stress testing to manage risk.
- How to use VAR to improve a bank's performance.
- VAR as a regulatory measure of risk and capital.

This book is aimed at risk management practitioners, general bank management, consultants, students and other people who have an interest in understanding VAR and its use in banks and, specifically, in trading. The book is intended to be accessible to non-mathematicians, even though all the key statistical concepts surrounding VAR are dealt with in sufficient detail to allow the reader to calculate VAR without further assistance. Therefore, the book is designed to be read without any prior knowledge of statistics. Care has been taken to provide a clear description of all mathematical notation used.

This book makes use of several worked examples which the reader may wish to replicate himself. Spreadsheets of all the major examples are provided with the book, showing exactly how each calculation in the text has been performed. It is suggested that the interested reader should try to replicate the examples initially without reference to the spreadsheets provided. The reader will gain more by working through the calculations himself and only using the spreadsheets when presented with an insurmountable problem, or, hopefully, to confirm a correct calculation.

The following is a brief overview of the contents of the book.

Introduction

A high-level introduction to risk in banking and particularly market risk. Pre-VAR market risk measures are described and explained, along with their pros and cons. Value at risk is then introduced. The remedies that VAR provides for some of the problems of pre-VAR risk measures are also explained. VAR is not the Holy Grail of risk measurement. Its strengths and weaknesses are introduced, leading on to a discussion of the need for stress testing.

Covariance

This chapter introduces the basic method of calculating VAR for linear positions. The building blocks of VAR: volatility, holding period and correlation are described. Example VAR calculations are presented for a single asset and then for a portfolio. The application of the covariance method to options is described and the problems this presents are discussed.

Calculating VAR using Simulation

The two other main methods of calculating VAR are described in this chapter: historical simulation and Monte Carlo simulation. Historical simulation faithfully reflects actual historical experience when calculating VAR. Monte Carlo simulation uses randomly generated price change events to model asset price change behaviour. There are now many methods of calculating VAR but all are combinations or variations on the three methods described in this book. This chapter also presents worked examples and compares the results produced by the three different methods.

Measurement of Volatility and Correlation

Volatility and correlations are included in all VAR calculation methods, either explicitly or implicitly. This chapter begins by explaining what volatility and correlation are. It then goes on to describe the most common volatility and correlation models used in the banking industry. The final part of the chapter presents the results of an empirical study of the effectiveness of different volatility models when calculating VAR at 95% and 99% confidence levels.

Implementing Value at Risk

With the different VAR calculation methods explained it is time to consider how VAR is implemented in practice. This chapter describes the overall approach to implementing VAR, describing the decisions and trade-offs that need to be made. The chapter then continues to describe an approach to implementing VAR for the main asset classes and product types encountered in trading organisations.

Stress Testing

Stress testing is an essential complement to VAR for managing market risk. This chapter explains why stress testing is so vital. Different methods of stress testing (e.g. scenarios analysis) are reviewed. The characteristics of effective stress testing are discussed and described.

Managing Risk with VAR

This chapter brings VAR and stress testing together into a single framework for managing market risk. The development of VAR and stress test limits is discussed along with a discussion of how to determine a bank's risk appetite in relation to VAR and stress testing.

Risk Adjusted Performance Measurement

This chapter explains how VAR fits into the overall management of a trading business. The concepts of shareholder value and the required return are introduced. Different measures of performance are then reviewed. The derivation of risk capital is discussed and illustrated with examples. The derivation of risk capital requires the introduction of measures of credit and operational risk. The chapter finishes with a description of the methods of allocating capital, again with examples.

Regulatory Reporting and VAR

The regulators have had a central role in the development of VAR, first responding to and then encouraging the banking industry to adopt VAR as a core measure of market risk. This chapter describes how regulators have adopted VAR and what banks must do to qualify to use VAR as their regulatory measure of market risk.

Acknowledgements

I am indebted to a number of people for their reviews and comments on various parts of this book. In particular I would like to thank Con Keating for his constant encouragement and help throughout the writing process. The book has benefited greatly from Con's comments and suggestions. Amongst the numerous people who have given their time in reviewing early drafts I would like to thank: Roger Barnes, Nick Bingham, Paul Bowmar, Stuart Chandler, Brian Hird, Rupert Macey-Dare and Barry Schachter.

1
Defining risk and VAR

INTRODUCTION

Banking is about managing risk and return. A simple statement, the achievement of which continues to present a major challenge to most banks around the world. This is surprising, given that few would disagree with this statement. Why does it present banks with such a challenge? Firstly, financial institutions face a multitude of risks, which are not easy to quantify and are even more difficult to control. Secondly, quantifying return on capital turns out not to be a straightforward equation.

In addition to the above, commercial pressures to deliver an ever increasing return, tend to encourage financial institutions to take ever more risk. There is regular and ample evidence of this. Most recently, the collapse of confidence in the Far Eastern economies, their currencies and stock markets, in October 1997, sparked a period of intense volatility in the world's financial markets. Stories abound of losses running into hundreds of millions of dollars in America's large investment banks. America's investment banks are, by general agreement, amongst the most advanced in terms of their measurement and control of risk – what hope then for the rest of us?

This book develops a framework for risk management based on value at risk (VAR) and stress testing. Taken together these two techniques, when applied correctly, can prevent a bank suffering embarrassing losses and can also help to reduce a bank's earnings volatility. The importance of reduced volatility of earnings will be clear by the end of the book. Before defining VAR it is worth describing the purpose of risk management, so that VAR can be placed in a wider context.

WHAT IS RISK MANAGEMENT?

The objective of risk management is twofold:

1. To improve a bank's financial performance.
2. To ensure an institution does not suffer unacceptable losses.

This might suggest that risk management is mainly about control. Not so. Risk management is as much about understanding the types of risk a bank faces as it has to do with controlling them. After understanding comes measurement. Unless risks are comprehensively and accurately quantified (within certain tolerances) there is nothing to control. Finally, it is the responsibility of risk management to communicate and educate senior management as to the nature and scale of risks being taken by the bank. Therefore risk management consists of the following basic activities:

- Understanding the risks being taken by an institution.
- Measuring the risks.
- Controlling risk.
- Communicating risk.

This book concentrates mainly on the measurement of market risk and the market risk measure VAR. In discussing the measurement of risk it is hoped that the reader's understanding of market risk will increase. Before introducing VAR, however, it worth spending a short while understanding the many different risks a bank faces.

DEFINING RISK

Risk only has any true meaning to the extent that it results in financial loss, either directly, or indirectly. Financial institutions face many risks which may, if not controlled, give rise to financial risk. The four main categories of risk are:

1. Market Risk

Market risk is the risk of loss resulting from a change in the value of tradable assets. For example, if a bank holds a position of one million ounces of gold then it is exposed to the risk that the value of gold decreases. There are several different classes of assets (interest rates, currencies, equities and commodities) and an almost infinite variety of financial products, all of which create exposure to market risk.

This book focuses on ways to quantify and thereby control market risk, namely VAR and stress testing.

2. Credit Risk

Credit risk is the risk of financial loss suffered when a company that the bank has dealt with (a counterparty) defaults, or when market sentiment determines that a company is more likely to default.

When a bank lends money to a counterparty it has an exposure to the default of that counterparty. Equally when a bank trades a swap, option, or other financial instrument, it has an exposure to the counterparty equal to the future value of the instrument transacted. Although not the main focus of the book, the quantification of credit risk is outlined in Chapter 9.

In addition to actual default, financial institutions are exposed to changes in market sentiment about the likelihood of default. If a bank buys a bond issued by a corporate its value will reflect the credit worthiness of the company. If the market feels that the credit worthiness of the company has decreased then the value of the bond will fall. This is often treated as market risk by traders and is called spread risk. As the credit rating of the company changes, the difference between the yield on the corporate bond and the corresponding government bond (the spread), will also change.

It is beyond the scope of this book to describe credit risk quantification methodologies, however, the reader may wish to read further into the subject of the quantification of credit risk. Credit risk measures, similar to VAR, have now been developed by banks such as J P Morgan (Masters, 1997), which are based on the volatility of the price of corporate bonds due to a change in the perceived credit worthiness of the issuer, or due to an actual credit event, i.e. a default.

3. Operational Risk

Operational risk is a broad category of risk which can result in the bank losing money, examples of operational risk include the following:

- *Control failure*   This is one of the biggest risks in all banks. Barings is a prime example of a failure of controls; its collapse was due primarily to a failure to control the market exposures being created within a small overseas branch of the bank.

- *Liquidity risk*   The risk of loss due to the bank requiring more funding than it can arrange.

- *Money transfer risk*   The risk of loss arising from failed or incorrect settlement.

- *Model risk*   The risk of loss arising from an institution's inability to value a financial instrument correctly.

- *Systems risk*   Failed or late systems projects cost banks a great deal of money, as do systems which fail to function reliably.

Operational risk is hard to quantify, as every loss is different and significant losses only happen rarely. Nonetheless some attempt must be made to assign a value to the various risks listed above. Two broad approaches to quantifying operational risk are discussed in Chapter 9.

4. Reputation Risk

Reputation risk is the risk of financial loss resulting from the loss of business attributable to a decrease in the institution's reputation. Although loss of reputation can be a slow attrition, it more often results from an error of judgement or execution in a major piece of corporate business. If the market perceives that the institution failed to handle successfully a significant piece of business then it is only natural that the bank's customers will consider using a different bank in future. On occasion, severe damage is done to an institution's reputation by a few individuals acting irresponsibly and at worst, unlawfully.

Chapter 8 shows how market, credit and operational risks can be brought together as a single number – risk capital – in the measurement of risk adjusted performance. This is of critical importance as it is essential for management's ease of understanding to have a single overall risk figure. One of the problems with traditional risk measurement techniques was that there were too many of them.

TRADITIONAL MEASUREMENT OF MARKET RISK

The quantification of market risk is not a new thing. Ever since positions were first marked to market, traders have wanted to understand the risk they are taking, particularly in terms of hedging parameters. Traders used and still use measures of market risk which are closely related to how their products are traded. The discussion below illustrates the traditional measures of interest rate risk.

The value of all interest rate (non-option) products is the present value of the future cash flows that make up the instrument. The present value of any cash flow is dependent on the maturity of the cash flow and the relevant interest rate (yield) at that maturity. Consider a two year interbank loan for $1m, paying a fixed rate of interest of 7%, semi-annually. Table 1.1 shows how the value of this interbank loan is calculated.

The present value of each cash flow is given by:

$$PV = \text{cash flow} \times \text{discount factor}$$

The discount factor, assuming annual yields, is given by:

Table 1.1 Present value of a loan

Cash flow ($)	Maturity (Years)	Yield (%)	Discount factor	PV ($)
35,000	0.5	6.0	0.9713	33,995
35,000	1.0	6.5	0.9390	32,864
35,000	1.5	7.0	0.9035	31,622
1,035,000	2.0	7.5	0.8653	895,619
			Present value of loan	994,100

$$\text{Discount factor} = \frac{1}{(1 + r)^n}$$

where: r = annual interest rate (divided by 100)
n = number of years

A trader whose position consists of this loan, is exposed to market risk, which, in this case, is interest rate risk.[1] The challenge with interest rates is to work with the whole yield curve. The value of the loan, as can be seen from Table 1.1, is dependent on the yields at all relevant maturities.

How then should we model the risk? A typical portfolio of interest rate assets will contain thousands of cash flows maturing on many hundreds of different dates. Each individual maturity date will have a unique yield associated with it. Therefore the value of the portfolio will be potentially dependent on several hundred yields. Each yield can be thought of as a risk factor that the portfolio is exposed to. The potentially large number of risk factors clearly presents practical problems. What is needed is a way to approximate the behaviour of all the yields together, i.e. the behaviour of the yield curve. The challenge then is to model how the yield curve changes, or moves. An analysis of yield curve movements shows that yield curve movements can be described by a relatively small number of characteristic movements:

- Parallel shift.
- Twist about a single maturity, often taken to be one year.
- Wave, or dip.

There are further minor shifts, which are normally ignored. Figure 1.1 shows, somewhat stylistically, how these yield curve movements look. For most markets, the first two movements, the parallel shift and the twist, taken together, account for between 80% and 90% of all yield curve movement. Given the relatively small residual risk, most banks model their interest rate risk around the first two

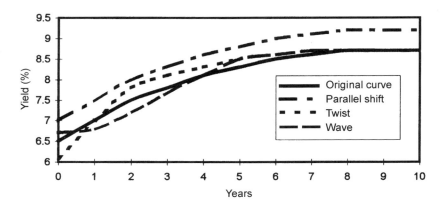

Figure 1.1 Yield curve movements

movements, ignoring the third and other minor shifts. Of the two, the parallel shift is the dominant movement, accounting for approximately 80% of yield curve movement by itself. A separate risk measure is used for each of the two main yield curve movements:

- The change in the present value of a portfolio due to a parallel basis point movement in the yield curve, known variously as PVBP, VBPM, PV01, etc. The use of a one basis point parallel shift in the curve is a *de facto* industry standard.

- The portfolio value change due to a yield curve tilt or twist. For what is often confusingly called 'yield curve risk' there is no *de facto* industry standard yield curve movement.

Both these risk measures are 'sensitivity' measures, as are the majority of traditional risk measures. Sensitivity risk measures quantify the profit and loss (P&L) impact on a portfolio of a specified change in a risk factor.[2] Both the above measures quantify the sensitivity of the portfolio value to specified shifts in the yield curve.

Outright Interest Rate Risk

The term 'Outright interest rate risk' expresses the exposure of a portfolio to a change in the overall level of interest rates, i.e. a parallel shift in the yield curve. This is measured by the VBPM risk measure. Returning to the loan we considered previously, we can now determine its sensitivity to a parallel shift in the yield curve. Table 1.2 shows the calculation of the VBPM for the loan.

Table 1.2 says that for a one basis point upwards parallel shift in the yield curve the loan would be worth $176 less. Note that the probability of a one basis point

Table 1.2 Value of a basis point move

Cash flow ($)	Maturity (Years)	Yield (%)	Shifted yield (%)	PV original ($)	PV shifted ($)
35,000	0.5	6.0	6.01	33,995	33,993
35,000	1.0	6.5	6.51	32,864	32,861
35,000	1.5	7.0	7.01	31,622	31,618
1,035,000	2.0	7.5	7.51	895,619	895,453
			Present value of loan ($) 994,100		993,925
			VBPM of loan ($)		−176

move in rates is not identified as any part of measuring the outright interest rate exposure. Therefore we are given no feel for the likelihood of losing $176.

Yield Curve Risk

To measure yield curve risk, some banks use a twist around the one year maturity point, other banks simply tilt the yield curve upwards, starting at the beginning and increasing the shift by one basis point for each successive year. A little thought will show that a yield curve tilt is in fact a combination of a twist plus a parallel yield curve shift. The fact that a curve tilt is a combination of two types of yield curve movement does not invalidate it as a measure of the sensitivity of the portfolio to a twist in the yield curve, the important thing is to ensure that the yield at each maturity is shifted by more than the preceding maturity.

A yield curve twist will have the greatest impact on an interest rate portfolio that has significant maturity mismatches, i.e. long and short positions at different maturities. Consider a bond portfolio with two bonds as illustrated in Figure 1.2: the trader has purchased a Eurobond with a maturity of three years and has hedged it (i.e. sold a government bond) with a hedge maturity of one year. The trader has 'duration'[3] hedged the original position, i.e. the value of the portfolio is not affected by a parallel shift in interest rates. This is done by ensuring that the right number of bonds are sold as a hedge, so that the VBPM of the hedge and the original position are equal even though the maturities may be different.

Figure 1.2 shows that the VBPM of both of the positions are equal to $100, thus the VBPM of the portfolio is zero. Table 1.3 shows the sensitivity of this portfolio to a twist in the yield curve.

Table 1.3 shows that, because there is a maturity mismatch between the original position and the hedge, the portfolio will lose money if the yield curve twists. This means that for a twist of the type specified in Table 1.3, the value of the portfolio will reduce by $200. The goal of yield curve measures such as this is to control the

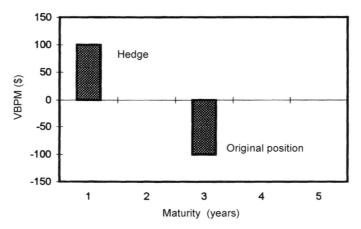

Figure 1.2   Duration hedged bond portfolio

amount of maturity mismatch that it is possible to create in the portfolio. Note that, as with VBPM, no feel is given by the yield curve measure of how likely it is that the bank will lose $200. It is extremely unlikely that a shift identical to the one specified in Table 1.3 will occur.

Why do we need VAR?

Traditional measures of risk came from the trading floor originally and are consequently designed to make sense to the trading community. Traditional risk measures reflect the way different financial instruments are traded. Taken one-by-one each risk measure is easy to understand. As each product group may have one or more risk measures, this can lead to a large number of risk measures being required to measure all the market risks a trading operation is exposed to.

Table 1.3   Impact of yield curve twist

Maturity (Years)	Curve twist (Basis points)	Position VBPM ($)	Value change ($)
0	−1	0	0
1	0	100	0
2	1	0	0
3	2	−100	−200
4	3	0	0
5	4	0	0
		Portfolio value change ($)	−200

Imagine the risk manager reporting the exposure of the bank to the chief executive officer (CEO). He dutifully gives the numbers associated with perhaps a dozen key risk measures. The CEO may have difficulty in assessing the overall riskiness of the bank's positions. He may ask: 'How much money can I lose in total? Is the bank safe?' The risk manager armed only with traditional risk measures will have difficulty answering these questions.

In addition to the difficulty with aggregating risk across trading areas with sensitivity-based measures, it is also not possible to use traditional risk measures to compare the riskiness of one trading activity with another. Another significant problem with traditional risk measures is that they give no feel for the probability that the amount identified will be lost. It is left to the trader, or manager, to use his experience and judgement – something that gets more difficult the further up the corporate ladder you go, as day-to-day contact with the markets is lost.

One aspect of portfolio management that is just as important to senior management as to traders is diversification. Diversification is the extent to which risk is reduced in a portfolio by the investment being spread over a number of assets, or asset classes. Traditional risk measures neither describe nor quantify diversification within a bank's portfolio.

There are many questions that traditional sensitivity-based risk measures cannot easily answer, here are a few:

- How much could I lose on a normal day – and with what probability?
- How much could I lose in extreme circumstances (stock market crash)?
- What is my overall exposure across all products, asset classes and currencies?
- If we are fully utilising our limits to the Far East, what kind of daily revenue volatility could we expect from this area of trading?
- What diversification benefits does the bank obtain as a whole from having an equities and an interest rate trading area?
- Which trading area is taking the most risk?
- Do our existing limits allow the bank to take more risk than we can afford?
- Are our trading operations making sufficient return when compared to the risk they are taking?

The following chapters will provide the reader with tools to answer all these questions.

VALUE AT RISK – A DEFINITION

Enough of the preliminaries! It is time to introduce value at risk. VAR is a statistical measure of the risk that estimates the maximum loss that may be experienced on a portfolio with a given level of confidence. VAR always comes with a probability that says how likely it is that losses will be smaller than the amount given. VAR is a monetary amount which may be lost over a certain specified period of time. The period of time is dependent on the period the portfolio is considered to be held constant. The following is a general formal definition of VAR:

Value at risk is the maximum amount of money that may be lost on a portfolio over a given period of time, with a given level of confidence.

VAR is typically calculated for a one day time period – known as the holding period – and is often calculated with 95% confidence. 95% confidence means that there is (on average) a 95% chance of the loss on the portfolio being lower than the VAR calculated. Thus the typical definition of VAR becomes:

The maximum amount of money that may be lost on a portfolio in 24 hours, with 95% confidence.

The holding period is one of the key parts of the definition. In the above definition, the holding period is one day, which is the holding period most commonly used. The holding period chosen will depend on how the resultant VAR is to be used, and can be calculated for any holding period. The holding period chosen has a significant effect on the VAR calculated, the longer the holding period the larger the VAR. This makes sense, as you would intuitively expect a larger change in price over a period of one month than over 24 hours.

95% confidence means that for about 5% of the time, the bank could expect to lose more than the number given by VAR. 5% of the time is one day in 20. When tossing a coin one expects to get a head 50% of the time, as long as a large number of throws is used. Out of a sample of 20 throws one might get 15 heads, rather than the expected 10. The same is true with VAR. The confidence levels will only be true if VAR is compared against the actual loss on a portfolio over a large number of days. It is possible, even probable, that at some point we will experience several days in a row in which the actual loss on a portfolio is in excess of the VAR figure.

One important thing the definition of VAR does not give any clue to, is that VAR takes account of the diversification effects present in the portfolio. We have all heard the old adage that one should not place all one's eggs in one basket. In other words, risk is reduced in a portfolio by spreading the investment over a number of assets. This risk reduction effect is fully taken into account when calculating VAR.

This brings us to one of the limitations of VAR. Although VAR tells us that a loss larger than a given amount, say '$X', will, on average, occur on one day in 20 (for VAR calculated with 95% confidence) VAR cannot tell us how big the loss that exceeds $X will be. VAR cannot tell us, therefore, what the maximum loss on a portfolio will be. Stress testing is needed to get closer to an answer for this. Therefore VAR is not sufficient by itself for effective market risk management.

VAR, as typically calculated, provides an accurate statistical estimate of the maximum probable loss on a portfolio when markets are behaving normally; this is discussed further in Chapter 5. On a fairly frequent basis, financial markets do not behave 'normally' this is demonstrated by more extreme price changes occurring in real life than are expected using standard statistical assumptions. VAR is not designed to cope with abnormal (extreme) price changes. Stress testing is typically used to supplement VAR for this reason. Taken together VAR and stress testing provide the basis of a comprehensive market risk measurement framework.

STRESS TESTING

If VAR covers so called 'normal' market behaviour then the impact of extreme price changes can be ascertained by using stress testing. Stress testing consists of applying pre-determined price changes to the assets making up a portfolio and working out the value change of the portfolio as a result of these price changes. Stress testing is described and discussed in Chapter 7.

One of the questions senior and trading management would like answered is 'What is the maximum loss we can sustain on our portfolio?' A little thought will show that for some products, such as options, it is not possible to identify a maximum loss. If we sell an option we are liable for almost unlimited loss. For many portfolios, therefore, it is not possible to identify the maximum loss. Nonetheless we must attempt to quantify how much could be lost on our portfolio in extreme market conditions. This can be arrived at by applying extreme price changes to our portfolio, by reference to, but not limited by extreme price changes experienced in the past. This is further discussed in Chapter 6.

Identifying the probability of such extreme events occurring is problematic. It may be possible to derive a probability from history. The other problem is that the behaviour of the market will almost certainly have changed since the last extreme event. Therefore, analysis of distant past events only has limited validity for today's market. In practice, risk managers and traders must use a combination of historic probability and their own subjective judgement as the likelihood of such an event in today's market.

The main job of stress testing is to identify scenarios which would cause the bank a significant loss. The job of the risk manager is then to get senior and trading management to think about these scenarios and to decide whether they are willing to accept the level of risk implied by the losses that would result from the scenarios identified given current market conditions.

AN ASSESSMENT OF VAR

One of the major advantages of VAR is that it is a risk measure that can be applied to *all* traded products. Therefore, it is a standard risk benchmark which allows the risk being taken by different trading areas to be compared directly. As VAR can be used to measure the risk on any product it can be combined across different trading areas to give a single figure for the risk being taken by all trading areas combined. Neither of these things can be achieved with traditional sensitivity-based measures of risk.

There are two other things that VAR can do which traditional risk measures cannot. The first is that VAR gives an estimate of the likelihood of a loss greater than a given figure occurring, i.e. VAR has a probability associated with it. This is far more useful than VBPM, which gives no feel for how likely the specified change in market prices is to occur. The second thing is that VAR takes account of how price changes of different assets are related to each other. This allows the reduction in risk through diversification (i.e. holding positions in a number of assets) to be measured.

However, VAR is no panacea, it only effectively measures market risk when the market is behaving 'normally'. This means that VAR is a measure of the day-to-day, or 'business-as-usual' risk on the portfolio, with a given level of confidence. VAR does not deal adequately with the fairly frequent extreme price moves observed in the financial markets. Therefore, VAR must be combined with stress testing to provide a more comprehensive market risk measurement framework.

In addition to the internal requirement for better risk measurement techniques, there is also an external dimension to VAR. It is now a global *de facto* risk measurement standard and is expected, if not quite required, by most regulatory bodies in G10 countries. It should also be noted that there are potentially significant benefits for banks stemming from the use of VAR. Regulators now allow banks to use VAR as the basis for calculating the bank's regulatory capital requirement. The required regulatory capital is appreciably less if calculated using VAR in place of the standard method. This means that the bank's actual capital can be leveraged more highly.

Rating agencies also expect banks to have implemented comprehensive VAR systems and to be able to demonstrate how it is used as a risk management tool in the bank. Regulators, as well as rating agencies, are more concerned with the demonstrable *process* of risk management than they are in the precise definition or method of calculation of VAR that a bank has chosen (unless there is something deficient about it).

One of the ways regulators and rating agencies expect banks to use VAR is as the basis for risk adjusted performance measurement (RAPM), though banks should need no encouragement to measure risk versus return. The last chapter in this book introduces the concept of measuring return on risk capital. Risk capital is the day-to-day level of risk that the bank is running. VAR is a key component of the bank's risk capital. It is perhaps through the use of RAPM that banks can derive the greatest benefit from VAR.

NOTES

1. The bank is exposed to interest rate risk only as long as it is a US$-based bank. Otherwise there is also a potential currency exposure, which would normally be hedged through US$ funding.
2. This is not realised profit and loss but the P&L resulting from revaluing the portfolio using a slightly changed yield curve.
3. Duration hedging refers to the use of the 'modified duration' of a bond position. The modified duration quantifies the sensitivity of the position, or portfolio, to a parallel shift in interest rates and is therefore essentially the same risk measure as VBPM.

2
Covariance

INTRODUCTION

This chapter introduces the reader to the first widely used and still most popular way of calculating value at risk. The chapter is structured to take the reader through a series of VAR calculations, progressively introducing the basic building blocks of all VAR models and the assumptions and decisions that need to be made, regardless of which VAR calculation method is adopted.

This chapter uses historic price movements of various assets. Unless otherwise stated, the history of prices used is from the period 25 November 1991 to 26 November 1996. The price histories were sourced from Datastream.

COVARIANCE FOR A SINGLE POSITION

Let us assume that we intend to build up a portfolio of assets and that we start by buying $1m worth of gold. We wish to know how much money we could lose on this position over the period of one day. To calculate the potential one day loss we need the volatility of gold price changes. The one-day volatility of the gold price changes is given to us as 0.55% (for the US dollar (USD) price of gold).

Therefore, we can calculate a value at risk number, i.e. the potential loss on the position over a one-day time horizon as:

$$VAR = V \times P$$

where: V = volatility
         P = position value ($)

Thus giving a VAR of $1,000,000 \times 0.0055 = \$5,500$

Therefore we could lose $5,500 on our position of $1m of gold over a 24-hour period.

The next thing you may want to know is what level of confidence we can place on the $5,500 figure. The level of confidence is defined statistically and requires an understanding of the frequency distribution of price changes.

The Normal Distribution

One view of statistics is that it is about describing and quantifying expectations or expected results. Expected results for many things fall into a range rather than a single value. One classic example is that of the expected height of an adult male human. The average height is 5′9″ but the probability of any one adult male being 5′9″ is low. The height of a male adult will lie in a range either side of the average or mean height of 5′9″. The range of possible heights and the probability of being a certain height is shown in Figure 2.1(a).

Figure 2.1(a) is a bar chart showing the percentage of the male population that have the heights shown along the horizontal axis. People's heights are said to be 'normally' distributed, this means that the frequency distribution graph has the classic bell shape, as shown in Figure 2.1(b). Many naturally occurring series have a distribution that is approximately normal.

One of the key assumptions made when calculating VAR using the covariance method is that returns (i.e. percentage price changes) in financial markets are also approximately normally distributed. The distribution of price changes for gold is shown in Figure 2.2.

A normal curve has been superimposed over the gold price distribution for comparison. By comparing the normal curve and the bars one can see that the distribution of gold price changes is a reasonable match to a normal distribution. It is clear, however, that not all the price changes are contained within the normal curve shown on the chart. The gold distribution displays the classic features of financial asset price change distributions, i.e. the tall central peak and 'fat tails'. A distribution with fat tails has a higher frequency of extreme price moves than a truly normal distribution. The extent to which price changes are normally distributed is discussed in Chapter 4.

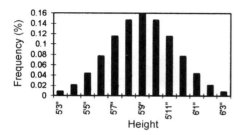 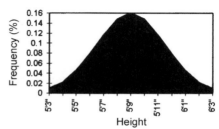

Figure 2.1 (a) Height distribution and (b) normal distribution

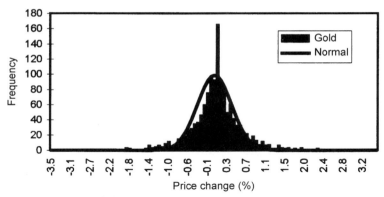

Figure 2.2   Gold vs normal distribution

The presence of fat tails in financial asset price changes means that VAR is not a sufficient risk measurement tool by itself. Thorough deterministic stress testing must be used to complement VAR. Stress testing investigates the potential loss on a portfolio due to a wide variety of price change scenarios and is described in Chapter 6.

Describing Volatility

Covariance VAR models assume normality, i.e. that percentage price changes in financial markets are normally distributed. This assumption allows volatility to be described in terms of standard deviations (SD). Volatility is usually described in terms of a percentage change with the standard measure of volatility being the percentage change equal to one standard deviation.

The critical question with respect to volatility is: 'What confidence can I have that future price changes will not be greater than the volatility quoted?'. A one standard deviation measure of volatility gives a confidence level of 68% that the absolute (i.e. positive or negative) value of future price changes will not exceed the given volatility. This is shown in Figure 2.3. The area, or proportion, of price

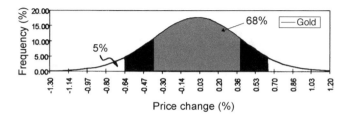

Figure 2.3   1 and 1.65 standard deviations

changes covered by one standard deviation is shown as the shaded area. The wider area, coloured black shows the price changes covered by 1.65 standard deviations. 1.65 standard deviations give a confidence level (called a confidence interval) of 90%. This means that 5% of upward price changes will be outside the 1.65 standard deviation number and 5% of downward price changes will be outside the 1.65 standard deviation number. Therefore, the negative percentage price change corresponding to 1.65 standard deviations gives a 95% confidence that a downward price change will not exceed this number. When measuring VAR we are only concerned with potential losses, not profits. Therefore, we only consider the downward percentage of price changes not covered by the multiple of standard deviations being used. This is often referred to as a 'one tailed' confidence interval.

In the gold example above, volatility was given as 0.55%. This was in fact a standard volatility quote, i.e. a one standard deviation measure.[1] Therefore, we can have a confidence level of 84% (1 SD = 68% of all price changes; taking only downward movements, 1 SD = 84%) that the loss will not exceed $5,500. When calculating VAR most banks use a one-tailed confidence interval of 95% or more. 95% confidence is given by 1.65 SDs; 99% confidence is given by 2.33 SDs.

Therefore, for the above example of a position of $1m of gold, if we want a VAR number with a 95% confidence interval we must multiply the volatility by 1.65. This gives a VAR of:

$$VAR = 1.65 \times 0.0055 \times 1,000,000 = \$9,075$$

This VAR has a 95% confidence that the loss will not exceed this figure in a 24-hour period. This should be rounded up to $9,100, as to quote any VAR number with several significant figures implies a level of accuracy and certainty that it is not possible to give. See Chapter 4 for a discussion on the accuracy of VAR calculations.

THE HOLDING PERIOD

The holding period is the time horizon over which VAR is calculated, i.e. the period of time over which the potential loss on the portfolio is being calculated. VAR increases with the holding period because volatility grows approximately in proportion to the square root of holding period (see Chapter 4 for a more in depth discussion of this). For example, if a bank changed its holding period from 1 day to 10 days its VAR number would be multiplied by the square root of 10, i.e. 3.16. Therefore the choice of holding period is critical to the VAR calculation.

The holding period is chosen by banks dependent on how they use VAR and what it represents to them. Many banks choose one day as the holding period. There is an argument to say that the holding period should equal the liquidation period of the different instruments in the bank's portfolio. The commonest rationale behind the choice of one day is because it is believed that the majority of liquid positions held by banks can be liquidated within one day. This does not take account of the liquidation time required for illiquid positions or large positions held by banks. The cost of liquidating a portfolio is discussed further below.

A second way of defining the holding period is: the time required to hedge away the bank's market risks (after all, swaps cannot simply be liquidated as they are not tradable securities). Consider a portfolio that had a single outright position of $1m of a 5-year Eurobond hedged with $1m of a 5-year government bond.[2] In theory at least, the position is duration hedged, i.e. there is no exposure to changes in 5-year interest rates. In practice, however, this portfolio is now subject to the spread risk (a type of basis risk) between Eurobonds and government bonds. This is the risk that the yield spread between government bonds and Eurobonds changes. So, although the new basis risk is normally a smaller risk than the original risk (dependent on the correlations), there exists a new basis risk in place of the original outright position risk. The original risk has merely been exchanged for a different, if smaller, risk. Therefore, it does not make sense to choose the holding period by considering the time required to hedge a portfolio as risk will not be eliminated by hedging, just reduced.

Another view is that the holding period represents the period of time over which the composition of the portfolio remains broadly constant. For most banks with significant trading operations the composition of their global portfolios do remain broadly similar over the period of one day and quite possibly longer. At the local business unit level the composition of the local portfolio often changes during the day and can look significantly different from one day to the next. Therefore basing the holding period on the period of time over which the portfolio remains constant does not make much sense as this period will differ depending on the level at which you are considering the portfolio, i.e. globally or locally.

Perhaps the main reason why a one-day holding period is chosen by banks is because P&L is measured on a daily basis. Thus daily VAR allows comparison with daily P&L.

Banks choose the holding period dependent on how they use the number, with holding periods chosen from one day (RiskMetrics[TM]) to one year (Bankers Trust) with various rationales given to defend the choice made. A one-day holding period yields a meaningful result to trading operations; i.e. using past price change history as a guide, VAR is the potential loss on the portfolio over a 24-hour horizon, assuming the size and composition of the portfolio remain constant. VAR calculated with a one-day holding period is a good measure of the day-to-day riskiness of the portfolio; in fact this is a good definition of VAR.

LIQUIDITY AND VAR

It is normally possible to liquidate positions in 'liquid' assets in a period of less than one day. Some assets can be liquidated almost instantaneously, such as currencies, government bonds and liquid exchange traded securities – such as futures. However, for all assets there is a limit as to what value of position can be liquidated in one day. For any asset there is a size of position that could not be liquidated at the quoted price or at all. That position size is dependent on the normal market size (NMS – normal amount or size of the asset traded) and other factors, such as the total value of the asset issued and the daily turnover.

It is unlikely that any bank will have a trading portfolio which consists only of assets of a size and liquidity that can be liquidated inside one trading day. Therefore, as most banks use a one-day holding period, the resultant VAR number does not predict the potential loss on the portfolio that may be suffered if the portfolio were to be liquidated.

For some purposes it is necessary to be able to calculate the potential loss involved in selling (liquidating) a portfolio. Lawrence, Robinson and Stiles (1996) propose an approach to calculating the minimum cost of liquidating a portfolio. Their approach is based on minimising both the transaction costs involved in liquidating a position and the potential loss on the portfolio whilst it is being liquidated, i.e. minimising the liquidation time. For example, it may make sense to liquidate a highly volatile asset in the shortest possible time, regardless of the effect the sale (or purchase) would have on the quoted price.

Liquidity in Times of Market Stress

During a period of severe market stress it is almost certain that holding periods for many products will change and become longer. An example of this was during the 1994 fall in the bond markets. In February when the market suddenly fell, it became almost impossible to sell Eurobonds. Liquidity did not return until the markets had stabilised. In this particular market disturbance, both the holding period extended out to at least two weeks and at the same time severe price changes were experienced. The impact of periods like this are best investigated through stress testing (see Chapter 6); VAR cannot predict maximum losses in markets experiencing severe stress.

VAR FOR A PORTFOLIO

So far in this chapter, we have considered two of the three key drivers of VAR: volatility and the holding period. The third key constituent to any calculation of VAR is portfolio diversification. Portfolio diversification describes the extent that the risk in a portfolio is reduced by holding a diversity of assets. This is the age-old concept of not putting all one's eggs in one basket.

When calculating VAR we are simply concerned with calculating the potential for loss on a portfolio taking account of any diversification of risk in a portfolio caused by holding positions in several assets. Correlations between assets are used to describe how the price changes in assets are related to each other. If the prices of the two assets always move in line with each other then there is a correlation of 1 between them. If their prices always move in an opposite direction then they have a correlation of −1 (correlations are always between −1 and 1).

To illustrate the risk reduction effects of diversification, consider a portfolio that can hold only two assets, A and B. The portfolio can contain any proportion of A or B. Asset B is twice as risky as asset A, but offers twice the return. Imagine that a portfolio manager has been given the portfolio to manage, which when given to him is 100% invested in Asset A. The portfolio manager wishes to increase the potential return on the portfolio but does not wish to increase the risk on the portfolio substantially.

Figure 2.4 shows the effect of diversifying the portfolio with increasing amounts of Asset B. As can be seen, even though Asset B is twice as risky as Asset A, the risk of the portfolio can be significantly reduced as the proportion of Asset B is increased – up to a certain point depending on the correlation. The diversification effect (risk reduction) increases as the correlation reduces.

If we now introduce the portfolio return into the diagram we have an illustration that is familiar to portfolio managers. For the same portfolio as above, Figure 2.5 plots risk (VAR) versus expected return for various correlations. Each curve shows the risk-return combinations available to the portfolio manager[3] and is known as a 'minimum variance frontier'. Figure 2.5 provides the link with Markowitz's portfolio selection model. Markowitz (1952, 1959) showed how to maximise the expected return from a portfolio for any given level of risk. The maximum expected

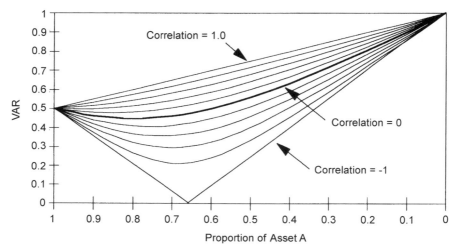

Figure 2.4 Effect of portfolio diversification (each line represents a change of correlation of 0.2)

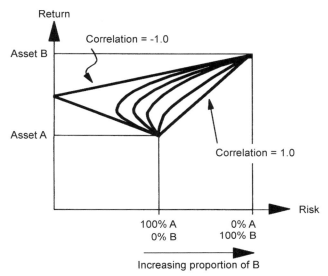

Figure 2.5 Risk versus return

return for the portfolio will occur along the part of the minimum variance frontier which has a positive slope (sloping up and to the right). This part of the curve is called the 'efficient frontier' and represents the maximum expected return on the portfolio for any given level of risk.

When calculating VAR, risk managers are normally only concerned with calculating the variance, or volatility, of a trading portfolio. Of course, portfolio managers and traders will be applying Markowitz's portfolio selection model to maximise their expected return for a given level of risk.

Returning to the impact of correlation on VAR, traders are most often concerned to know how much risk remains in a hedged trading position. Traders often make money from executing a transaction, as opposed to taking a position in an asset as an investment. Therefore, traders often wish to minimise the risk on the portfolio of assets they hold as a result of undertaking customer transactions. Figure 2.6 shows the VAR for a trading portfolio consisting of $100m of a Eurobond, duration hedged (i.e. portfolio VBPM of 0) with a government bond. In other words the portfolio consists of a long position of the Eurobond (i.e. a purchased Eurobond) and a short position in a government bond (i.e. a sold government bond). If the prices of the two bonds moved perfectly in line with each other they would have a correlation of 1 and the portfolio would be risk free. However, as mentioned in Chapter 1, the portfolio is subject to spread risk and the two bonds are not perfectly correlated, though they are likely to be highly correlated in most mature markets.

Figure 2.6 shows how the VAR of the portfolio reduces as the correlation increases. Note that the VAR has increased to half its maximum (VAR of 350) when the correlation has reduced from 1 to 0.75. This shows that hedged portfolios

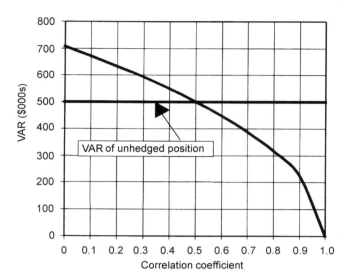

Figure 2.6   Hedging effect of correlation

are very sensitive to small changes in high correlations. It should also be noted that a correlation of at least 0.5 is required to reduce the VAR of the portfolio, i.e. 'hedging' with an instrument with a correlation of less than 0.5 will increase the VAR. In practice a government bond does not provide a perfect hedge for a Eurobond as the correlation between these two classes of assets is less than one, though typically higher than 0.8.

Calculating VAR for a Portfolio

The VAR of a portfolio is simply the volatility of the portfolio. In effect, therefore, when calculating VAR for a portfolio we wish to combine the price change distributions of each of the assets in the portfolio, into a single value change distribution of the portfolio. The formula below shows how the volatility of a portfolio of Assets A and B can be calculated; VAR can be calculated as the portfolio volatility (multiplied by the current market value of the portfolio).

$$\sigma_P = \sqrt{a^2.\sigma_A^2 + b^2.\sigma_B^2 + 2a.b.\rho_{AB}.\sigma_A.\sigma_B}$$

where: σ_P = volatility of the portfolio
         a, b = proportion of Assets A and B in the portfolio (fractions)
         σ_A, σ_B = volatilities of Assets A and B
         ρ_{AB} = correlation between Asset A and Asset B
Note that $a.\sigma_A$ = VAR of single Asset A as shown in the first section of this chapter.

From the equation above it can be seen that the third term will be 0 if the correlation between the two assets is 0 (i.e. Assets A and B are independent). In this case VAR is the square root of the sum of the squares, i.e.:

$$\sigma_P = \sqrt{a^2.\sigma_A^2 + b^2.\sigma_B^2}$$

The equation above can be expanded for as many assets as are present in the portfolio:

$$VAR_P = \sqrt{\sum P_i^2.\sigma_i^2 + 2\sum_i \sum_j P_i.P_j.\sigma_i\sigma_j.\rho_{i,j}}$$

where: i and j are the set of pairs of assets or risk factors in the portfolio.
P is either the proportion or position of the ith asset.

In practice, however, VAR for a portfolio is calculated using the following matrix formula:

$$VAR_P = \sqrt{V.C.V^T}$$

where: VAR_P = VAR of the portfolio
V = row vector of VARs for each individual position
C = matrix of correlations
V^T = transpose of matrix V

Example: calculation of VAR for a portfolio

Consider the following portfolio, which is referred to as Portfolio 1 throughout the remainder of the book:

Asset	Position ($m)
Gold	2
Sterling	3
Rand	1

VAR is calculated for Portfolio 1 using the historical simulation and Monte Carlo simulation approaches in Chapter 3. The volatilities of the three assets, with 95% confidence, are:

Asset	Volatility (%)
Gold	0.9128
Sterling	0.9920
Rand	1.8498

Now the vector, 'V', of VARs for the individual positions can be calculated:

Asset	Vector 'V' of position VARs ($)
Gold	18,256 (2,000,000 × 0.009128)
Sterling	29,761
Rand	18,498

The correlation matrix for the three assets below shows that the three assets are essentially uncorrelated, this will give a high diversification of risk:

Correlations	Gold	Sterling	Rand
Gold	1	0.0405	0.0912
Sterling	0.0405	1	0.0479
Rand	0.0912	0.0479	1

Using the matrix equation above, the VAR for Portfolio 1 can be calculated as follows:

$$VAR_P = \sqrt{\left\{ (18,256 \ 29,761 \ 18,498) \left\{ \begin{array}{ccc} 1 & 0.0405 & 0.0912 \\ 0.0405 & 1 & 0.0479 \\ 0.0912 & 0.0479 & 1 \end{array} \right\} \left\{ \begin{array}{c} 18,256 \\ 29,761 \\ 18,498 \end{array} \right\} \right\}}$$

This gives $VAR_P = \$41,470$, or $41,000 to two significant figures. See the appendix to this chapter for a review of matrix multiplication.

This means that on this portfolio it is expected that a loss greater than $41,000 can be expected on 5% of days, i.e. one day in 20. As this is a statistical measure it will require a considerable number of days before one could look at the actual experienced profit and loss to see whether this is a fair value of VAR. It may be the case that several losses of this magnitude are experienced straight away or not for a long time. In practice the composition of any trading portfolio is likely to change daily (in fact almost constantly during the trading day) and therefore the VAR is different for each end of day position.

It is informative to see the effect that different correlations have on the VAR of the above portfolio. The table below presents different correlation scenarios:

Correlation scenario	VAR ($'000s)
Actual correlations	41
All correlations of 1	66
Correlations of −1 between gold and Rand	31

From the above table it can be seen that correlations of 1 increase the VAR. This is because correlations of 1 between all three assets means that there is no diversification effect taking place; the three assets effectively become one asset from a risk perspective. Correlations of 0 imply that the risk associated with the three assets are entirely independent. Introducing correlations of −1 between gold and Rand means that gold is hedging the Rand position, as Rand has twice the volatility of gold and half the position size of gold.

In practice correlations of −1 are fairly rare but correlations of close to 1 are common within product categories. There are very high correlations between bonds with different maturities, for example there is a correlation of 0.99 between the yields of 5- and 7-year USD treasuries. There are also high correlations across some currencies. For example, the correlation between French and German 10-year government bonds is approximately 0.8. This is due in no small part to the efforts made by the French and German governments to meet the convergence criteria for a single currency. These high correlations give a good indication of which assets (instruments) will act as effective hedges.

EXTENDING COVARIANCE TO COPE WITH OPTIONS

There are two problems with using covariance to calculate VAR for options. The first problem is that the assets considered so far in this chapter have a single risk factor, i.e. the asset itself. This is not so for options, for which there are several risk factors. The second problem which is not so tractable, is that options have a skewed distribution with respect to the asset underlying the option. This is illustrated in Figure 2.7 which shows the skewed distribution[4] for the written option considered in the worked example below.

Figure 2.7 shows the distribution for an option which is one month from expiry. If the option remains at-the-money (underlying asset has same value as the strike of the option) the gamma (see below) will increase as the option approaches expiry. This would have the effect of further increasing the skew in the distribution. The skew can have a marked effect on the VAR. There is more risk associated with writing options than with taking positions in the underlying asset; this is reflected in the negatively skewed distributions for written options. For a written option the skew increases the risk and VAR, whereas the skew reduces the risk and VAR for a purchased option.

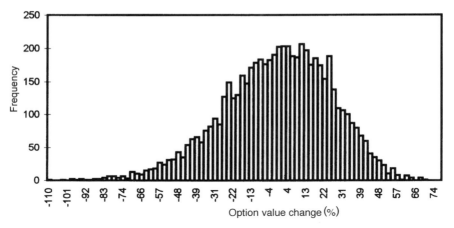

Figure 2.7   Distribution for a written option

A Sensitivity-based Approach to VAR

This section describes the sensitivity-based approach to calculating VAR for an option. In practice, VAR is commonly implemented using this approach for all instruments though a full implementation is not possible for options with the covariance method. For a fuller description of the sensitivity based approach see Chapter 5.

An option's price is sensitive to changes in three market risk factors: the price of the asset underlying the option (the 'underlying'), implied volatility and the risk free rate.

Implied volatility is similar to but not the same as the experienced historic volatility of the USD/Rand exchange rate. It is the volatility that is implied by an option's price for a given price of the underlying asset – in this case the USD/Rand exchange rate. The implied volatility reflects more than just the current price volatility of the underlying asset. Implied volatility reflects market *expectations* of the volatility of the underlying as well as supply and demand. Options are often traded on volatility with the implied volatility becoming the effective price of the option. Note that this volatility is different from the estimates of historic volatility used in VAR calculations.

Just how sensitive an option is to the three market risk factors is dependent on the structure of the option and, in particular, the price or rate at which the option was struck compared to current market prices and the remaining time to expiry. Managing risk for options has always involved the 'Greeks', or sensitivity of the option price to small changes in each of the risk factors. The various generic risk factors associated with options and the sensitivities used to measure and manage these risks are described in Table 2.1.

Table 2.1 Option risk factors and the 'Greeks'

Risk factor	Sensitivity (the 'Greeks')	Sensitivity description
Price of the underlying asset	Delta and gamma	Delta is the sensitivity of the option price to a change in price of the underlying asset.
		Gamma is the sensitivity of the option price to the square of the change in price of the underlying asset.
Implied volatility (The volatility of the underlying asset implied by the option's price. Implied volatility is quoted in the market as is any other price/rate.)	Vega	Vega is the sensitivity of the option price to a change in implied volatility.
Risk free interest rate (The re-investment rate with no default risk – normally the interest rate on government debt corresponding to the remaining time to expiry.)	Rho	Rho is the sensitivity of the option price to a change in the risk free rate.

Some of the sensitivities, particularly delta and gamma, are similar to measures of risk used with other financial instruments. Delta is analogous to the value of a basis point move (PVBP) of a bond, and gamma is analogous to the convexity of a bond. The relationship of an option's price to changes in implied volatility and the risk free rate are linear, i.e. vega and rho are approximately constant (for constant underlying price and time to expiry). This is not so for an option's sensitivity to changes in the price of the underlying asset.

There is a convex relationship between an option's price and changes in the underlying, in much the same way as there is a convex relationship between a bond's price and changes in yield (the curve is far more pronounced with options). The relationship between the option price and the price of the underlying asset is shown in Figure 2.8, and is for a currency option with the option price calculated using the Black–Scholes[5] equation.

Delta by itself is not sufficient to model the convex relationship between the option price and the underlying. To achieve a closer match a second sensitivity, gamma, is required. Gamma describes the rate of change of delta and is therefore a second order derivative of the option price with respect to the underlying.

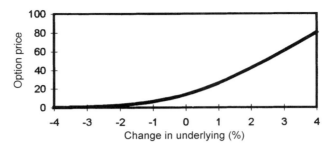

Figure 2.8   Call option price vs change in underlying

It should now be clear that an option cannot be represented as a single risk factor as with the products considered so far in this chapter. The covariance approach to options is to represent an option as a collection of separate positions in each of the risk factors described above. Volatilities and correlations can be derived for each of these risk factors.

The equivalent position of each risk factor is determined by the 'Greeks' for the option. This works as long as the 'Greeks' are expressed as fractions. For example, if an option has a delta of 0.5 then the option's value change, for a small change in the underlying price, will be half that for an equivalent position in the underlying asset, i.e. a position equal to half the notional of the option. A worked example of this is given below.

The use of positions in risk factors cannot cope with gamma. Therefore, the convexity of the option price is lost with the covariance approach. This is a critical shortcoming. As previously stated, most banks use an alternative approach to calculating VAR for portfolios containing options. Various methods have been put forward for extending the covariance approach to cope with gamma in vanilla option portfolios. One method, published by J P Morgan (Zangari, 1996), uses the Cornish–Fisher expansion. The Cornish–Fisher expansion is applied to the skewed portfolio return distribution to calculate the standard deviation of the portfolio containing options. It should be noted that this type of extension of the covariance approach will only work with vanilla options. It will not work with complex options, such as digitals or barriers, which can have multiple peaks in the price change distribution.

Worked Example

The sensitivity-based method described above can be illustrated by considering a foreign exchange option. In order to hedge the Rand exposure in Portfolio 1, a trader may wish to sell (write) a Rand option. If he sells an at-the-money (ATM) option (i.e. an option with a strike equal to the current exchange rate) then it will have a delta of 0.5. Therefore, to be delta hedged, he needs to write an option with a nominal principal of twice as much as the Rand position in the portfolio, i.e. an

Table 2.2 Rand option — risk factors

Greek	Risk factor	Value (fraction)	Position ($m)	Volatility (%)
Delta	Rand currency	0.50429	1.0086	1.85
Gamma	—	0.00673	—	—
Vega	Implied volatility	0.02287	0.0457	11.23
Rho − USD	USD risk free interest rate	0.00224	0.0045	0.33
Rho − Rand	Rand risk free interest rate	−0.00725	−0.0145	0.90

option with a nominal of $2m should be written as there is $1m of Rand in Portfolio 1.

The trader wishes to hedge the exposure for one month, perhaps corresponding with a period of uncertainty in South Africa, i.e. the option has an expiry date of one month from the present. The risk factors for this option are shown in Table 2.2.

Notice first of all that, as this is a foreign exchange option, there are two rhos, one for USD and one for Rand. The asset positions are arrived at by multiplying the fractional 'Greeks' by the nominal amount of the option, i.e. $2m. Note that a risk factor position cannot be created for gamma as it has the same underlying risk factor as delta. As the relationship between the gamma and the underlying asset is different (i.e. dependent on a squared change in the underlying price) from the delta the two positions cannot be combined.

The volatility of each risk factor is also shown in Table 2.2. Notice that the volatility of the implied volatility is much higher than the other volatilities; this can lead to implied volatility becoming a major factor in the calculated VAR. Apart from the information given in Table 2.2, correlations are required to calculate VAR. It was found that the four risk factors listed were largely uncorrelated, with the exception of the risk free rates, where there was found to be a weak correlation of 0.3. The risk factor positions for rho and the implied volatility are so low that they have virtually no impact on calculated VAR. The VAR for the option using the covariance approach was calculated to be $19,350. This can be compared against the VAR calculated for the same option using the Monte Carlo approach (see Chapter 3) which gave a value of $24,600. The difference (20%) is due to the fact that the standard covariance approach cannot take account of gamma.

SUMMARY

The covariance approach to calculating VAR is a statistical model that assumes that price changes are normally distributed. This is generally a reasonable assumption for non-leveraged products (though the assumption should be verified for all assets in a given portfolio). For options and other structured products that have optionality built into them, the covariance approach is not appropriate. Various methods of extending the covariance approach have been proposed, however, banks who need to calculate VAR for portfolios including options typically use either Monte Carlo simulation or historical simulation.

The above discussion and examples of the calculation of VAR using the covariance approach show that VAR is dependent on three main factors: price change volatility, the holding period and the correlations between assets. In practice volatility is measured with a given level of confidence, typically 95%. The holding period is most often chosen to be one day, i.e. the resultant VAR calculation represents potential losses on a portfolio over a period of one day. Correlations describe how the price changes of different assets move in relation to each other. Correlations also describe the diversification of risk present in the portfolio.

VAR measures the potential loss on a portfolio in normal trading conditions. However, it is clear that financial markets suffer a large number of extreme price movements when compared to the statistical expectation of such movements as expressed by a normal distribution. VAR is not an appropriate risk management technique for dealing with large price shocks. VAR must be supplemented by stress testing (see Chapter 6).

One of the main advantages of covariance is that it is a 'closed form' analytical solution to the calculation of VAR. This means that it is quick and easy to calculate as the calculation can be replicated for simple portfolios on a spreadsheet. See spreadsheet Covar1.xls on the disk.

NOTES

1. Note: volatility is usually quoted as a one standard deviation annual change.
2. Assumes that the two bonds have the same characteristics, i.e. same coupon, coupon frequency and payment dates.
3. Note that the *x*-axis shows increasing risk (VAR) and also an increasing proportion of Asset B in the portfolio.
4. Skewed distributions have a tail which is longer on one side than the other. The option distribution is negatively skewed as the extended tail is on the left.
5. Note that, in fact, it is the Garman Kohlhagen version of the Black–Scholes equation which has been used as this version is appropriate for currency options. The model will be referred to as Black–Scholes throughout this book.

APPENDIX: MATRIX MULTIPLICATION

Some simple notation needs to be established before the rules for matrix multiplication can be given. Consider the following 2×2 matrix:

$$A = \begin{bmatrix} a_{11} & a_{12} \\ a_{21} & a_{22} \end{bmatrix}$$

The subscripts indicate the way each element of a matrix is referenced, first by row and then by column. Thus each element of a matrix can be denoted a_{ij} where the subscript i refers to the row and j to the column.

We can now progress to the rules for matrix multiplication with the use of an example. Consider two matrices:

$$A = \begin{bmatrix} a_{11} & a_{12} & a_{13} \\ a_{21} & a_{22} & a_{23} \end{bmatrix} \quad \text{and} \quad B = \begin{bmatrix} b_{11} & b_{12} \\ b_{21} & b_{22} \\ b_{31} & b_{32} \end{bmatrix}$$

We wish to find the product of these two matrices, a third matrix C. The rules for matrix multiplication are as follows:

- The number of columns in A must equal the number of rows in B.
- The resultant matrix will have the same number of rows as A and the same number of columns as B.
- The ij^{th} element of C is equal to the 'row-on-column' product of the ith row in A and the jth column in B. This is the critical rule to remember.

Therefore C is a 2×2 matrix, with each of the elements calculated as follows:

$$A.B. = C = \begin{bmatrix} (a_{11}b_{11} + a_{12}b_{21} + a_{13}b_{31}) & (a_{11}b_{12} + a_{12}b_{22} + a_{13}b_{32}) \\ (a_{21}b_{11} + a_{22}b_{21} + a_{23}b_{13}) & (a_{21}b_{12} + a_{22}b_{22} + a_{23}b_{32}) \end{bmatrix} .$$

3
Calculating VAR using simulation

INTRODUCTION

This chapter describes the two main simulation approaches to calculating VAR – historical simulation (sometimes called the full valuation approach) and Monte Carlo simulation. The main advantage of these techniques over covariance is that they can both cope with any type of option. This chapter gives brief overviews of the two methods and then goes through worked examples to illustrate the approaches.

The Problem with Covariance

Covariance has a number of important benefits, not least that it is easy and quick to calculate. The problem with covariance, however, is that it is a model of the financial markets which makes strong assumptions about the way financial products behave. The biggest assumption made is that price changes in the financial markets are normally distributed. Although this is a reasonable, though not entirely accurate, assumption for many linear products it is not a reasonable assumption for portfolios containing even a small quantity of options, as was shown in the previous chapter. As with all models, covariance fails to resemble perfectly the real world in certain situations.

HISTORICAL SIMULATION

Historical simulation provides an approach to calculating VAR that is not model based, although it is still a statistical measure of potential loss. As the maths is simple it is far more easily accepted by management and the trading community. This is because it is easy to understand how the VAR number was arrived at. The main benefit, however, of historical simulation is that it can cope with options in a

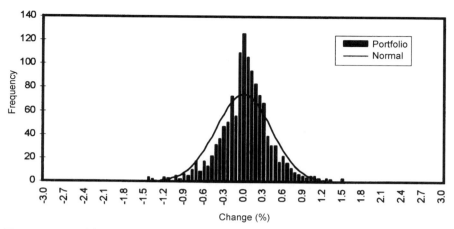

Figure 3.1   Portfolio vs normal distribution

portfolio. Historical simulation can cope with all vanilla exchange traded and over-the-counter (OTC) options.

In terms of representing actual market behaviour, historical simulation is superior to covariance. The historical simulation method does not assume that price changes are normally distributed. This is a significant advantage of the historical simulation method of calculating VAR. Figure 3.1 shows a comparison between the actual distribution of value changes for Portfolio 1 versus the equivalent normal distribution. It displays the classic characteristics of financial price change distributions. Historical simulation captures the characteristics of the price change distribution of the portfolio, as VAR is calculated from the actual distribution of portfolio value changes. As a result of this, where a portfolio distribution has fat tails, it will tend to produce a slightly higher VAR number than the VAR calculated by the covariance method.

Banks that have complex option portfolios prefer to use Monte Carlo or another numerical simulation for their option portfolios. This is partly because such numerical simulation approaches are being used to value the portfolios in the first place. Complex options and portfolios of options often have gamma profiles that only occur in certain highly specific price scenarios. It is possible that the price scenario that would cause a substantial loss has not been encountered in the price history used to generate VAR by historical simulation. This is particularly likely if a relatively short period of prices history is used, such as 100 days or less. Monte Carlo simulation generates a very large number of price change scenarios, or events, which are applied to the portfolio. There is, therefore, a much greater chance that any specific loss causing scenario will be included in the distribution of portfolio value changes. The problem of important price change events not being in the historical data set used is especially acute for barrier options. Barrier options have a price function which moves from close to zero to a given value as an underlying price barrier is crossed.

Calculating VAR using Historical Simulation

Historical simulation takes a portfolio of assets at a particular point in time and then revalues the portfolio a number of times, using a history of prices for the assets in the portfolio. The portfolio revaluations produce a distribution of profit and losses which can be examined to determine the VAR of the portfolio with a chosen level of confidence. As can be imagined, this approach becomes very computationally intensive when the portfolio contains a large number of products and when a reasonable length of historical prices is used.

There are a few different ways to calculate VAR using historical simulation. The simplest way is to revalue the portfolio using a specified history of prices. The portfolio value is then calculated for each day. The portfolio values can then be placed into percentiles. The VAR can then be read off from the percentile corresponding to the required confidence level.

The problem with this approach is that, as the value of the portfolio changes, the percentage value changes in the portfolio no longer refer to the original portfolio value. Also, over the given history, the prices of the assets making up the portfolio will change in relation to one another. This means that the composition of the portfolio is changing throughout the length of the price history used. Revaluing the portfolio using actual asset prices will not give the correct result. What is actually required is a history of portfolio value changes based on *today's* portfolio with *today's* portfolio value and composition.

The correct method of calculating VAR using historical simulation is to use a history of percentage price changes and apply these to today's portfolio, as follows:

- Obtain percentage price change series for every asset or risk factor needed to revalue the portfolio.
- Apply price changes to the portfolio, to generate a 'historical' series of portfolio values changes.
- Sort the series of portfolio value changes into percentiles.
- The VAR of the portfolio is the value change corresponding to the required level of confidence

Each of these steps is discussed and illustrated below for Portfolio 1 (i.e. the same portfolio that was used in the previous chapter on covariance).

Historical Price Series

Figure 3.2 shows 100-day historical price series for Sterling and Rand from our portfolio (exchange rates against the US dollar). Notice that the percentage change price series is required rather than the absolute exchange rate. The relative volatilities of Sterling and Rand can be clearly seen from the two graphs. The effect of

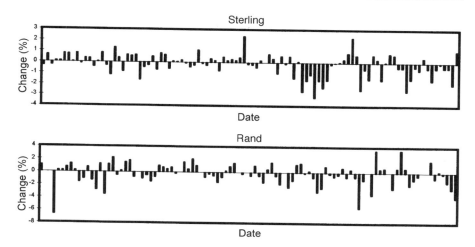

Figure 3.2 Historical price series for Rand and Sterling (a) Sterling – change in $ exchange rate; (b) Rand – change in $ exchange rate

diversification can also be seen. The two graphs show quite different patterns of price change; if they were highly correlated it would be clearly visible from the graphs.

There are two key questions to be answered with respect to setting up the required historical price series:

1. What length of price series should be used?
2. What should be done about products for which no price history exists?

The length of the time series is the biggest decision that must be made when using the historical simulation approach to calculating VAR. Historical simulation assumes that the future is adequately represented by recent history. It is essential, therefore, to ensure that a bank or trading area is happy with the VAR characteristics given by the length of the time series chosen. Chapter 4 shows that the choice of the length of price history (the observation period) is one of the most important decisions to be made when implementing VAR. Chapter 4 describes the behaviour of VAR models with different observation periods. In practice, the length of history used, varies significantly between market practitioners. Some banks use just 100 days of price history, others use three or more years.

Using fewer days data than there are risk factors in a portfolio can sometimes lead to an erroneous VAR calculation. This problem is further explored in the Appendix to this chapter. It should be noted that although correlations are not explicitly calculated in the historical simulation method, they are nonetheless present in the historic price series.

New assets create an interesting problem as it is impossible to obtain a price history. It should also be noted that this problem does not apply only to historical simulation. If there is no price history it will also not be possible to calculate a volatility or correlations between this new asset and other assets. In practice, a price series can be borrowed from an existing asset with similar characteristics until an adequate price history has been accumulated. In a large diverse portfolio this is an acceptable practice.

If historical simulation is being used for a portfolio containing options then a history of implied volatilities must be obtained. It is unlikely that histories for all the implied volatilities required can be created. However, the Monte Carlo simulation approach to creating price histories can be used to create the missing series.

Apply Price Changes to a Portfolio

Having created a history of percentage price changes for each component of the portfolio, the price changes can now be applied to each portfolio component to generate a 'history' of portfolio value changes. Table 3.1 shows the results of this process for the first 20 days of historical prices.

The first portfolio value change is given by:

Table 3.1 Generating a history of portfolio value changes

Gold (% change)	Rand (% change)	Sterling (% change)	Portfolio change ($000s)
0.06	1.10	−0.35	1.7
−0.12	0.00	0.65	17.1
0.47	0.00	−0.32	−0.3
−0.28	−6.67	0.11	−69.0
0.57	0.26	0.11	17.2
−0.55	0.26	0.78	14.9
0.20	0.79	0.72	33.5
0.09	1.32	0.03	15.7
−0.41	0.27	0.79	18.3
0.38	−1.61	−0.16	−13.2
0.17	−1.06	0.37	4.0
0.61	0.78	0.34	30.2
−0.07	−1.32	−0.44	−27.9
0.16	−2.86	0.05	−23.8
−0.26	1.26	0.84	32.6
0.59	−3.58	−0.34	−34.1
−0.01	1.23	−1.20	−23.9
0.23	2.25	1.32	66.6
0.07	−0.51	0.42	8.8
0.53	0.25	−0.86	−12.5

$$\text{Value change} = ((0.06 \times 2{,}000{,}000) + (1.1 \times 1{,}000{,}000) +$$
$$(-0.35 \times 3{,}000{,}000))/100$$
$$\text{Value change} = \$1{,}700$$

A more generalised formula is as follows:

$$V = \sum_i f(\delta_i, \alpha_i)$$

where: V = value change of the portfolio

f = function that determines the value of a portfolio component; for straightforward assets such as contained in Portfolio 1, the value of the component is arrived at simply by multiplying the price by the quantity of the asset. For other products, such as options, a valuation model must be used.

α_i = sensitivity of portfolio component to risk factor, i

δ_i = percentage price change in risk factor, i

Determine VAR

Once a series of portfolio value changes has been generated, VAR can be determined. The first step is to sort the portfolio value changes into percentiles. A percentile contains 1% of the value changes. The portfolio value changes must first be sorted and then placed into percentiles. Table 3.2 shows the portfolio value changes given in Table 3.1 sorted into percentiles 5% wide. In practice VAR would not be derived from only 20 days of history.

As discussed above, the minimum number of observations used by banks in practice is 100 days of history. As there are only 20 observations it is not possible to distinguish confidence levels other than with 5% steps. There are statistical functions which will interpolate confidence levels at finer intervals but with so few observations, spurious accuracy would result.

In the example used here VAR with 95% is given as $34,000 (quoting VAR to greater than two significant figures overstates the accuracy that is possible). VAR calculated for the whole of the five-year history available gives a VAR of $43,000. As would be expected, the two results are significantly different. It would have been pure chance if the 20-day sample had the same statistical characteristics as the full five-year data set.

The VAR calculated by historical simulation can be compared with the VAR calculated on the same data set using the covariance method. Covariance VAR calculated on Portfolio 1 was $41,000. It is a good test of any VAR calculation to compare the VAR calculated to VAR calculated using another method. In this case the results are within 5% of each other. As it is probably impossible to calculate VAR with greater than 90% accuracy, these results validate each other. Also remember that historical simulation will tend to produce a higher VAR than covariance due to the fat tails of the typical value change distributions of financial portfolios.

Table 3.2 Deriving VAR for Portfolio 1

Confidence level (%)	Portfolio change ($'000s)
100	−69.0
95	−34.1
90	−27.9
85	−23.9
80	−23.8
75	−13.2
70	−12.5
65	−0.3
60	1.7
55	4.0
50	8.8
45	14.9
40	15.7
35	17.1
30	17.2
25	18.3
20	30.2
15	32.6
10	33.5
5	66.6

MONTE CARLO SIMULATION

Historical simulation showed how to generate VAR by simulating portfolio valuation changes resulting from revaluing the portfolio using the actually experienced history of asset price changes over a chosen period of time.

As long as price histories for the assets in a portfolio are available for an appropriate length of history then historical simulation is a particularly effective way of calculating VAR. However, if a sufficient history of price changes is difficult to come by, historical simulation may be rendered difficult to implement. There is also an argument which says that the history of actual prices is a limited set of events from which to derive VAR. This last argument is certainly answered by Monte Carlo simulation.

A set of price changes for assets in a portfolio on a particular day can be thought of as a single portfolio event. Monte Carlo simulation involves artificially generating a very large set of events (correlated asset price changes) from which VAR is derived. A large number of events are generated from random numbers; these events are then applied to a portfolio and VAR is determined from the resulting set of portfolio value changes in exactly the same way as with historical simulation.

Monte Carlo simulation is preferred as a solution to calculating VAR versus the covariance approach, as options can be dealt with properly. As discussed in Chapter

2, covariance cannot deal with gamma or exotic options for which the option price is derived numerically. These problems are overcome with the Monte Carlo approach as they are with historical simulation.

It should be noted that the Monte Carlo simulation approach makes the same fundamental assumption about market behaviour as the covariance approach, i.e. that asset price changes are normally distributed. As stated before, this is a reasonable assumption for many assets; however, there are assets, such as those found in emerging markets where this assumption is less valid. The actual behaviour of the assets that make up the majority of a bank's portfolio should be examined carefully to ensure that normality is a reasonable assumption.

The remainder of this chapter describes the process of calculating VAR using Monte Carlo simulation. Figure 3.3 shows the Monte Carlo method as a process

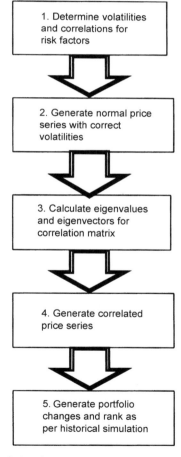

Figure 3.3 Monte Carlo simulation for VAR

flow. Each of the steps shown in the figure are described in the following sections. Step 1 is exactly the same as for the covariance method, i.e. volatilities and correlations are calculated for every risk factor in the portfolio. Where volatilities and correlations cannot be observed from historical series they must be approximated by borrowing the information from similar assets (i.e. making an educated guess at the volatilities and correlations required).

Monte Carlo Simulation for a Single Asset

The process of generating a set of portfolio valuation events is best considered in two stages. The first stage is to generate a set of normally distributed price changes with the correct volatility for a particular asset. As with the chapter on covariance, the VAR of a $1m position in gold will be derived first. The second stage of the process is to generate correlated asset price changes, this can be done using eigenvalues and eigenvectors. This process is described in the section on generating correlated price changes. Generating a set of price changes for a single asset involves the following steps:

- Generate random numbers.
- Convert to a set of normally distributed price changes.

The first step in generating a set of normally distributed price changes is to generate a set of random numbers. There are a wide range of commercially available computer-based programs to do this, including standard functions within spread-sheets. There is a whole branch of maths associated with the generation of true random numbers but this need not concern us here. We require a random number generator that enables a series of price changes to be generated with the volatility and correlations displayed by the actual asset. Random number generators usually ask for a range within which the random numbers are required. The process described here requires random numbers between 0 and 1.

The next step is to convert the set of random numbers generated into a normally distributed set of random numbers. A standard set of random numbers will be uniformly distributed across the number range chosen, i.e. 0 and 1. This number range is chosen so that the next step can assume that the random numbers are points on a cumulative normal distribution, i.e. each random number represents a cumulative probability for a normal distribution. The set of random numbers is then converted into a normally distributed set of random numbers by applying the inverse of the cumulative normal distribution function to each random number.[1] This process can be understood intuitively with the help of Figure 3.4 which shows that if evenly spread random numbers are fed in to the function represented by the 'S' shaped curve, then the output will have a greater number of readings in the middle than at the tails, i.e. a normal distribution. The output, i.e. the x-axis, are normally distributed price changes.

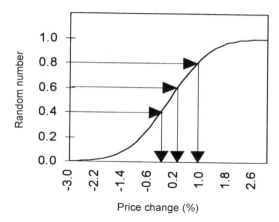

Figure 3.4 Cumulative normal distribution

The cumulative distribution function is given in the Appendix to this chapter. As with the generation of random numbers, the inverse cumulative normal function is widely available for computers and spreadsheets. The process described above typically assumes a standard normal distribution. Therefore, the price changes generated will have a standard deviation (volatility) of 1. The price change series generated must display the same volatility as the asset being modelled. Therefore, the price changes generated must be multiplied by the standard deviation of the asset under consideration.

Table 3.3 shows this process for 10 random numbers. The third column is arrived at by multiplying the 'normalised' random numbers by the daily volatility of gold (1 standard deviation), as used in the covariance example in Chapter 2, i.e. 0.5532%.

To save computation time and to ensure an even distribution each price change generated should be duplicated but with the opposite sign. The duplicate but opposite price changes are known as antithetics; their use will ensure a perfectly symmetrical price change distribution is created.

From this point, the process is identical to the historical simulation method. The price changes generated are applied to the portfolio, in this case $1m of gold. VAR is then the percentile portfolio value change equal to the required confidence level.

Convergence

The VAR given by the Monte Carlo approach should be identical to that given by the covariance approach for linear portfolios, i.e. portfolios without options. The only potential problem is one of convergence. As the random numbers are different each time the simulation is run so is the VAR that is calculated, i.e. the simulation does not give the same value every time. The only way to ensure that a reasonable

Table 3.3 Converting random numbers to price changes

Random numbers (0–1)	Inverse normal function	Gold price change (%)
0.223	−0.764	−0.422
0.002	−2.954	−1.634
0.618	0.301	0.166
0.569	0.174	0.096
0.872	1.135	0.628
0.425	−0.190	−0.105
0.142	−1.070	−0.592
0.397	−0.261	−0.144
0.579	0.199	0.110
0.726	0.601	0.333

estimate of VAR is produced from each run is to use a large number of events. 10,000 events is often taken as a bench mark number of events. However, convergence should be checked by running the simulation on a typical portfolio a number of times. Table 3.4 shows the statistics generated for gold, by running the simulation 20 times with only 1000 events or price changes.

The expected value of VAR for $1m of gold is $9,100 (from the covariance calculation in Chapter 2). As can be seen from Table 3.4 the *mean* VAR produced from 20 runs of the simulation is $9,000 (to 2 significant figures), which is close to the expected value. There is, however, no guarantee that the mean would be this close for a second 20 runs of the portfolio. More importantly, the VAR produced by individual runs varied from $8,500 to $9,800. With the maximum VAR generated being over 9% from the mean. Clearly 1000 events is not sufficient. Table 3.5 shows the same statistics for 20 simulation runs using 10,000 events.

Table 3.5 shows that the standard deviation, or standard error, of the simulation has converged to approximately 1% of the mean value. This is an acceptable error or tolerance level. Also the mean VAR derived is exactly the same as that given by the covariance approach, i.e. $9,100. When determining the number of runs required it should be noted that there is not a directly proportional relationship between the number of runs and improved convergence. Improvement in convergence is proportional to the square root of the multiple of runs used; for

Table 3.4 Convergence statistics for 20 runs with 1000 events

Analysis	$	Distance from mean
Mean VAR	−8,996	
Standard deviation	345	
Max VAR	−8,474	−5.8%
Min VAR	−9,822	9.2%

Table 3.5 Convergence statistics for 20 runs with 10,000 events

Analysis	$	Distance from mean
Mean VAR	−9,098	
Standard deviation	106	
Max VAR	−8,863	−2.6%
Min VAR	−9,280	2.0%

example, doubling the number of runs will improve convergence by the square root of 2. As a general rule convergence should be investigated for typical portfolios to ensure the simulation is sufficiently accurate. A 1% standard error is normally taken to be sufficiently accurate.

Monte Carlo for a Multi-asset Portfolio

In the previous section, the process required to generate artificial price change series with the required volatility was described. This section shows how this process is extended to multi-asset portfolios. For multi-asset portfolios the price changes must be correlated. Correlated price changes are generated using a mathematical technique based on eigenvectors and eigenvalues. The process involves the following steps:

- Calculate eigenvectors and eigenvalues.
- Generate correlated price changes for all assets.

Understanding Eigenvectors and Eigenvalues

Eigenvectors and eigenvalues describe the behaviour of how the price changes of a group of risk factors move in relation to each other. For those with an engineering background eigenvectors are the principal components of the correlation matrix. For many correlation matrices there is no intuitive meaning to eigenvectors. In the case of a yield curve, however, eigenvectors do have a common sense meaning. Consider the correlation matrix in Table 3.6 which shows a correlation matrix for successive futures contracts.

Table 3.6 shows the classic features of a yield curve correlation matrix. The correlations close to the diagonal are very high and drop-off with the distance from the diagonal. Yield curves are often thought about in terms of the principal components of their movement with the first three principal components usually being thought of as:

Table 3.6   A correlation matrix for the first 11 interest rate futures contracts (Sterling)

Contract	1st	2nd	3rd	4th	5th	6th	7th	8th	9th	10th	11th
1st	1	0.86	0.69	0.56	0.49	0.42	0.37	0.33	0.29	0.27	0.28
2nd	0.86	1	0.94	0.85	0.78	0.71	0.64	0.59	0.51	0.48	0.47
3rd	0.69	0.94	1	0.97	0.91	0.87	0.81	0.74	0.67	0.63	0.6
4th	0.56	0.85	0.97	1	0.98	0.94	0.9	0.84	0.77	0.73	0.7
5th	0.49	0.78	0.91	0.98	1	0.98	0.96	0.91	0.86	0.82	0.89
6th	0.42	0.71	0.87	0.94	0.98	1	0.99	0.96	0.92	0.89	0.86
7th	0.37	0.64	0.81	0.9	0.96	0.99	1	0.99	0.96	0.93	0.91
8th	0.33	0.59	0.74	0.84	0.91	0.96	0.99	1	0.98	0.97	0.95
9th	0.29	0.51	0.67	0.77	0.86	0.92	0.96	0.98	1	0.99	0.97
10th	0.27	0.48	0.63	0.73	0.82	0.89	0.93	0.97	0.99	1	0.99
11th	0.28	0.47	0.6	0.7	0.89	0.86	0.91	0.95	0.97	0.99	1

1. Parallel shift.
2. Yield curve tilt.
3. Twist or hump.

Note that this is a mathematical model of yield curve movement and is not intended to suggest that yield curves actually move in this way. The principal components taken together effectively 'model' the average yield curve move. It is unlikely that any specific yield curve move will be the same as any eigenvector or combination of eigenvectors.

When the first three eigenvectors are calculated for the above correlation matrix it can be seen that they correspond well to the first three principal components named above. Figure 3.5 shows the first three eigenvectors for the correlation matrix in Table 3.6.

Eigenvalues give the relative weighting or importance of each eigenvector. There are eleven eigenvectors in total for the correlation matrix above, however the first three have by far the most importance as measured by the eigenvalues. The weighting of the first three eigenvectors are: 55%, 24% and 12% respectively. As can be seen from Figure 3.5, the first eigenvector corresponds to a parallel shift in the yield curve. The 55% weighting associated with the first eigenvector supports the use of the value of a basis point move (PVBP – a parallel shift in the curve) as the main measure of risk in an interest rate trading environment.

Note also that the eigenvector corresponding to the parallel shift is generated by the high correlations adjacent to the diagonal of the correlation matrix. Given the high relative importance of the first eigenvector, it then becomes clear that the correlations next to the diagonal are the most important and drive the resultant VAR. Thus, information describing the behaviour of the yield curve is concentrated in the correlations close to the diagonal.

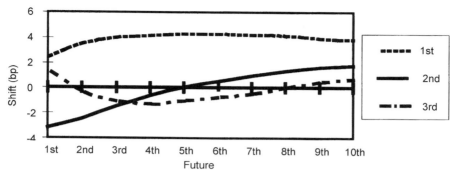

Figure 3.5   First three eigenvectors

Calculating Eigenvectors and Eigenvalues

It is outside the scope of this book to go through the fairly complex maths associated with the derivation of eigenvectors and eigenvalues. There are standard computer-based solutions available for the generation of eigenvectors and eigenvalues. One of the standard techniques used is the Jacobi method. The Jacobi method is well described in Teukolsky *et al.* (1994).

Eigenvectors and eigenvalues can be determined for all correlation matrices, however, some correlation matrices will produce negative eigenvalues and such matrices need to be 'cleaned' before they can be used to generate price change series. Negative eigenvalues indicate that the correlation matrix is faulty or non-sensical. Non-sensical correlation matrices will give an erroneous VAR. Non-sensical correlation matrices result from faulty measurement of correlations. Avoiding faulty measurement of correlations and cleaning non-sensical correlation matrices is discussed in the appendix to this chapter.

The eigenvalues and eigenvectors for the correlation matrix for Portfolio 1 (given in Chapter 2) are shown in Table 3.7.

Table 3.7 shows the vertical eigenvector for each asset along with an eigenvalue for each asset. Looked at in this way, each eigenvector consists of a number of elements with one element for each asset. This visualisation of eigenvectors helps in understanding the equation for producing correlated random price changes.

Table 3.7   Eigenvalues and eigenvectors for Portfolio 1

	Eigenvalues	Eigenvectors Gold	Sterling	Rand
Gold	0.908	0.687	0.622	0.375
Sterling	1.123	0.075	0.453	−0.888
Rand	0.969	−0.723	0.638	0.265

Generating Correlated Random Price Changes

A series of correlated random price changes are generated for each asset, using the following equation:

$$x_k = \sum_i^Z \sqrt{\lambda_i}.x_{norm}.v_{ki}.\sigma_k$$

where: x_k = correlated random price change for asset k with a normal distribution and the volatility of the asset k

$\sqrt{\lambda_i}$ = square root of the eigenvalue for the ith asset

x_{norm} = random price change from a normally distributed series (see above for producing a series of random numbers with a normal distribution)

v_{ki} = the kth element of the eigenvector for the ith asset

σ_k = volatility of the kth asset

For example, for gold in Portfolio 1, the first two correlated random price changes would be generated as shown in Table 3.8 (remembering that the standard deviation (volatility) for gold is 0.5532). For sterling, using the same random numbers and a volatility of 0.6012 the price changes generated are shown in Table 3.9.

The correlated price changes generated are then applied to the portfolio of assets in the same way as for historic simulation. VAR is also determined as for historic simulation, i.e. the portfolio value changes are sorted and the percentile corresponding with the desired level of confidence is the VAR of the portfolio.

Calculating VAR with Monte Carlo Simulation

VAR for a linear portfolio (portfolio containing no options) calculated with the Monte Carlo simulation should be identical to that calculated with the covariance

Table 3.8

Normalised random price changes	Calculation of correlated price change	Correlated price change of gold
1 −0.5 1.5	$(\sqrt{0.908} \times 1.0 \times 0.687 \times 0.5532)+$ $(\sqrt{1.123} \times -0.5 \times 0.622 \times 0.5532)+$ $(\sqrt{0.969} \times 1.5 \times 0.375 \times 0.5532)$	0.486
2 −0.5 −0.1	$(\sqrt{0.908} \times 2.0 \times 0.687 \times 0.5532)+$ $(\sqrt{1.123} \times -0.5 \times 0.622 \times 0.5532)+$ $(\sqrt{0.969} \times -0.1 \times 0.375 \times 0.5532)$	0.522

Table 3.9

Normalised random price changes	Calculation of correlated price change	Correlated price change of Sterling
1 −0.5 1.5	$(\sqrt{0.908} \times 1.0 \times 0.075 \times 0.6012)+$ $(\sqrt{1.123} \times -0.5 \times 0.453 \times 0.6012)+$ $(\sqrt{0.969} \times 1.5 \times -0.888 \times 0.6012)$	−0.890
2 −0.5 −0.1	$(\sqrt{0.908} \times 2.0 \times 0.075 \times 0.6012)+$ $(\sqrt{1.123} \times -0.5 \times 0.453 \times 0.6012)+$ $(\sqrt{0.969} \times -0.1 \times -0.888 \times 0.6012)$	−0.006

approach. In fact, calculating VAR using the covariance technique is a good check on the accuracy of the implementation of the Monte Carlo technique. If the two methods give different results for a linear portfolio then something is wrong with the implementation of one, or both, of the methods.

The VAR for Portfolio 1 calculated using the Monte Carlo approach gives a mean VAR of $41,440 over 20 runs using 9,000 price change events. This compares to $41,470 with the covariance model. These results are 0.07% apart. The standard deviation of the VARs produced over the 20 runs was $943 with maximum and minimum VARs being within ± 6% of the mean result. In practice a convergence of ± 5% is typically required.

VAR for Options

Taking the same Rand option as considered in Chapter 2 on covariance, i.e. a sold at-the-money (ATM) option for delivery of $2m worth of Rand with one month to expiry. In Chapter 2 we had calculated the VAR as $19,000 and had noted that the covariance technique could not cope with option gamma. The approach used to incorporate options was to include option sensitivities (the 'Greeks') in the covariance calculation as pseudo assets.

With Monte Carlo simulation the same sensitivity-based approach can be used. The approach of using sensitivities, instead of positions, is often used with Monte Carlo and the historical simulation techniques to reduce the number of risk factors required to represent the portfolio. The use of sensitivities allows thousands of options with the same basic characteristics (i.e. same underlying asset) to be reduced to the three/four risk factors or option sensitivities. This technique can massively reduce the computational effort required to calculate VAR. However, some accuracy will be sacrificed, as discussed below.

To do this, each of the sensitivities (the 'Greeks', see Chapter 2 for a brief description) are treated as separate assets, or more correctly, as separate risk factors. A percentage price change series is created for each of the option's underlying risk factors. The change in the option price can then be approximated using the following equation, which is a Taylor series expansion of the option pricing function.[2] A price change series can be created as long as the volatility of each risk factor is known along with the correlations (this information is also required for the covariance approach).

$$\Delta P_o = \delta.\Delta u + \frac{\gamma}{2}.\Delta u^2 + V.\Delta v + \rho.\Delta r + \theta.\Delta t$$

where: ΔP_o = change in option value
 $\delta.\Delta u$ = delta times the change in value of the underlying asset
 $\frac{\gamma}{2}.\Delta u^2$ = half the gamma times the square of the change in the value of the underlying asset
 $V.\Delta v$ = vega times the change in the implied volatility of the underlying asset
 $\rho.\Delta r$ = rho times the change in the risk free rate
 $\theta.\Delta t$ = theta times the change in time being considered, in the case of VAR with a one-day holding period, the change in time is one day. However, as the value change of the option with time is a known quantity it should be left out of the calculation.

The covariance estimate of VAR for the option included all the risk factors but could not account for gamma. Therefore if the Monte Carlo simulation is run using all the 'Greeks' except gamma then it should give the same result as the covariance estimate. Table 3.10 shows that this is in fact true. However, as can be seen in Table 3.10, significantly different VARs are produced dependent on which terms of the Taylor expansion are chosen. If a sensitivity approach is used then all the 'Greeks' should be used (this generally excludes theta).

From Table 3.10 you will note that the inclusion of the gamma sensitivity adds hardly anything to the calculated VAR. This is because the basic sensitivity approach does not represent options well when they are ATM (strike price same as underlying

Table 3.10 Option VAR using different approximations

Approximation	VAR ($'000s)
Black–Scholes	−21,245
Delta	−18,691
Delta plus gamma	−18,922
All 'Greeks' – except gamma	−19,338
All 'Greeks'	−19,553

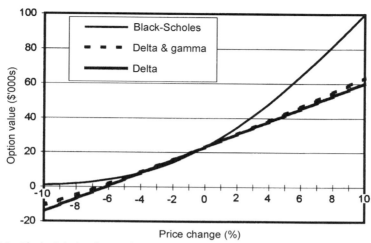

Figure 3.6 Black–Scholes vs 'Greek' approximation

price). The VAR using the Black–Scholes formula which correctly models this option's price behaviour is $21,245 or 9% greater than the 'All Greeks' approximation. This difference would increase for ATM options as they approach the expiry date. The fact that the basic sensitivity approach does not model an at-the-money option's price behaviour well is shown by Figure 3.6 which shows the change in value of the option using Black–Scholes, delta by itself and delta and gamma together as valuation approximations. Figure 3.6 shows that a delta/gamma approximation is only a reasonable approximation for this option over a fairly narrow range of changes in the exchange rate. Therefore, for a volatile currency, such as Rand, a basic sensitivity-based approach can give a very misleading VAR.

VAR for a Delta Hedged Portfolio

The differences in VAR shown above for a single option can be accentuated even more in certain portfolio structures. Consider a portfolio consisting of $1m of Rand, which the trader wishes to hedge against changes in the USD/Rand exchange rate. He decides to hedge the portfolio by selling a currency option. He sells the option described in the section above. As the option is at-the-money it has a fractional delta of 0.5. Therefore selling a Rand/USD currency option with a notional $2m will make the portfolio insensitive to small changes in the Rand/USD exchange rate, i.e. the portfolio is delta hedged. Table 3.11 shows the VAR calculated by Monte Carlo simulation using the same sensitivity approximations for the option as in the previous section.

Table 3.11 gives some interesting results. Again, the VAR calculated using the Black–Scholes formula is greater than the 'All Greeks' approximation. This time the difference is larger; the Black–Scholes VAR is 44% greater than the VAR

Table 3.11 VAR using different approximations –
Rand position ($1m) delta hedged with an option

Approximation	VAR ($)
Black–Scholes	−7,366
Delta	−158
Delta plus gamma	−392
All 'Greeks' – except gamma	−5,116
All 'Greeks'	−5,206

calculated using the sensitivity-based approach. This demonstrates again the shortfall of the sensitivity-based approach for certain option portfolios.

Other interesting results can be seen in Table 3.11. Looking at the delta and delta plus gamma figures it can be seen that the inclusion of gamma makes little difference to the VAR. As noted previously, the two rho sensitivities only have a marginal impact on the VAR. This leads us to the conclusion that the vega risk factor is of greater importance than gamma in this portfolio. Vega is the risk factor dependent on the volatility of the implied volatility; the volatility of the implied volatility for this option is estimated at 6.8%. This is an order of magnitude greater than the volatility of the exchange rate. Therefore, even though the vega sensitivity of the option is small, i.e. only 1/20 of the delta, if the portfolio is delta hedged vega can become the most significant risk factor in the portfolio.

Improving the Sensitivity Approximation

Like most approximations, the basic sensitivity approach to calculating VAR can be improved. The sensitivity approximation described so far fails to capture an option's price behaviour because it is sampling that behaviour at a single point. A much improved estimation of VAR can be obtained by using weighted sensitivities. At this point it should be noted that this is only necessary for delta and gamma; the other sensitivities behave in a linear manner.

First, delta and gamma are measured for various changes in the price of the underlying asset. Then weighted deltas and gammas can be used in the Monte Carlo simulation by interpolating between the various deltas and gammas depending on the price change under consideration.

For example, for the option discussed in this chapter, Table 3.12 shows delta and gamma at three points, i.e. at-the-money (where it is now) and then for a 1% change in the underlying exchange rate either side of the current position. If an exchange rate change of 0.75% is encountered then delta and gamma used will be the sum of 0.75 times the +1% delta and gamma plus 0.25 times the 0% delta and gamma. If a

Table 3.12   Delta and gamma for various changes in the underlying exchange rate

% change	−1	0	1
Delta	0.001441	0.001681	0.001922
Gamma	0.000022	0.000022	0.000022

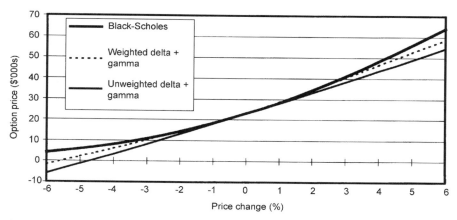

Figure 3.7   Weighted vs unweighted 'Greeks'

price change of greater than 1% is encountered then the 1% sensitivities are used.

The linear interpolation between the points described here could be improved upon as well if so desired. However, this is unlikely to yield any worthwhile improvement in accuracy. Figure 3.7 shows the improvement yielded by the use of weighted 'Greeks'. The anticipated improvement in the VAR calculated is borne out by Table 3.13 which shows that the various approximations of VAR are now all much closer to the Black–Scholes figure than with unweighted delta and gamma. The All 'Greeks' approximation is now within 3.5% of the Black–Scholes VAR.

Table 3.13   Option VAR using weighted 'Greeks'

Approximation	VAR ($)
Black–Scholes	−21,245
Delta	−21,286
Delta plus gamma	−21,514
All 'Greeks' − except gamma	−21,778
All 'Greeks'	−21,989

As a word of caution, the choice of points at which to measure the sensitivities is critical. An inappropriate choice can lead to the calculated VAR being just as far from the true VAR as when using unweighted sensitivities.

SUMMARY

This chapter has introduced and described the two main simulation approaches to calculating VAR: historical simulation and Monte Carlo simulation. Both these simulation approaches have the ability to cope with any type of option which gives them a major advantage over the covariance approach. However, the two simulation techniques differ fundamentally in the assumptions they make about the way financial instruments behave. In particular, historical simulation makes no assumptions about the form of price change distributions for financial assets, whilst Monte Carlo simulation assumes price changes are normally distributed, just as with the covariance approach.

This chapter has also explored sensitivity based techniques for reducing computational power required and a method for improving the accuracy of sensitivity-based approximations, i.e. the use of weighted deltas and gammas.

It should be noted that Monte Carlo simulation is just one method of simulating asset price changes. Monte Carlo simulation is based on random numbers which gives rise to a potential problem with the technique. As the events generated by a Monte Carlo simulation are random, there is no guarantee that the events required to produce an accurate VAR are actually generated. This is normally considered to be a minimal problem given that a large number of events are used. An alternative approach to Monte Carlo simulation is to *deterministically* generate the events to be tested. A deterministic approach avoids the possibility that required events are not generated. Deterministic approaches also avoid the convergence problems associated with a randomly generated set of events. Deterministic simulations are outside the scope of this book, however, for further information a good starting place is the work of Stein (1987) using Latin Hypercube sampling.

NOTES

1. The inverse cumulative distribution function assumes that it is converting cumulative probabilities from a standard normal distribution, i.e. a normal distribution with a mean of 0 and a standard deviation of 1.
2. Taylor series expansions can have an infinite number of terms for each of the risk factors. In practice the terms with higher powers often add little accuracy and are thus disregarded. The Taylor expansion given here is that classically used for vanilla options. Only the first two terms with respect to the underlying are used. As the other risk factors are all linear with respect to the option price only the first term for each needs to be included.

APPENDIX

The Cumulative Normal Distribution Function

Where a ready-made computer-based solution is not available, the cumulative normal distribution function can be estimated to four decimal places using the polynomial approximation given below (Abramowitz and Stegun, 1972):

When $x \geq 0$:

$$N(x) = 1 - N'(x).(ak + bk^2 + ck^3)$$

When $x < 0$:

$$N(x) = 1 - N(-x)$$

where: $N(x) =$ cumulative normal distribution value for x
$N'(x) = 1/\sqrt{2\pi}.e^{x^2/2}$ (This is the standard normal distribution function)
$k = 1/(1 + \gamma.x)$
$\gamma = 0.33267$
$a = 0.4361836$
$b = -0.1201676$
$c = 0.9372980$

For a Monte Carlo simulation we start with the cumulative probability, $N(x)$, and need to find x. This can be done by using an iterative trial and error numerical procedure for x, such as the Newton–Raphson technique.

Derivation of Eigenvectors and Eigenvalues

It is not recommended that the reader attempts to derive eigenvectors and values directly himself. Instead, a technique such as the Jacobi method should be used. However, for those interested, eigenvectors and eigenvalues can be found as follows[1]:

Eigenvalues can be found by solving the following equation for the correlation matrix:

$$\text{Determinant } (A - \lambda.I_n) = 0$$

where: $A =$ correlation matrix (an $n \times n$ matrix)
$\lambda =$ eigenvalue matrix
$I_n =$ identity matrix (with dimensions $n \times n$)

An $n \times n$ matrix will have n eigenvalues, one for each asset. With certain correlation matrices the eigenvalues produced will involve the square root of negative numbers and will yield unusable eigenvalues involving complex numbers. The matrix cleaning procedure described below will alter the correlation matrix to remove the faulty information contained within the matrix.

Eigenvectors can be found by finding the non-trivial solutions of the set of simultaneous equations denoted by:

$$(A - \lambda_i.I)v_i = 0$$

where: $v_i = $ the eigenvector for eigenvalue and asset, i.

Non-sensical Correlation Matrices

Chapter 3 mentions that non-sensical correlation matrices will be created on occasion, particularly when correlations are invented. In fact non-sensical correlation matrices can be created if any of the four rules below are broken. The fact that a correlation matrix is non-sensical is indicated by it having negative eigenvalues. To use more formal mathematical terminology, in order to be valid, a correlation matrix must be positive semi-definite. That is to say:

$$V.C.V^T \geq 0$$

where: $V = $ row vector of VARs for each individual position
              $C = $ matrix of correlations
              $V^T = $ transpose of vector V

You will recognise this equation as part of the equation for calculating VAR for a portfolio, introduced in Chapter 2. If VAR is the volatility of the portfolio, the equation above is the variance of the portfolio. Therefore, for the correlation matrix to be valid, the above calculation must not give a negative variance.

As an illustration, consider an equivalent way of stating the VAR matrix formula to calculate the VAR of a portfolio:

$$\text{Portfolio VAR} = \sqrt{\sum P_i^2.\sigma_i^2 + 2\sum_i \sum_j P_i.P_j.\sigma_i\sigma_j.\rho_{i,j}} \geq 0$$

For a simple three-square correlation matrix and taking care to avoid the square root of negative numbers, the equation above implies that:

$$P_1^2\sigma_1^2 + P_2^2\sigma_2^2 + P_3^2\sigma_3^2 + 2(P_1\sigma_1 P_2\sigma_2\rho_{12} + P_1\sigma_1 P_3\sigma_3\rho_{13} + P_2\sigma_2 P_3\sigma_3\rho_{23}) \geq 0$$

Now set all position amounts and volatilities equal to one, then:

$$2(\rho_{12} + \rho_{13} + \rho_{23}) \geq -3$$

Now let $\rho_{12} = \rho_{13} = -1$ then $\rho_{23} \geq 0.5$. Therefore, $\rho_{23} < 0.5$ is not possible. The reader can confirm this with the Covar.xls spreadsheet.

Correlation matrices which produce negative eigenvalues are the result of problems with the way in which the correlations were derived. Positive semi-definite correlation matrices will be produced as long as none of the following rules are broken; the price change history from which the correlations are calculated must:

1. Contain no missing days of data.
2. Have more days (or samples) of data than the number of risk factors in the correlation matrix, otherwise it will be possible to construct risk free portfolios. Interested readers could try to demonstrate this fact to themselves with a small portfolio of two assets.
3. Have the same number of days of data for all risk factors, otherwise the correlations may not be consistent.
4. Have correlations derived from price change series in which the prices were recorded at the same time. One of the commonest reasons for non-sensical correlation matrices is sampling timing problems with the underlying price series.

These rules are likely to be broken if correlations are taken from external sources, estimated from other data (e.g. spread volatilities) and almost certainly when correlations are 'invented' to reflect a risk manager's view of market behaviour, in lieu of available price change histories.

Cleaning Correlation Matrices

If the rules above are broken (and they often are in practice) then the correlation matrix can be cleaned using the following process to remove negative eigenvalues. It should be noted this process effectively removes information from the resultant correlation matrix as negative eigenvalues are set to zero. If the eigenvalue has a high value (perhaps representing a weighting of greater than 10%) then the risk manager must decide whether he is happy to lose this information or whether it would be better to clean the original time series from which the correlation matrix was derived. Negative eigenvalues can be handled as follows:

- Set negative eigenvalues to zero.
- Calculate new correlation matrix. The new correlation matrix is then used in place of the original.
- Generate new eigenvalues and eigenvectors from the new correlation matrix.

This process effectively scales up the valid eigenvalues and eigenvectors to make up for the negative eigenvalues that have been removed.

In the above process, the new correlation matrix can be calculated from the following equation, after setting all negative eigenvalues to zero:

$$C = E.\lambda.E^T$$

where: $C =$ new correlation matrix

$E \,\&\, E^T =$ matrix of eigenvectors and its transpose

$\lambda =$ eigenvalues matrix, i.e. a matrix with the eigenvalues on the diagonal

The new correlation matrix, C, is unrealistic if its diagonal elements are not equal to 1. If this is the case the new correlation matrix must be normalised using the following equation:

$$C' = 1/\sqrt{D}.C.1/\sqrt{D}$$

where: $C' =$ normalised new correlation matrix

$1/\sqrt{D} =$ a diagonal matrix with diagonal elements equal to $1/\sqrt{(D_i}$ where D_i is the ith diagonal element of the matrix C.

In practice correlation matrices are often *not* positive semi-definite when the matrix contains correlations across different markets. One possible, though not theoretically sound, solution to this problem is to take care measuring correlations within individual markets and then assume that there is a zero correlation between markets.

NOTE

1. There are many sources for examples of the derivation of eigenvalues and eigenvectors, e.g. Teukolsky *et al.*, 1994. Another more general introduction to mathematical techniques for engineers is Jordan and Smith (1994).

4

Measurement of volatility and correlation

INTRODUCTION

When calculating VAR we are trying to model the way financial assets behave. In particular we are trying to capture the behaviour of price changes – volatility – and the extent that the prices of any pair of assets change together – correlation. As with all models, they approximate the real world. Or to put it another way, in order to make the calculations tractable, certain simplifying assumptions are made about the real world. To ensure that the end result has meaning it is critical that we investigate the effect of the assumptions made on the calculated VAR.

Much has been written on the assumption of normality which is the single biggest assumption made by most VAR models. Less has been written on whether this assumption invalidates the VAR model when tested against real price change series. This chapter discusses the assumption of normality and its impact on the effectiveness of VAR models. It also introduces the need for stress testing to cope with rare events that VAR is not designed, or expected, to cover.

One of the requirements of VAR models is that they respond to changes in price change behaviour of the assets in the portfolio. There are a variety of different ways of measuring volatility, all of which respond differently to changes in behaviour. This chapter describes the main volatility measurement methods, their behaviour and which method should be used depending on the objective.

NON-NORMALITY

The assumption of normality is the largest assumption made in many VAR models, particularly the covariance and Monte Carlo models. As with naturally occurring distributions, financial price change histories are not perfectly normally distributed. The assumption of normality is used as it allows for the easy quantification of volatility at any required confidence level, simply by multiplying the one standard deviation value of volatility by the required factor.

The normality assumption specifically implies that successive price changes are independent of each other and that there is as much probability of an upward change in prices as there is of a downward one, i.e. the distribution of price changes is symmetrical around the mean. The first requirement states that financial asset prices changes are not serially correlated, i.e. that the price change on a given day is not dependent on the previous day(s) price changes. Neither of these requirements are in fact satisfied for financial assets.

Non-normality can be largely characterised by two types of behaviour, kurtosis and skew. Kurtosis describes the extent to which distributions are taller and have fatter tails than a standard normal distribution. Skew describes the extent to which a distribution leans to one side, i.e. is not symmetrical around a mean of zero. Both these behaviours are described below.

Fat Tails

One of the most often commented on aspects of financial price series is that they contain many 'outliers', i.e. price changes of a magnitude of several standard deviations. These large outlying price changes, when taken together, are known as 'fat tails'. In Figure 4.1 the tail of the price change distribution for gold for the five years to 26 November 1996 is shown. The kurtosis displayed by gold is typical of that found in financial asset price change distributions.

The greatest downward move is 5.9 standard deviations from the mean. The probability of a 5.9 standard deviation price change is less than 1 in 500 million observations, or days. The five years of data contains 1,305 daily price changes so the probability of such a large move occurring in this sample is almost zero. In fact there are several extreme price changes in this sample.

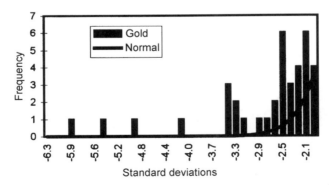

Figure 4.1   Gold distribution – tail

The probability of a 3 SD or larger move is approximately 0.25%. Therefore in an average period of five years of price changes it would be expected that there would be approximately three moves greater than 3 SDs; in fact there were a total of 20 such price moves. If the historic data sample had only a few observations (say 100 or 200) it could be claimed that it was an unrepresentative sample but with five years of data this is extremely unlikely to be the case. Because the number of outliers is so large in comparison to what would be expected in a truly normal distribution, financial price change distributions are said to have 'fat tails', i.e. more price changes experienced at the tails of the distribution than are expected.

Fat tails have the effect of increasing the volatility of the asset. For example if price moves of greater than 3 SDs are stripped out of the distribution for gold, the standard deviation is reduced from 0.553% to 0.475%. Therefore the fat tails have a significant effect on the volatility of the asset and the resultant VAR. This does not mean that VAR calculated using the assumption of normality properly takes account of 'fat tails'. The standard deviation, as illustrated above, is effectively overstated due to extreme price movements. However, this does not mean that 1.65 SDs will be overstated, relative to a 'trimmed' distribution (extreme price changes removed) which will depend on the density (number of readings) and shape of the fat tail. At 95% confidence (1.65 SD) the volatility may be over or understated. However, at 99% confidence, 2.33 standard deviations will almost always understate the volatility, as a normal distribution really has a very low density at this point, whereas financial price change series almost always have significantly heavier tails than a normal distribution.

Skewed Distributions

Another type of non-normality that is experienced in the financial markets is a skewed distribution. A skewed distribution is one in which the distribution is not symmetrical around the mean. Figure 4.2 shows a negatively skewed distribution, with a characteristically long tail to the left. Skewed distributions are sometimes caused by a prolonged move in the value of an asset in one direction. Prolonged 'bull' and 'bear' markets may create a skewed distribution. Persistent upward or downward moves in the value of an asset will certainly cause the distribution to be skewed.

Skews in financial asset distributions are often temporary phenomena, rather than a fundamental aspect of the asset's behaviour (with the exception of options, which are always skewed). It should be noted that VAR calculated using historical simulation does not assume that the portfolio distribution is symmetrical. Therefore, any natural skew in a distribution will be taken into account in the resultant VAR. Another approach is to assume that a skewed distribution *is* due to a temporarily trending market. With this view the skew should be removed from the asset's distribution. The skew can be removed by using antithetics which are merely the opposite of all price changes in the historical series. Using antithetics

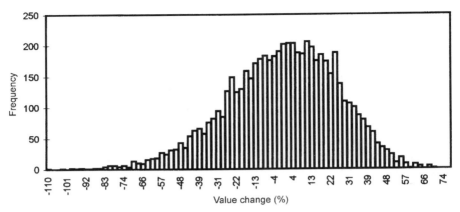

Figure 4.2 Distribution for a sold option — negative skew

doubles the number of price change samples available and will ensure that any skew is removed. The use of antithetics will transform the original distribution to a symmetrical distribution with a mean of zero. Therefore using antithetics will build in the assumption of a zero mean.

Assuming a Zero Mean

The actual mean is not normally used in the calculation of VAR using the covariance or Monte Carlo methods, i.e. the standard deviation is measured from the mean, whether zero or not. This builds in the assumption that the mean of price change distributions is zero. The mean of the daily price change distribution of most financial price series is very close to zero, therefore this is a reasonable assumption. The error introduced by this assumption is small as long as the mean is close to zero.

For longer holding periods the mean is far less likely to be zero. For equities and commodities the mean will be positive as their prices will tend to increase over time (i.e. have a positive price drift); for other assets a non-zero mean may result from a longer-term change in relative value of one currency versus another, i.e. an imbalance in the two economies. Therefore, for longer time horizons the volatility measure should take account of the actual mean of the distribution. For example, if a distribution has a mean price change of 0.5 and a 95% confident measure of volatility of 2, then the volatility to be used in calculating VAR should be $0.5 - 2 = -1.5$.

Modelling Actual Distributions

There is no reason why it has to be assumed that financial price change distributions are normally distributed. A normal distribution is assumed because it has been found to lead to reasonably accurate VAR models. Assuming normality also has the important advantage that the distribution can be described easily by measures such as the standard deviation. For most traded financial assets (not including options) the assumption of normality is unlikely to lead to significant errors in the calculation of VAR.

Any potential errors resulting from the assumption of normality become increasingly insignificant for portfolios as the number of assets in the portfolio grows, except for portfolios containing options. A portfolio of assets effectively dilutes the non-normality of individual assets. Thus the portfolio will move towards a normal distribution as the number of non-option assets increases; this is a function of the central limit theorem (see most standard texts on statistics) and works better across asset classes than within a single, highly-correlated asset class such as bonds. Therefore, it can be dangerous to assume normality for a portfolio of highly-correlated assets.

In all cases where non-normality is suspected, the actual historical price change data series must be examined to determine the nature of the non-normal behaviour. The mean will be the most important piece of information along with the kurtosis and skew, which have values of 0, 3 and 0 respectively, for a standard normal distribution. For most financial asset distributions the kurtosis is normally at least twice that of the standard normal distribution and can be as high as 100 times greater. Subsequent sections in this chapter will argue that most financial assets do display a degree of abnormality but that the experienced lack of normality does not significantly impact the accuracy of the resultant VAR calculations.

If, after analysis, it is found that the assumption of normality is not acceptable, then an alternative distribution model can be used if the asset represents a significant proportion of the bank's portfolio. One sophisticated distribution modelling technique is the Ramberg et al. (1979) method, which creates a model of an actual distribution. If a distribution fitting technique is used then the standard deviation used in the covariance calculation is replaced by a price change corresponding to the required level of confidence. Alternatively, the price change corresponding to the required level of confidence can be read directly from an actual distribution (historical simulation – see Chapter 3). If this approach is used then no assumptions are made with regard to the form of the distribution. It should be noted that using a more sophisticated distribution model, such as the RTDM model mentioned above, will inevitably increase the computations required to calculate VAR. A trade-off must be made between increasing the accuracy of the VAR model and the reduction in ease of calculation of the VAR model.

Options and Normality

It should be noted that the assumption of normality is not reasonable for options and other structured derivatives containing optionality. Options and structured derivatives have very definite non-normal distributions which must be modelled correctly in order to produce a reasonable estimate of VAR. For complex structured derivatives, such as multi barrier options, it is unlikely that it will be possible to fit an analytically solvable distribution model to the actual distribution. Most banks calculate VAR for such products by generating a price change distribution either from historical price series of the underlying assets and revaluation of the option (historical simulation) or using a Monte Carlo simulation. The price change distribution can be generated either by using the valuation model of the product, or by using risk factor ('Greek') approximations (see Chapters 2, 3 and 5 for examples of this).

VAR and Stress Testing

The non-normal behaviour of financial markets has several implications for the limitations and use of VAR numbers. The large number (relative to statistical expectation) of extreme price moves in the financial markets means that using VAR alone as a means of deciding whether the bank is adequately capitalised is not sufficient. The impact of extreme price changes can only be properly investigated through the use of deterministic stress testing (see Chapter 6); VAR is a good measure of the underlying day-to-day riskiness of a portfolio. The impact of extreme price moves is a separate risk management technique and is an essential companion to VAR.

VAR calculates the potential loss on a portfolio with a given degree of confidence in what can be described as normal continuous markets, i.e. in a financial market that is not subject to frequent price movements of several standard deviations. In a time of market stress, VAR ceases to provide the required level of certainty with regard to the size of potential losses. If there is a market crash VAR cannot be taken as a guide as to how much money may be lost. The 1987 equities crash in London was a 20 SD event. Having enough capital to survive even a 6 SD move would not have been sufficient.

MEASURING VOLATILITY

Thus far, volatility has been presented as a given number in the chapters on calculating VAR. In order to build an effective VAR model it is essential to understand volatility and the behaviour of volatility models. The correct choice of volatility model will be one of the most important factors in determining the effectiveness of your VAR model.

Describing Asset Returns

Before discussing different volatility models, it makes sense to think briefly about asset returns and the connection with the calculation of VAR. When calculating

VAR we want to estimate the maximum negative return (loss) on a portfolio with a given degree of confidence. The following discussion shows why VAR for a single asset is taken to be equal to the volatility of the asset (multiplied by the position value).

Consider an equity, whose value is expected to increase over time but there is no certainty as to its value tomorrow. The return on an asset can be expressed mathematically to take account of both the uncertainty in tomorrow's price and its expected return over a period of time:

$$R = \mu.\Delta t + \epsilon.\sigma.\sqrt{\Delta t}$$

where Δt is the period of time over which the return is being measured. If we now assume we are interested in returns over one day then:

$$R = \mu + \epsilon.\sigma$$

where: $R =$ return on asset (will have same units as μ and σ). For the purposes of calculating VAR, we will define the return on an asset as the percentage price change of the asset. For clarity, the rest of this book refers to percentage price changes, rather than returns, which can be defined in numerous ways.

$\mu =$ the expected return on the asset.

$\sigma =$ the volatility of the return (one standard deviation), also expressed in the same units as the return, i.e. percentage price changes.

$\epsilon =$ a random draw from the return distribution of the asset. If assumed to be normally distributed, then ϵ is drawn from a normal distribution with a standard deviation equal to the return volatility for the asset.

Assuming that returns are not skewed, the mean value of the return distribution will be equal to the expected return of the asset. For example, if an equity generally increases in value by 10% each year, then the expected daily return is 10/260 = 0.038% (assuming 260 working days in a year). This is also the *mean* of the return distribution. If we know that the annual volatility of the equity is 20% then the daily volatility of the equity is:

$$\frac{20}{\sqrt{260}} = 1.24\%$$

As can be seen from this example, the daily expected return is tiny when compared with the daily volatility. Therefore, when calculating VAR for a one-day time horizon, it is reasonable to assume that the mean is zero and is usually assumed to be so. Now the above equation reduces to:

$$R = \epsilon.\sigma$$

As ϵ is a random draw from a normal distribution we can now move to calculate VAR for a single asset. It is a property of the normal distribution that if ϵ is equal to -1.645 then we know that 95% of returns will be less than $1.645 \times \sigma$. Thus we have demonstrated how the above equation allows us to calculate VAR.

Note that the volatility in the equations above is the volatility of returns or percentage price changes – not the volatility of the asset price.

Many institutions implement VAR using the assumption that asset returns are log-normally distributed rather than normally distributed. This means that the natural logarithm of the asset returns are normally distributed. There is a fair wealth of studies to indicate that this is in fact true. Nonetheless, it makes little difference to the calculation of VAR unless the volatility of the asset is particularly large and the time horizon being used is long. Therefore this chapter assumes that asset returns are normally distributed; the empirical study, described at the end of this chapter, indicates that this assumption works just as well as the assumption of log normality for the calculation of daily VAR.

VAR for Longer Time Horizons

Assuming that the mean is zero would clearly not be a reasonable assumption when calculating VAR for a longer time horizon. The mean should not be assumed to be zero and should be taken into account when calculating VAR.

From the first equation given above, it can be seen that the annual return for an asset can be worked out from the one-day return; the mean value can be scaled up by the number of working days. The volatility can also be scaled up by the square root of the number of days. The equation implies that the change in an assets value is simply proportional to time and will grow indefinitely as shown in Figure 4.3.

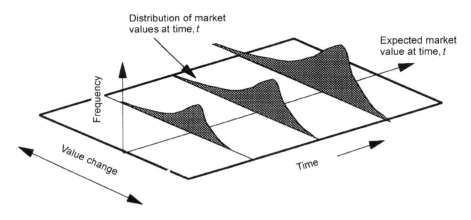

Figure 4.3   Volatility increases with time

This is not true for many assets. Both the value of many assets and their volatility are subject to 'mean reversion'. Mean reversion is a behaviour that means that an asset's value will vary in a range about an observable long-term average, rather than grow indefinitely. Interest rates are a prime example of a class of risk factors which are subject to mean reversion.

The impact of mean reversion is that volatility (and therefore VAR) cannot be scaled up from one day volatility to one-year volatility. In practice it is usually a reasonable approach to scale by the square root of time, for scaling up from one-day to 10-day volatility. As the ratio of scaling period to original period becomes larger so does the potential error introduced. As a rule of thumb a ratio of up to 10 will give a sufficiently accurate result. Therefore, the 10-day volatility could be worked out from the one-day volatility, as follows:

$$Vol_{10\,day} = \sqrt{10}.Vol_{1\,day}$$

Therefore, the 10-day volatility of gold = $0.5536\% \times 3.1623 = 1.75\%$. This method tends to underestimate volatility out to about 20 days and overestimate volatility for longer periods due to mean reversion.

Measuring the 10-day volatility directly from the data series is a more accurate method. This method, although more accurate, requires a much longer price history than the scaling approach described above. The 10-day volatility can be measured directly from the price series, as long as there are sufficient 10-day periods in the price series. As a rule of thumb at least 30 non-overlapping periods should be used, which implies a minimum of 300 days of data. Therefore, the problem with directly measuring volatilities over longer time horizons is the number of price changes required. Non-overlapping periods are required to reduce auto-correlation in the volatility estimate.

One technique used to generate more independent price changes from a small sample set is called bootstrapping. The reader should be aware that this technique destroys mean reversion and is therefore not applicable unless mean reversion is known not to be significant in the return distribution of the asset under consideration.

Volatility Models

There are a number of different ways of measuring volatility, all of which behave differently and which therefore directly impact on the behaviour of the VAR model. The following commonly used volatility models are discussed:

- Standard deviation.
- Simple moving average.
- Percentile method/historical simulation.

- Exponentially weighted moving average.
- GARCH.

Standard Deviation

The standard deviation measure of volatility is the method most directly associated with the normal distribution. The standard deviation measures the dispersion of the distribution, i.e. the average distance of a price change from the mean value. The formula can be given in several ways:

$$\sigma = \sqrt{(X - \bar{X})^2}$$

where: $\sigma =$ standard deviation.
$X =$ the percentage price change series, i.e. $X = x_1,\ x_2,\ x_3 \ldots x_n$ where x_n is one price change from the series.
$\bar{X} =$ the mean of the series (a bar denotes the 'average' or mean value of a series of numbers)

The equation can also be written:

$$\sigma = \sqrt{\frac{\sum(X - \mu)^2}{n}} \quad \text{for the whole population, or}$$

$$\sigma = \sqrt{\frac{\sum(X - \mu)^2}{n-1}} \quad \text{for a sample of the whole population}$$

where: $\mu =$ mean value of series
$n =$ number of percentage price changes in the series

The first equation assumes that the data used to calculate the standard deviation is the whole population and the second equation assumes that the standard deviation is being calculated on a sample of the whole population. In practice there will be very little difference between the volatilities calculated by the two methods. Those people who believe that volatility is constantly changing will prefer the first equation, those that believe that there is some longer term 'true' volatility, will prefer the second method. Subsequent sections in this chapter discuss whether volatility is in fact constant for financial asset series, or not. From these equations it can be seen that the standard deviation is the square root of the average of the squared distances of each percentage price change from the mean.

Figure 4.4 shows how VAR behaves when the standard deviation is used as a measure of volatility. The Rand/sterling exchange rate is used throughout the discussion on volatility models. The graph shows the percentage price changes in

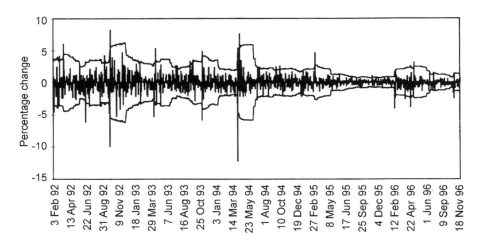

Figure 4.4   Rand/Sterling exchange rate – VAR vs price change (standard deviation – 50-day observation period)

the exchange rate, plotted as the columns, versus the VAR (shown as an upper and lower band around the price changes over a four-year period). The VAR band is calculated with 95% confidence. The standard deviation was calculated from a rolling observation period of 50 days.

The observation period is the number of days (or samples, if a longer horizon is being used) that are used to calculate volatility. Later discussions in this chapter will show that the choice of observation period is one of the most critical factors in determining the behaviour and effectiveness of a VAR model.

In Figure 4.4, the days on which the price change exceeded the VAR estimate can be seen as columns going through the VAR bands. Figure 4.4 shows clearly that the standard deviation measure of volatility increases significantly after a large change in the exchange rate and stays at the new level until the large price change drops out of the observation period.

Figure 4.4 also shows the VAR bands moving up and down as periods of low and high volatility are encountered in the series. The standard deviation is assumed to be an estimate of the true level of volatility which is a constant. Which one of these two views works best for VAR models is discussed with examples in the section below and is based on an empirical analysis of VAR estimates with various assets over a period of time.

Simple Moving Average

The moving average measure of volatility is the same as the standard deviation except that the mean is assumed to be zero. Given that the mean of most price series will be close to zero, the moving average will give a very similar answer to the

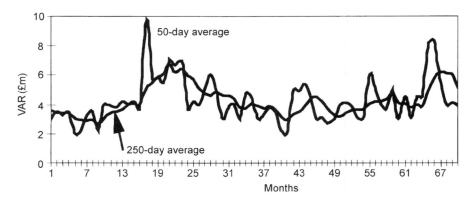

Figure 4.5 Un-weighted moving average

standard deviation and behaves in an almost identical manner. The moving average equation for calculating volatility is:

$$\sigma = \sqrt{\dfrac{\sum\limits_{t=n}^{t=1}(X_t)^2}{n}}$$

where: X_t = percentage price change for day, t ($t = 1$ is the previous day's price change, $t = 2$ is the price change from two days ago, etc.)

n = the number of days over which the moving average is being measured

Figure 4.5 illustrates the behaviour of the moving average measure. The moving average volatility is shown using two different observation periods. It can be seen that the 50-day observation measure responds much faster to changes in the underlying series, whereas the 250-day measure effectively has a delay built into it. Also, the longer the observation period the greater the smoothing effect will be with longer observation periods giving a volatility measure that is far more stable and resistant to short-term changes in the underlying series. The impact of the behaviour illustrated here on VAR models is discussed in the section on empirical analysis of VAR model accuracy (see pages 89–101).

Percentile Method/Historical Simulation

The percentile method is perhaps the most straightforward and makes absolutely no assumption about the form of the underlying series distribution. This method of deriving volatility does not use any equations at all! Volatility is found in exactly the same way as VAR is found in the historical simulation method.

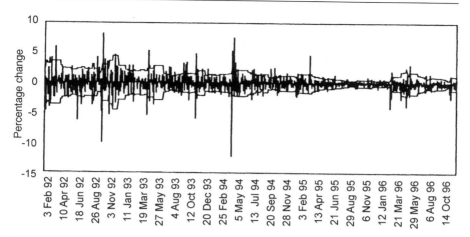

Figure 4.6   Rand/Sterling exchange rate – VAR vs price change (historic – 50-day observation period)

The percentage price change series is simply sorted into order and then divided into percentiles. The volatility is then taken as the price change corresponding to the confidence level required. Figure 4.6 illustrates the behaviour of this method of deriving volatility.

Figure 4.6 shows the characteristic plateaux in VAR created by this volatility model. This method is favoured by those who believe that the assumption of normality compromises the overall VAR model. A number of institutions who use a covariance VAR model use the percentile method to derive their volatilities, thus getting rid of an important part of the normality assumption in their VAR calculations.

Non-constant Volatility

Thus far, the volatility models examined assume that volatility is constant over time and the models therefore assign an equal weight to each day's return. It is generally well accepted, however, that volatilities and correlations in the world of finance are not constant over time, but are almost constantly changing. In fact, financial markets display irregular but frequent step changes in volatilities and correlations, i.e. a period of low volatility followed by a period of high volatility. This is known as volatility clustering. In a volatility cluster, a large return is likely to be followed by more large returns, this means that serial correlation *is* present in financial asset return series. Part of the assumption of normality is that of independence of returns, i.e. that there is no serial correlation in financial asset return series. Return clustering is clearly visible in the Rand/GBP series used throughout this chapter, as it is with most assets.

One explanation for clustering of returns in financial assets is that economic news has an immediate impact on that day's return and a decreasing effect on the returns of subsequent days, i.e. the impact 'decays', normally over a fairly short period of time. This explanation is not entirely consistent with the efficient markets theory which suggests that any new information is immediately reflected in market prices, i.e. there should be no impact on subsequent day's returns.

The presence of serial correlation between returns has important consequences for the estimation of volatility. It means that recent returns will provide more information about the current level of volatility than will older returns. This suggests that one approach to obtaining a volatility model that accurately measures the current level of volatility would be to give a higher weighting to recent returns. With the models discussed so far, only the observation period can be altered and perhaps made shorter to capture only recent behaviour; however, all the methods described above give the same weighting to each return.

The next two volatility models discussed do not assume constant volatility. Both the exponentially weighted model and GARCH assume that serial correlation is present in financial asset return series. As a result, both models weight recent returns more highly than older returns. Therefore, both the exponentially weighted and GARCH models of volatility are *conditional* on recent returns.

Exponentially Weighted Moving Average

The exponentially weighted moving average (EWMA) volatility model has been made famous by J P Morgan. EWMA is an important aspect of the RiskMetrics^{TM} VAR model. EWMA employs a 'decay factor' that is used to weight each day's percentage price change. More recent days receive a heavier weighting than older days. It should also be noted that EWMA is non-parametric, i.e. it does not assume that price changes are normally distributed.

J P Morgan use EWMA as they recognise that volatility is not constant over time and they want a method that will respond quickly to changes in volatility. The equation for deriving volatility using EWMA is:

$$\sigma = \sqrt{(1 - \lambda) \sum_{t=n}^{t=1} \lambda^t (X_t - \mu)^2}$$

where: $\lambda =$ the decay factor. The decay factor determines both the degree of weighting of recent returns and also the speed with which the volatility measure will return to a lower level after a large return. A lower decay factor gives a higher weighting to recent returns and will also allow the volatility measure to quickly drop back to its previous level after a large return.

   $n =$ Number of days used to derive the volatility. As the weighting of each day's price change will never reach zero, n could be set to infinity, see Figure 4.7. In practice, the weightings rapidly reduce to close to zero. With decay factors of 0.94 and 0.97, using the last 50 and 100 days respectively will give good results. $t = 1$ for the previous day's change.

$\mu =$ The mean value of the distribution, which is normally assumed to be zero for daily VAR.

The equation for exponentially weighted volatility can also be stated as:

$$\sigma = \sqrt{\lambda\sigma_{t-1}^2 + (1 - \lambda)X_t^2}$$

This form of the equation is directly comparable to the GARCH equation (see the section on GARCH below). The choice of decay factor is critical and is the main factor determining the performance of the model. Figure 4.7 shows the effective weightings for each day's change for decay factors of 0.94 and 0.97.

J P Morgan's RiskMetrics^{TM} uses a decay factor of 0.94 for its daily volatility and 0.97 for its monthly volatilities. As can be seen from the weightings, a decay factor of 0.94 effectively uses an observation period of about 30 days. The relative weightings of days after this are very low. Whereas with a decay factor of 0.97 the effective observation period is closer to 100 days. A decay factor of 0.97 will, therefore, give a longer-term average volatility. The choice of 0.94 for daily volatilities emphasises that J P Morgan want a measure that is only capturing very recent volatility behaviour in the underlying series. The total number of days of data needed for a given level of accuracy for EWMA is given by:

Required number of data points = log(required accuracy) / log(decay factor)

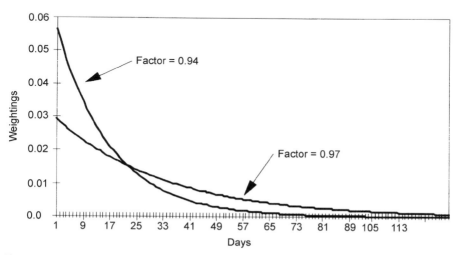

Figure 4.7 Exponential weighting factors

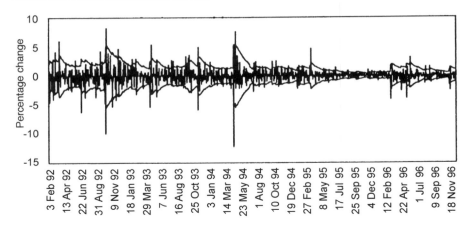

Figure 4.8   Rand/Sterling exchange rate – VAR vs price change (exponential – decay factor 0.94)

Figure 4.8 shows the behaviour of the exponentially weighted measure of volatility with a decay factor of 0.94. It can be seen that EWMA fits much more closely to the underlying series and responds to changes in the underlying series very quickly. For a discussion of whether the use of EWMA produces a more accurate VAR model see the section describing an empirical investigation below.

GARCH

GARCH (generalised autoregressive conditional heteroskedastic) has been used extensively in the financial markets and there are many variations of it. The GARCH method presented here is the original method as first proposed by Bollerslev (1986); subsequent variations have not added significantly to the accuracy given by this original version. The equation for the basic GARCH $(1,1)$[1] model is:

$$\sigma = \sqrt{\omega + \beta\sigma_{t-1}^2 + \alpha X_{t-1}^2}$$

where: σ_{t-1} = volatility for the previous day
α, β and ω are estimated parameters. $\alpha + \beta$ is called the 'persistence' and must not be greater than one (see the discussion of mean reversion below).

Estimating the GARCH parameters is not a simple process. The estimation involves maximising the likelihood function, one of the best known techniques for this is given by Berndt *et al.* (1974). Just as with the Monte Carlo VAR method the calculation of the GARCH parameters must be made to converge on stable values.

This typically requires three years of data. In a typical implementation the GARCH parameters would be recalculated once per month. For a large number of assets this is a significant amount of computation. It is also worth noting that the presence of extreme price changes in the data series can cause problems for the maximum likelihood function, resulting in a lack of convergence.

Perhaps the most interesting and useful feature of the GARCH model is that it embodies 'mean reversion'. Mean reversion refers to the fact that the value of some financial assets will vary about some longer-term value. It is known that interest rates and particularly interest rate spreads display this characteristic. In addition, volatilities also display this behaviour. The two GARCH parameters α and β, taken together (persistence), will determine how long a single price change will affect future forecasts of volatility. The higher the persistence, the longer the price change will affect future volatility estimates. A high persistence number also implies a higher average volatility. Figure 4.9 shows the behaviour of the GARCH model for the Rand/Sterling exchange rate. It also shows that the GARCH model responds even more aggressively to changes in the underlying series than the EWMA model. Also, the mean reversion can clearly be seen towards the right-hand side of the diagram; there is a period during which the volatility in the underlying series reduces to close to zero. Unlike the EWMA model, however, the GARCH-based VAR does not follow the underlying series down. Instead, the GARCH-based VAR stays up at a longer-term mean value and refuses to go below it.

Figure 4.10 compares the behaviour of the EWMA and GARCH models; the mean reversion can be clearly seen. Also, it can be seen that the GARCH model reacts more violently to a change in the underlying series and then comes back down afterwards faster than the EWMA method, though it does not go down as far.

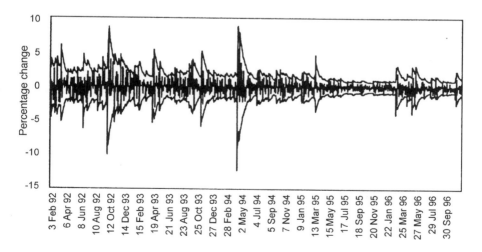

Figure 4.9 Rand/Sterling exchange rate – VAR vs price change (GARCH (1,1))

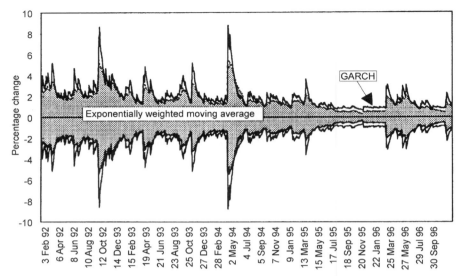

Figure 4.10 Rand/Sterling exchange rate (GARCH (1,1) versus exponential (0.94) − 95% confidence)

By comparing the equations for EWMA and GARCH

$$\sigma = \sqrt{\lambda \sigma_{t-1}^2 + (1 - \lambda)X_t^2}$$

$$\sigma = \sqrt{\omega + \beta \sigma_{t-1}^2 + \alpha X_{t-1}^2}$$

it can be seen that β in the GARCH equation is equivalent to the decay factor (λ) in the EWMA equation and that α in the GARCH equation is equivalent to $(1 - \lambda)$ in the EWMA equation. Therefore, EWMA is a special case of GARCH where the persistence is equal to one and $\omega = 0$. The above discussion on persistence would imply that EWMA would produce a higher average volatility; in fact this is not necessarily the case. It is the ratio of the β to the α that determines the speed with which volatility will forget past events. This can be seen from the discussion of the decay factor (λ) in the section on EWMA above. As $\lambda(\beta)$ tends towards one, $1 - \lambda(\alpha)$ gets smaller and the volatility will become more of a longer-term average.

MEASURING CORRELATION

Introduction to Correlation

Correlations are just as critical in VAR calculations as volatility. One of the important aspects of VAR is that it is a risk measure that captures the degree of diversity in a portfolio, i.e. the extent to which risk is reduced by holding positions in a varied portfolio of assets. Correlations embody the degree of diversification within a portfolio. A simple non-mathematical definition of correlation is as follows:

The extent to which the price changes of two assets occur at the same time.

Correlation is normally expressed as a correlation coefficient between 1 and −1:

- A correlation of 1 indicates that the price changes are perfectly correlated and always occur together. If two assets have a correlation of 1 they behave as if they are the same asset.

- A correlation of 0 means that there is no relationship between the price changes of the two assets, i.e. they are entirely independent of one another.

- A correlation of −1 means that the price changes of one asset are always the opposite to that of the other asset.

Timing Errors

It is important to stress that to get a meaningful correlation the price change of the two assets must be taken at exactly the same time. Timing errors are the commonest cause of spurious correlations. With only two assets it may be possible to ensure that price change readings are taken at the same time. However, with a large portfolio, typically containing several hundred assets, timing errors are a serious problem. This problem is most commonly solved by calculating correlation based on price changes over a five-working day period. Because the time period and therefore the price changes are so much larger, the timing errors caused by taking readings a short time apart become insignificant.

For example, consider the correlation of changes in swap interest rates with changes in government bond rates. It is expected that the correlation between the two will be high. When correlations are measured from daily changes this is often found not to be the case. The correlation was measured between swap and government bond rates for the Irish Punt. The correlation based on daily changes was found to be 0.42. This immediately sets the alarm bells ringing as the correlation seems too low. When the correlation was measured again, using five-day changes, the correlation was found to be 0.85. Therefore, timing errors *halved* the measured correlation.

Timing errors are the usual source of non-sensical correlations, giving rise to correlation matrices which are not positive definite (see the Appendix to Chapter 3 for methods of dealing with this problem).

A good feeling for the correlation between two assets can be obtained by graphing the price changes in the two assets. Figure 4.11 shows the correlation between the percentage price changes in the Rand/Sterling exchange rate and the percentage price changes in gold (price expressed in sterling).

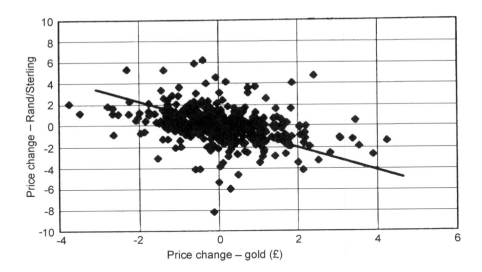

Figure 4.11   Correlation – gold vs Rand/Sterling

   This discussion of the estimation of correlation coefficients assumes that there is
a linear relationship between the percentage price changes. Of course, it is possible
to use a relationship which is curved; however, it is unlikely that this will add to the
accuracy of your estimate of VAR. In Figure 4.11 a straight line has been drawn
through the ellipse of points. The gradient of this line is the correlation coefficient.
Roughly speaking, the correlation coefficient is approximately:

   1 – the minimum width of the ellipse / maximum width of the ellipse.

The sign will need to be adjusted depending on the sign of the gradient of the line
drawn through the ellipse. The gradient of the line in Figure 4.11 is negative and
therefore so is the correlation coefficient. In Figure 4.11 the ellipse is fairly broad
around the superimposed line; this indicates a low correlation. An alternative way
of thinking about this is that in this case the straight line drawn through the ellipse
explains relatively little of the total ellipse of points. In fact the correlation
coefficient is −0.28. This is a low correlation and is statistically close to 0 (see the
discussion below on measurement error).
   Figure 4.12 shows the correlation between two parts of the German yield curve.
Correlations down the yield curve, from about two years onwards, tend to be high.
This also explains why a parallel shift in a yield curve is known to explain such a
large proportion of yield curve movement. Figure 4.12 shows a typical ellipse for
highly-correlated instruments. The correlation is in fact 0.94, which is high, but not
unusually so for two points on a yield curve.

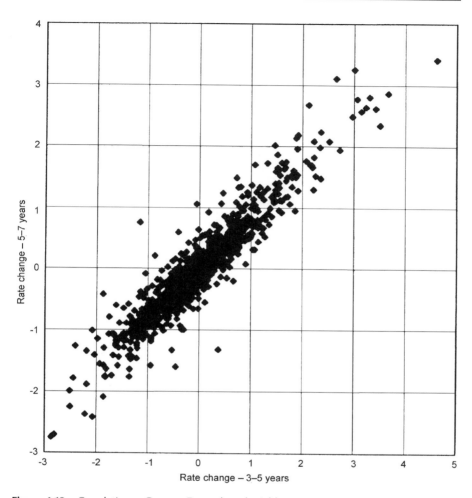

Figure 4.12 Correlation – German Deutschmark yield curve

Market Stress and Correlations

Scatter diagrams will form a symmetrical ellipse when markets are behaving normally. As with volatility, however, correlations behave differently during times of market stress. Examination of scatter diagram will occasionally reveal a distorted ellipse. Figure 4.13 is an imaginary scatter diagram for two equity markets.

It shows an ellipse which is essentially circular except for the protrusion in the bottom left of the diagram. This scatter diagram indicates that these two assets

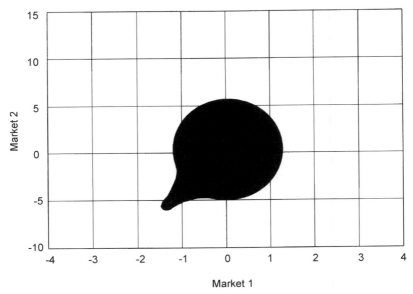

Figure 4.13 Correlation between equity markets

display two distinct types of behaviour in relation to each other. Most of the points on the scatter diagram form a circle – indicating that there is little or no correlation between the two equity markets. The protrusion indicates a second type of behaviour: that if there is a crash in one equity market it is often accompanied by a crash in the second. This reflects what we know about equity markets. If there is a severe downward adjustment in one of the major markets, particularly the American market, it often causes a world-wide drop in other equity markets. In practice this should not concern us too much and we should assume there is a zero correlation between the two markets for two reasons:

1. The protrusion shown is exaggerated, it is very difficult to find a correlation graph showing this degree of distortion to the ellipse. This is because there are not enough severe price movements to cause the degree of distortion shown in Figure 4.13, i.e. they are very rare events.
2. If we remember that VAR is about estimating the potential loss on a portfolio when the market is behaving normally, it should be clear that VAR is not designed to capture this type of behaviour. The effect of severe market moves should be investigated with the use of stress testing, as such moves will not be captured by VAR. Therefore, we should ignore the distortion and take the correlation between the two markets as zero, i.e. they are uncorrelated.

Calculating Correlation

As with volatility, there are a variety of ways to calculate correlation. The methods described here assume a linear relationship between two assets. The basic equation for calculating correlation is:

$$\rho_{x,y} = \frac{COV_{x,y}}{\sigma_x.\sigma_y}$$

where: $\rho_{x,y}$ = correlation between assets x and y
$COV_{x,y}$ = covariance between assets x and y
σ_x = volatility of asset x
σ_y = volatility of asset y

The covariance for assets x and y is the average of the product of the deviations for each pair of price changes. Covariance is calculated from the following equation:

$$COV_{x,y} = \frac{1}{n}.\sum_{i=1}^{n}(x_i - \mu_x)(y_i - \mu_y)$$

Correlations can also be calculated using other methods, such as the moving average and exponentially weighted methods. The behaviour of the correlations calculated using different methods is exactly the same as already described for volatilities. Therefore, there are exactly the same decisions to be made about the length of the observation period to be used. See the section 'An Empirical Analysis of VAR Model Accuracy' below for a full discussion of the most appropriate observation period.

J P Morgan's RiskMetrics[TM] uses an exponentially weighted measure of correlation to match its volatility calculation method. The equation for deriving correlations is the same as the standard equation above. The volatilities put into the equation are exponentially weighted, as is the covariance. The exponentially weighted covariance is calculated as follows:

$$COV_{x,y} = \sqrt{(1-\lambda)\sum_{t=n}^{t=1}\lambda^t X_t.Y_t}$$

where: X_t and Y_t are the percentage price changes on day t for assets x and y. Note that the mean of the distributions for assets x and y are assumed to be zero.

Implementing Correlations

Many institutions trade thousands of individual assets across different classes of assets. Modelling correlations for large diverse portfolios presents particular challenges. Most institutions do not consider it practical to calculate the correlation between every pair of assets. Thus correlations are implemented in a hierarchical manner which takes account of trading patterns and the practicalities of measurement.

Consider an interest rate trading operation, trading in 15 different currencies. In most implementations of VAR (see Chapter 5) each of the 15 yield curves is split down into approximately a dozen risk factors with each risk factor representing exposure to a particular maturity. Thus in total there might be 180 (15 × 12) risk factors in this trading operation. If interest rate options are traded as well, then the number of risk factors would be at least doubled to take account of the term structure of volatility. This is just interest rate trading; consider how many other risk factors would be required for the other asset classes of equities, currencies and commodities. Just the interest rate correlation matrix (ignoring volatility) would be 180 × 180, i.e. 16,110 correlations.[2] In practice it would be impractical to calculate so many correlations and perhaps more importantly, it is not necessary to do so.

The precise method of implementing VAR for this imaginary trading operation would depend on the type of trades undertaken. If we assume that most of the trading is within a single currency, then the normal method would be to work out the correlations for all the maturities down each yield curve and then assume a single correlation between each yield curve. The single correlation would normally be chosen as the correlation of the mid-point on the yield curve around which the majority of trading takes place. Using a single correlation between yield curves would reduce the number of correlations needed to 171((6 × 12 − 6) + (7 × 15)).

This approach is fine as long as there is not extensive cross currency trading. It is possible that in some of the Deutschmark block currencies (such as the Netherlands and Belgium), positions are hedged with German futures as the German futures market is large, liquid and highly correlated with other Deutschmark block currencies. In this case it probably would not matter that a single correlation is used between, say the Belgium and German curves.

Another type of cross currency trading is spread trading. As an example, a trader may believe that the interest rate differential between Italian and German government bonds is too large and the spread will narrow soon. This view will be executed as a long position in Italian bonds and a short position in German bonds (or bond futures). If this type of spread play makes up more than a small percentage of trading then it is inappropriate to assume a single correlation between the Italian and German curves. Correlations must then be calculated for all the maturities at which cross currency spreads are traded.

The same approach is taken to correlations across asset classes. Therefore, a single correlation may be used to calculate VAR for a combined portfolio of interest rate and currency assets; the correlation between currencies and interest rates. Of course a great deal of information is lost in this process but as long as there is not extensive cross asset trading, this approach will give a reasonable result and will reflect the way in which each asset class is most often traded as if it were a separate market place. A hierarchy is thereby created, in which fewer and fewer correlations are used as the aggregation of VAR for the bank's overall portfolio gets higher and higher.

MEASURING 'SIGNIFICANCE' AND ASSOCIATED ISSUES

In statistics most numbers are estimates or an interpretation of the truth. The equations given in the sections above on calculating volatility and correlation give *estimates* of these parameters rather than absolute values. Given that these are estimates, we know that the actual value of a parameter will lie in a range much like the distribution of returns. In a price change distribution the expected price change is the mean of the distribution; however, we know that the actual price change will fall somewhere within the normal distribution if it behaves normally. This section shows how the confidence intervals around estimations of volatility and correlation vary with the length of the observation period, i.e. how many days (or samples) are used to derive the volatility or correlation.

Standard Error and Sample Size

The true value of many statistical measures is assumed to fall within a range. If we measure the mean of a series, the value calculated will vary depending on which particular sample set we take from the series, and will also depend on the size of the sample set chosen. If very small sample sets are taken, then one could imagine large variations in the value of the mean calculated; if larger sample sets are used then the variation in the measured mean will be smaller. Therefore, the mean of a distribution can be considered to lie within a range, the size of which will depend on the size of sample sets chosen.

The range of mean values can be thought of as having its own distribution. The standard deviation of this distribution is known as the standard error. If the form of the distribution is known then we can calculate the range within which the mean will fall with a specified level of confidence. The following sections show how to calculate the range within which measures of volatility and correlation lie. As a general rule, the standard error will reduce proportionally with the square root of the number of samples used.

It should also be noted that this section is predicated on the idea that longer term constant volatilities and correlations describe the behaviour of financial assets fairly. In the section on measuring volatilities, the notion that volatilities and correlations are not constant for financial assets was proposed as a more effective view of the financial world. Nonetheless, the following discussion adds to an understanding of volatility and correlation measurement.

Estimation of Confidence Intervals – Volatility

The confidence interval within which an estimate of volatility lies is given by the following equations (also known as the F-Test):

$$\text{Confidence Interval} = \sigma\sqrt{F(n-1, \infty)} \text{ to } \frac{\sigma}{\sqrt{F(\infty,\ n-1)}}$$

where: $F()$ is the inverse of the F probability distribution, and n is the number of days in the observation period.

Figure 4.14 shows the confidence intervals for an estimated measure of volatility of 1. As is expected, the range within which the value of volatility lies if we want to be 99% confident of its value is greater than if we only require 95% confidence.

Figure 4.14 shows how the estimation accuracy increases with an increase in the length of the observation period. In fact, the accuracy of the volatility estimate increases proportionally with the square root of the number of days in the observation period.

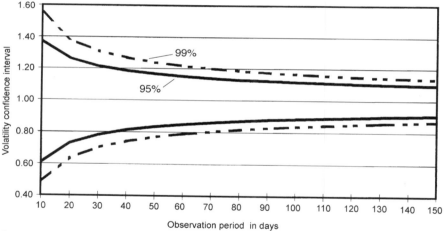

Figure 4.14   Volatility – 99% and 95% confidence intervals

Estimation of Confidence Intervals – Correlation

The confidence interval for the correlation coefficient is slightly more complicated. Significance tests and confidence intervals for the correlation coefficient, ρ, are most easily dealt with using the Fisher transformation, Z:

$$Z = \frac{1}{2}\ln\left(\frac{1+\rho}{1-\rho}\right)$$

where: $\rho =$ the correlation coefficient

$Z =$ the Fisher transformation, a normally distributed transformation of the correlation coefficient (also known as the Z-score).

Z is normally distributed with a variance $= 1/(n-3)$. The 95% confidence interval for Z is given by:

$$Z_{CI} = Z \pm \frac{1.95}{\sqrt{(n-3)}}$$

where: Z_{CI} is the specified confidence interval of the Fisher transformation.

However, we require the confidence interval for the correlation rather than Z. The confidence interval for the correlation coefficient can be found using the inverse Fisher transformation:

$$\rho_{CI} = \frac{e^{2Z'-1} - 1}{1 + e^{2Z'}}$$

where: ρ_{CI} is the specified confidence interval of the correlation coefficient

Z' is the inverse Fisher transformation.

Figure 4.15 shows the 95% confidence intervals for values of correlation between -1 and 1. It is instructive to note that the confidence interval is much wider when the correlation is low than when it is high. For high correlations (greater than 0.9) the magnitude of potential error in the estimate of correlation is low, whereas for a correlation of 0 the confidence interval is very wide, especially when few samples are used.

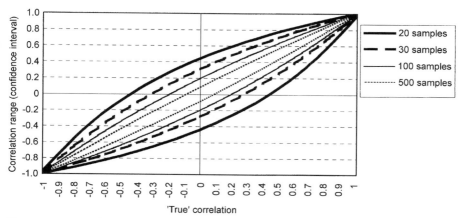

Figure 4.15 Correlation 95% confidence intervals for different numbers of samples

As discussed in the section on measuring correlations, in practice correlations are most often measured using changes over non-overlapping five-day periods. Therefore six months of price history will only give about 20 non-overlapping samples from which to measure correlation. The use of two years of price history will give approximately 90 samples. As can be seen from Figure 4.15, the accuracy initially increases rapidly with the number of samples as with volatility. However, to achieve materially improved accuracy after 100 samples requires several hundred samples to be used. 500 samples would represent nearly 10 years of price history.

The problem of insufficient data points can be solved using a mathematical technique known as bootstrapping (Efron and Tibshirani, 1993). Bootstrapping randomly samples five-day changes from the data set and thereby creates far more data points than would be available otherwise. It should be noted that bootstrapping does not work when deriving correlations for returns over longer time frames as mean reversion effects are lost in the bootstrapping process.

To distil the above discussion down to basics, we can see that correlations between 0.4 and −0.4 are statistically close to 0. This conclusion can save a lot of effort that could be spent on accurately measuring low correlations. Whereas, in fact, the effort should go into accurate measurement of high correlations as even a small change in high correlations can dramatically affect the calculated VAR.

Estimation Accuracy and Non-constant Covariance

The above discussion shows that to have a good level of confidence in the covariance VAR parameters of volatility and correlation, a fair amount of data is required. For volatilities, Figure 4.14 shows that to get an estimate of volatility that is accurate to ± 10% 150 days of data is required. For correlations, the story is slightly different. High correlations (greater than 0.9) require relatively few samples to produce an accurate estimate of correlation. For lower correlations, far more sample points are required. For a correlation of 0, Figure 4.15 shows that 500 samples are required to get an estimate with 95% confidence.

There is also another reason for deriving covariance parameters from large samples. Chapter 3 described the possibility of creating non-sensical correlation matrices that may potentially cause a VAR analysis to fail or be meaningless. One of the key stipulations for avoiding this was the requirement to have more days, or samples, of data than there are risk factors. In practice, even relatively small banks will have over 200 risk factors. This implies that correlations should be derived from at least 200 samples.

Running contrary to the requirement for using large data samples is the fact that in order to get a VAR model to have the right predictive behaviour it is necessary to use shorter, rather than longer, observation periods. Banks often use observation periods of 100 days or less. Therefore in practice, correlations and volatilities are often drawn from data with fewer samples than risk factors.

This goes directly against the requirements for longer observation periods given by the requirement to reduce estimation error and to ensure sensible correlation matrices. Of course, the confidence intervals calculated above for volatility and correlation assume that the volatilities and correlations are in fact constant. As volatility and correlation are not constant, the above measures of confidence for volatility are of more theoretical than practical importance.

With regard to the potential problem of producing non-sensical correlation matrices, in practice this problem can be worked around (see Appendix to Chapter 3), so this requirement can also be put to one side.

The extent to which a VAR model is theoretically sound if short observation periods are used is the subject of a long and not necessarily enlightening discussion. In the final analysis the success of a VAR model must be judged by its predictive behaviour, i.e. the percentage of portfolio value change exceptions that the model generates versus the expected, or desired, percentage.

CAN YOUR VAR MODEL BE RELIED ON?

Having calculated the bank's VAR the chief executive then looks you in the eye and demands to know what confidence he can place on the VAR number he has just received. VAR is calculated from positions, correlations and volatilities. Correlations and volatilities are statistical estimates of the behaviour of the assets making up the portfolio. Measures of correlation and volatility are both subject to the statistical estimation error as described above.

Estimation errors and the assumption of normality all potentially cause errors in the resultant VAR. However, the confidence levels discussed under the sections on measuring volatility and correlation all assume that there is a true constant volatility and correlation. This is simply not true for financial assets. As discussed below, volatilities and correlations are not constant over time, they change as the behaviour of the asset and financial markets change. This means that the standard error measures are not applicable to financial assets. This in turn leaves us in an awkward position of not being able to directly estimate the statistical error in the volatility and correlation estimates. So, how accurate is our calculated VAR?

In the final analysis the accuracy of a VAR model is determined by whether the percentage of days on which the portfolio's loss exceeds the previous day's estimate of VAR is acceptably close to the required value. This can be ascertained by 'back testing'.

Back Testing

To 'back test' a VAR model simply means that, for a given number of days, the loss on a portfolio is compared to the previous day's estimate of VAR. The number of days in which the loss on the portfolio exceeded the VAR estimate is the number of exceptions. The number of exceptions should be reasonably close to that expected given the target level of confidence. So, for a 1000 days and a 95% confidence level, the number of exceptions should be close to 50. The Basle requirements for the use of VAR as a regulatory capital measure gives a good description of back testing (Basle Committee, 1996) and specifies that banks wishing to use a VAR model to calculate regulatory capital must be able to undertake both of the following types of back testing.

Hypothetical Back Testing

Hypothetical back testing is the more useful of the two methods for checking the mathematical soundness of the VAR model and that the model has been implemented correctly. One of the problems with back testing is that the composition of a portfolio will change daily, thereby making it difficult to measure the performance of the VAR model on a consistent basis over a period of time. Hypothetical back testing involves freezing the portfolio from a chosen day and then applying a history of asset price changes to it, thus generating a history of gains and losses on the portfolio. The VAR on the portfolio is also calculated for each day. The number and percentage of exceptions can then be found by comparing each day's VAR estimate to the portfolio gain or loss on the following day.

Trading Outcome Back Testing

In this method the actual daily gains and losses for a trading area, again over a given period, are compared against the calculated VAR for the previous day. The percentage of exceptions can then be found and compared against the desired result as for hypothetical back testing. Trading outcome back testing is the ultimate measure of the success of the VAR model from the regulators and bank management's point of view.

It should be noted, however, that it has less statistical meaning than the hypothetical back testing. Daily trading profit and loss (P&L) is 'contaminated' with many items in addition to asset price changes. Trading P&L includes items such as:

- Commissions, fees and brokerage.

- Turnover spread, profit made from buying and selling securities during the day.

- P&L made from positions taken during the day which are hedged or cut-out before the end of the day. The composition of a portfolio is generally crystallised at the end of the day for the calculation of VAR.

In fact, it is unlikely that a trading operation will make a significant proportion of its P&L by taking positions and then waiting for prices to move. Of course this does occur where banks take a directional view of the markets and is a natural part of proprietary trading. P&L will be most uncontaminated by intra-day trading for institutions which do take longer-term directional views, such as hedge funds and fund managers. Intra-day trading activity should improve the portfolio's P&L over that resulting purely from price movements. As such, the percentage of trading P&L exceptions is a measure of the efficiency of the traders. Traders should be able to reduce the volatility of the experienced P&L on a portfolio and should be creating a portfolio P&L distribution with a positive mean. Therefore, it is expected that an efficient trading operation should ensure that the trading portfolio experiences less exceptions than would be expected. This is an interesting and useful measure of trading efficiency.

Measuring VAR Model Accuracy

The number of exceptions, over any given period of time, is given by the confidence level chosen for the VAR model; for example 50 exceptions are expected from 1000 days for a VAR model with 95% confidence. In practice, the number of experienced exceptions is unlikely to be precisely 50. The number of exceptions will lie in a range given by a binomial distribution. The binomial distribution describes the probability of a specified number of exceptions occurring in a given sample size (number of days for daily VAR). Figure 4.16 is the binomial distribution of the expected number of exceptions for a period of 1000 days for a VAR model with a confidence level of 95%.

As can be seen from Figure 4.16 the range of possible exceptions is quite wide. Therefore we need to decide how many exceptions we are prepared to accept before rejecting the VAR model. Standard statistics suggests the use of a decision test for whether a model should be accepted or rejected, i.e. a Type I error test. The Type I error test examines the chance of erroneously rejecting a valid model based on a given number of exceptions. To illustrate the point consider the case in which VAR was calculated for 1000 days and there were 53 exceptions. From Figure 4.16 it can

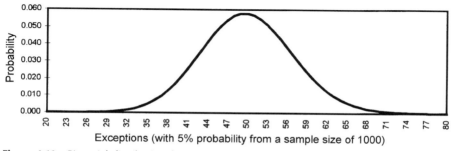

Figure 4.16 Binomial distribution for VAR exceptions

be seen that 53 exceptions is near the centre of the distribution. If we rejected the VAR model because it gave 53 exceptions versus the expected 50, it would seem likely that we would be erroneously rejecting a valid model. If the model gave 70 exceptions and was rejected, it can be seen from the distribution that it would seem far more likely that the model is invalid and there is therefore a low chance that we are erroneously rejecting a valid model. What we are doing here is seeing whether the actual number of exceptions differs significantly from our expectation. This test is one of a pair of standard statistical tests of significance:

- Type I – if a valid model has been erroneously *rejected* then a Type I error is said to have been made.
- Type II – if an invalid model has been erroneously *accepted* then a Type II error is said to have been made.

The two tests are mutually exclusive and therefore only one of these tests can be used. Basle specifies use of the Type I error check and it is therefore adopted henceforth in this book. Basle states that the regulators wish to be 95% confident that they are not committing a Type I error, i.e. erroneously rejecting a valid model. This tends to give the benefit of the doubt to the VAR model. Whether the number of exceptions produced by your VAR model satisfies Basle's 95% confidence can be ascertained using the Z-score for a binomial distribution:

$$Z\text{-score} = \frac{X - Np}{\sqrt{Npq}}$$

where: $X =$ number of exceptions
$N =$ number of days over which back test was conducted
$p =$ required confidence level – as a fraction
$q = 1 - p$

A one-tailed 95% confidence that the model will not be erroneously rejected is given by a Z-score of 1.645. For a two-tailed test, a Z-score of 1.645 will give a 90% confidence that the VAR model will not be erroneously rejected.

Under Basle, market risk regulatory capital is based on a bank's VAR. Therefore Basle is only interested in the under estimation of VAR. The regulators do not mind if the bank over-estimates VAR and thereby provides more capital than it needed to. Therefore, the test specified by Basle is a one-tailed test. This is indicated in Figure 4.17; a line is drawn beyond which Basle will reject a VAR model, Basle does not care how *few* exceptions occur.

From a bank's perspective, clearly the Basle requirement must be satisfied, however over estimation of VAR is not desirable for several reasons. As stated above, over estimation of VAR will result in excess capital being provided. Internally, as well, a bank will be concerned not to overestimate VAR. As time progresses more traders will be rewarded on the return they earn on economic capital; with VAR being a constituent part of economic capital, traders will be very

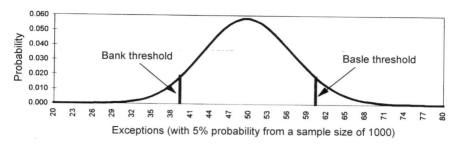

Figure 4.17   Number of exceptions and acceptance of a VAR model

concerned to ensure VAR is not being overestimated. Further, many traders' positions are already limited in terms of VAR, again the accurate calculation of VAR will be important. Therefore, from a bank's internal perspective, a two-tailed test is required as indicated in Figure 4.17.

Table 4.1 indicates the range of the number of exceptions that is acceptable for Basle and internally, for a 1000-day back test. It shows clearly that a much tighter range is required for 99% confidence. Given the number of extreme price moves in the financial markets and the way they clump together it can be seen that it will be much harder to satisfy the accuracy requirements for a 99% confidence level than for a 95% level of confidence. This is possibly another reason why a 95% confidence level is chosen by most banks. The difficulty in calculating VAR with 99% confidence is due to the lack of normality in the return distributions of financial assets.

Table 4.1   Acceptable number of exceptions for a back test over a 1000 day period

	95% confidence VAR	99% confidence VAR
Basle	Not applicable	0−14
Bank	39−61	6−14

AN EMPIRICAL ANALYSIS OF VAR MODEL ACCURACY

So far this chapter has presented a largely theoretical discussion of the extent of non-normality in financial markets, different volatility and correlation models. This section presents an investigation into the impact of these two factors on the accuracy of VAR models.

The starting hypothesis of the investigation is that lack of normality in financial assets does not significantly compromise the calculation of VAR. To test this hypothesis, five years of daily price change history was gathered for 15 assets,

Table 4.2

Assets tested

Yen/Sterling exchange rate
US$/Sterling exchange rate
Gold
S&P 500
Swedish 3-month LIBOR
Rand/Sterling exchange rate
Sterling 1-year LIBOR
Copper ($)
Mexican Peso/US$ exchange rate
DEM 3–5 year bonds (EFFAS)
US$ 3–5 year bonds (EFFAS)
UK 3–5 year bonds (EFFAS)
JP¥ 3–5 year bonds (EFFAS)
Malaysian equities (local currency)
Brazilian equities (local currency)

approximately covering the period January 1992–December 1996. The group of assets includes interest rates, commodities, equity indices and exchange rates. The collection of 15 assets is shown in Table 4.2.

The collection of assets tested is not large enough to provide conclusive proof of conclusions drawn here, but is indicative of results to be found in most normally diversified portfolios. As can be seen from Table 4.2, the sample includes assets that are likely to display a significant lack of normality. This was a deliberate selection criterion as assets such as copper and the Mexican Peso have suffered severe price moves in recent history. If the hypothesis is valid for this group of assets then there is a reasonable chance of it being generally applicable.

Description of Investigation

The investigation involved conducting a hypothetical back test, as described above, for each asset and finally for all the assets grouped together as a portfolio. For a single asset, VAR is calculated by multiplying the position of the asset by its volatility with the appropriate confidence level. If the position is assumed to be 'one', then the VAR for each asset then becomes equal to the volatility estimate. The investigation therefore concentrated on different volatility models and understanding their predictive characteristics. The portfolio investigation treated the portfolio in its entirety and assumed that its composition did not change over the period of the back tests.

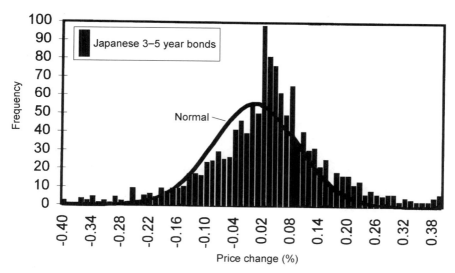

Figure 4.18   Japanese 3–5 year bonds (EFFAS)

The investigation was based on five years of data for all of the assets (November 1991–1996), with exception of Swedish LIBOR and Mexican Peso for which only two and three years of data, respectively, was available. The longest observation period used was 250 days, this means that the back tests could be performed for the last four years. Four years of data is slightly more than 1,000 days. Therefore, for convenience, all back tests were conducted over 1,000 days of price history with the exception of Swedish LIBOR and Mexican Peso. All the data series were sourced from Datastream except for the EFFAS (European Federation of Financial Analyst Societies) bond yield series which were sourced from Open Bloomberg. A series of back tests were undertaken using different volatility models and different observation periods, the results of these tests are described below. All of the assets selected had price change distributions that displayed a marked lack of normality over the historical period chosen; specifically all the assets have distributions with fatter tails than expected in a normal distribution.

In addition, other types of non-normality are displayed in some of the assets chosen. For example, the Yen EFFAS bond yield distribution displayed a significant negative skew as shown in Figure 4.18. Figure 4.19 shows the totally abnormal behaviour of Sterling 1-year LIBOR. The distribution for Sterling 1-year LIBOR appears to show a multi-modal distribution, displaying five peaks rather than a single central peak. It is clear that this asset is far from being normally behaved.

As was said at the beginning of this section, the really important question is whether it is possible to construct a VAR model with the required behaviour in terms of generating exceptions, not whether a particular asset can be assumed to have a normal distribution.

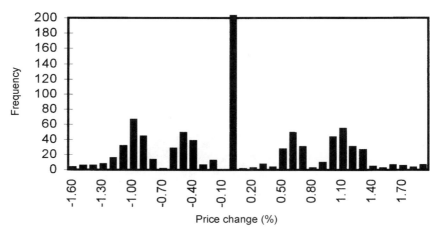

Figure 4.19   Sterling 1-year LIBOR

Effect of Varying the Observation Period

The first set of back tests undertaken used the standard deviation as a measure of volatility and used an observation period of one year (250 days). The model was set up to calculate VAR with 95% confidence (i.e. volatility was multiplied by 1.645). The results are presented in Table 4.3.

Table 4.3   Standard deviation – 250-day observation period

Asset	Exceptions %	Accept? 5
Yen/Sterling exchange rate	4.4	Yes
US$/Sterling exchange rate	3.0	No
Gold	4.1	Yes
S&P 500	4.1	Yes
Swedish 3-month LIBOR	10.3	No
Rand/Sterling exchange rate	3.2	No
Sterling 1-year LIBOR	3.1	No
Copper ($)	6.0	Yes
Mexican Peso/US$ exchange rate	3.4	No
DEM 3–5 year bonds (EFFAS)	5.0	Yes
US$ 3–5 year bonds (EFFAS)	3.8	No
UK 3–5 year bonds (EFFAS)	2.9	No
JP¥ 3–5 year bonds (EFFAS)	6.6	No
Malaysian equities (local currency)	3.8	No
Brazilian equities (local currency)	2.7	No

Table 4.3 shows the percentage of price changes in excess of the calculated VAR. For each asset a two-tailed Type I error test was used as described above in the section on hypothetical back testing. If the VAR model is rejected it means that we can be 95% certain that a valid model was not erroneously rejected. As can be seen, the volatility model used is only accepted as valid for five of the 15 assets. We can conclude that this volatility measure does not result in a VAR model with the desired characteristic of producing 5% exceptions.

The next series of back tests was conducted using a variety of shorter observation periods and again using the standard deviation measure of volatility. The results are given in Table 4.4.

Table 4.4 shows a marked improvement in the performance of the VAR model as soon as the observation period is reduced to 100 days or less. It is worth noting that there is no significant improvement in performance with observation periods of less than 100 days (100 days equates approximately to the last six months).

So why are shorter observation periods more effective? The answer is because volatility in financial markets is not constant and large price changes cluster together. Volatility models with shorter observation periods are more responsive to changes in volatility. This can be seen by examining graphs for the Rand/Sterling exchange rate in Figures 4.20 and 4.21. In Figure 4.20, with an observation period of 250 days, the periods of higher volatility in the exchange rate have virtually no effect on the calculated VAR. This means that when a period of higher volatility is encountered the VAR model gets caught out. The use of a longer observation period will also mean a higher average volatility; this can be seen by comparing the period of low volatility in Figures 4.20 and 4.21 (towards the right hand side). In Figure 4.20, with an observation period of 250 days, the volatility remains higher than in Figure 4.21.

By comparison with Figure 4.20, in Figure 4.21, with an observation period of 50 days, the VAR model can be seen to be far more responsive to changes in the underlying volatility. Clearly, to measure VAR with 95% confidence a responsive measure of volatility is required; this is given by shorter observation periods.

The next set of back tests tested all the models described in this chapter against the requirement to calculate VAR with 95% confidence. The EWMA model was tested using decay factors of 0.94 and 0.97. The results for these tests are summarised in Table 4.5. Table 4.5 shows that, for VAR calculated with a confidence level of 95%, the type of volatility model used does not really matter as long as a short observation period is used and it does not embody a significant degree of mean reversion. It is worth noting that the use of the exponentially weighted volatility model (with a decay factor of 0.94) did not give any significant improvement in performance over the standard deviation model with a short observation period.

The EWMA model with a decay factor of 0.97 failed for most assets because as the decay factor gets close to 1 the effective observation period gets longer and longer. A decay factor of 0.97 has an effective observation period of approximately

Table 4.4   Standard deviation – various observation periods

Asset	Observation days 250 Exceptions (%)	Accept?	Observation days 100 Exceptions? (%)	Accept?	Observation days 50 Exceptions? (%)	Accept?	Observation days 30 Exceptions? (%)	Accept?
		5		11		11		12
Yen/Sterling exchange rate	4.4	Yes	5.2	Yes	4.5	Yes	5.1	Yes
US$/Sterling exchange rate	3.0	No	4.0	Yes	4.2	Yes	4.7	Yes
Gold	4.1	Yes	4.8	Yes	4.8	Yes	4.8	Yes
S&P 500	4.1	Yes	4.4	No	3.6	No	3.9	No
Swedish 3-month LIBOR	10.3	No	10.7	No	7.0	No	8.5	No
Rand/Sterling exchange rate	3.2	No	3.1	Yes	3.9	No	4.3	Yes
Sterling 1-year LIBOR	3.1	No	4.1	Yes	4.6	Yes	4.7	Yes
Copper ($)	6.0	Yes	5.5	Yes	4.9	Yes	4.9	Yes
Mexican Peso/US$ exchange rate	3.4	No	5.3	Yes	4.8	Yes	5.4	Yes
DEM 3–5 year bonds (EFFAS)	5.0	Yes	5.8	Yes	5.0	Yes	5.0	Yes
US$ 3–5 year bonds (EFFAS)	3.8	No	4.4	Yes	4.3	Yes	4.3	Yes
UK 3–5 year bonds (EFFAS)	2.9	No	4.4	Yes	4.1	Yes	4.4	Yes
JP¥ 3–5 year bonds (EFFAS)	6.6	No	6.7	No	5.5	Yes	5.8	Yes
Malaysian equities (local currency)	3.8	No	4.3	Yes	4.1	Yes	4.2	Yes
Brazilian equities (local currency)	2.7	No	3.9	No	3.2	No	3.2	No

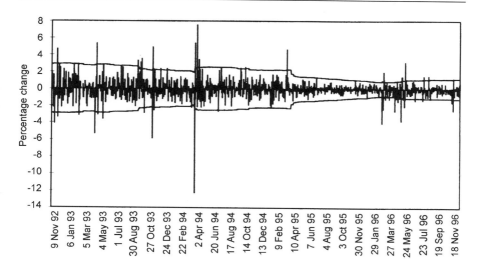

Figure 4.20 Rand/Sterling exchange rate – VAR vs price change (standard deviation – 250-day observation period, 95% confidence)

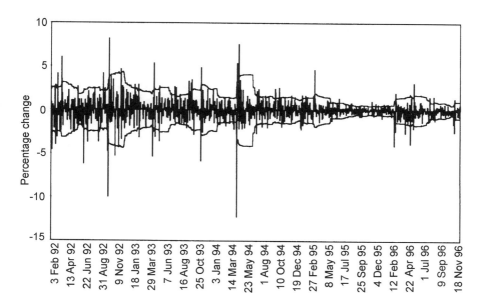

Figure 4.21 Rand/Sterling exchange rate – VAR vs price change (standard deviation – 50-day observation period, 95% confidence)

Table 4.5 Results of volatility model back tests – 95% confidence

Volatility model (two-tailed test)	Assets accepted
Standard deviation – 250 days	5
Standard deviation – 100 days	11
Standard deviation – 50 days	11
Standard deviation – 30 days	12
Exponential (0.94)	11
Exponential (0.97)	4
GARCH (1,1)	5
Historic 50-days	11

100 days. This results in the volatility staying higher for longer as shown in Figure 4.22. Figure 4.22 compares the behaviour of the EWMA model using decay factors of 0.94 and 0.97.

It is perhaps initially puzzling that the GARCH model produced such a poor result. A little thought yields the explanation that the GARCH model contains too much mean reversion to calculate VAR with 95% confidence. The calculation of VAR with 95% confidence requires a measure of volatility that is responsive to both upward and downward changes in volatility. For most of the 15 assets, the GARCH model produced only just above 3% of exceptions against the required 5%. The calculated VAR was breached so rarely because the volatility remained high even in times of lower volatility. This can be seen clearly in Figure 4.23 which gives a comparison of VAR calculated using the exponentially weighted model (decay factor 0.94) and the GARCH model.

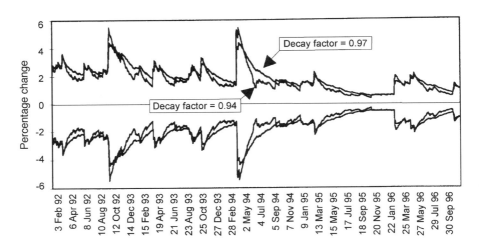

Figure 4.22 Rand/Sterling exchange rate (EWMA – comparison of decay factors)

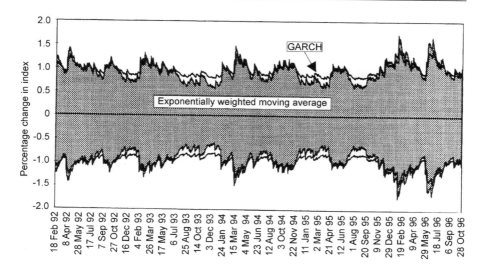

Figure 4.23   S&P 500 (GARCH (1,1) versus exponential (0.94), 95% confidence)

Figure 4.23 shows how the GARCH volatility remains high throughout; note also that the GARCH model's response to changes in short term volatility is asymmetrical. The GARCH model has only a limited response to a downward move, whereas it responds positively to upward changes in short term volatility.

The Basle Test

Producing a VAR model that meets your internal requirements is useful – but is not enough. It is generally accepted that the use of a VAR model for regulatory purposes will result in a lower capital requirement. To be useable for regulatory purposes a VAR model must satisfy the Basle criteria, as outlined in the Basle back testing framework (Basle Committee, 1996). That is, the VAR model must calculate VAR with 99% confidence and must be tested over at least 250 days using a minimum one-year observation period. See Chapter 9 for a fuller discussion on regulatory VAR.

A second series of back tests were undertaken to see what type of volatility model works best for the Basle requirements. The key requirement is for a 99% confidence level. It is intrinsically more difficult to estimate VAR with 99% confidence as the estimate is drawn from the tail of the price change distribution. Fat tails and lack of normality will affect the 99% confidence level far more than the 95% VAR.

There is an argument to say that trying to estimate VAR with 99% confidence is pointless. 99% VAR has no more value than 95% VAR except that 95% VAR is almost certainly more accurate. Of course the Basle committee wanted to set a rigorous capital target for banks to help ensure the stability of the financial markets. However, this can be achieved by several means, for example by requiring a higher multiple of the regulatory VAR number. At the time of writing, a multiple of three is specified by Basle.

Table 4.6 summarises the results of the back tests performed and the number of assets accepted when the volatility models were set up to calculate VAR with 99% confidence.[3] As for the 95% confidence level tests, a two-sided Type I error test was performed, i.e. it was assumed that banks are concerned about the over estimation of VAR just as much as they are concerned with the under estimation of VAR.

Table 4.6 shows almost the complete reverse of Table 4.5. Table 4.6 shows that all the low observation period volatility models perform very badly when estimating VAR with 99% confidence. The only models that performed well were the EWMA model with a decay factor of 0.97 and the GARCH model.

Although not a very satisfactory result, the standard deviation model with an observation period of 250 days was twice as successful as the shorter observation period models. This is the opposite of the findings for the estimation of VAR with 95% confidence. Is there a rational explanation for this reversal in behaviour?

With the shorter observation period models, the standard deviation VAR estimate closely follows the contour of the change in short-term volatility of the underlying price series. Over a short period of lower volatility the VAR estimate reduces rapidly. In fact it reduces so much and so fast that the VAR estimate gets caught out too often by short-term clusters of larger price changes.

When a longer observation period is used, the VAR model effectively has a longer term 'memory' and does not get caught out so easily by sudden changes in the underlying volatility. This was illustrated in Figures 4.20 and 4.21. This suggests the use of longer observation periods when measuring VAR with 99% confidence, which also ties in with the Basle requirement to use at least 250 days of data. Both the EWMA 0.97 and the GARCH model contain a longer-term memory and have a positive response to short-term increases in volatility. Both of these

Table 4.6 Results of volatility model back tests – 99% confidence

VAR method (two-tailed test)	Assets accepted
STDEV 250 days	8
STDEV 100 days	4
STDEV 50 days	5
STDEV 30 days	4
Exponential (0.94)	7
Exponential (0.97)	11
GARCH (1,1)	11
Historic 50-days	0

characteristics are needed to measure VAR effectively with 99% confidence. These characteristics can be seen in Figures 4.22 and 4.23.

Does this mean that we have to use a EWMA or GARCH model if we want to calculate VAR with 99% confidence? Table 4.6 would tend to suggest the answer is 'Yes', though note that GARCH performs no better than EWMA with a decay factor of 0.97. This suggests that the considerable extra amount of computational effort required by GARCH is not justified in terms of better performance.

Considering the standard deviation model, using an observation period of 250 days, the model could only be accepted for half the 15 assets, thus demonstrating the relative difficulty of measuring VAR with 99% confidence. On an asset by asset basis we would have to conclude that the standard deviation model VAR model was not working satisfactorily. However, all is not lost, for two reasons:

1. Remembering that a number of awkward assets were chosen deliberately, an examination of the VAR versus price change graph may reveal why the model failed and allow us to determine whether, in fact, the VAR model is at fault or whether the asset's behaviour is such that any VAR model would be expected to fail.

2. The second cause for hope is that although we have concentrated here on the estimation of VAR for single assets, in practice, banks wish to estimate VAR for large portfolios. In large portfolios the erratic changes in volatility are averaged out (central limit theorem – see any standard text on statistics). This portfolio effect makes it far easier to estimate VAR.

Figures 4.24 and 4.25 illustrate the first point. Figure 4.24 shows the price of the Brazilian equity index over the last five years, showing a very strong upward move. This upward drift shows up in Figure 4.25. In Figure 4.25 it can be seen that there are far more upward moves than there are downward moves. The VAR envelope appears to be shifted down the graph. From this it can be seen that it is likely that VAR would be underestimated. Table 4.4 shows that this is exactly

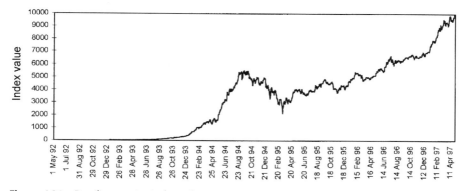

Figure 4.24 Brazilian equity index – history

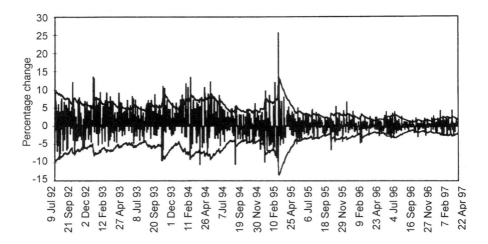

Figure 4.25   Brazilian equity index – VAR vs price change (exponential – 0.94)

what happened. All the standard deviation VAR models failed for the Brazilian equities index, when in fact there is nothing wrong with the VAR models – it is the unusual, non-stationary behaviour of the data series that caused an apparent failure in the model.

Figure 4.26 shows VAR versus the price changes for a portfolio made up of all 15 assets. Figure 4.26 shows that a far more constant volatility profile is generated for a portfolio than for a single asset. All VAR models with longer observation periods (250 days) satisfied the two-tailed Type I error test for the portfolio regardless of which volatility model was used. The following volatility models were tested:

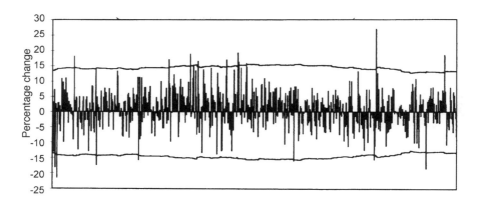

Figure 4.26   Portfolio – VAR vs value change (moving average – 250-day observation period)

- Standard deviation.
- Moving average.
- Exponentially weighted.
- Historical simulation.

Although often omitted from VAR methodology papers, there are a few worthwhile papers describing the results of back tests. One such is a paper by Hendriks (1996) of the Federal Reserve Bank who undertook an extensive back test on foreign exchange portfolios to determine the effectiveness of various VAR models.

The study undertaken by Hendriks involved looking at portfolios of foreign exchange positions. It should be noted that these positions behave in a linear fashion and the conclusions drawn from this study could not be applied to portfolios containing options or other leveraged products. Using five years of data Hendriks found that the covariance approach covered slightly more than 95% of actual price moves when a 95% confidence interval was chosen and 98.3% of actual portfolio value changes when a 99% confidence interval was chosen.

Useful observations can be made from Hendriks' study, even though the portfolios investigated only contained currency positions. It is reasonable to conclude, for portfolios that contain only linear instruments, that covariance is in fact an accurate method of calculating VAR, especially when a relatively low confidence interval of 95% is chosen. The level of uncertainty in the calculated VAR grows, as higher confidence intervals are chosen.

CONCLUSION

One of the most important messages from this chapter should be the need to back test theoretical VAR models. In many organisations much work and discussion takes place on the merits of GARCH versus other measures of volatility. Such theoretical discussions are rarely supported by thorough back testing (that would often prove the discussion to be a waste of time).

Managers implementing VAR should always insist that quantitative theories are back tested on a representative portfolio for the organisation, before effort is wasted implementing these theories, with perhaps no discernible benefit (except to make the model less comprehensible to people outside the risk management department). Always remember, the objective is to build a VAR model that produces an acceptable number of exceptions. The objective is *not* to build a model that accurately predicts volatility or correlation.

This chapter contains a number of theoretical concepts, an appreciation of which is essential when building a VAR model. However, putting theory to one side, the following practical conclusions can be drawn from this chapter and used when implementing VAR:

- The lack of normality of even fairly awkward asset series does not seriously compromise the ability to estimate VAR at the 95% confidence level.

- To build an effective VAR model, the choice of observation period is more important than the choice of volatility model.

- To estimate VAR with 95% confidence, an observation period of 100 days or less is far more effective than longer periods.

- To estimate VAR with 99% confidence, an observation period of 250 days or more is far more effective than shorter periods due to the longer effective 'memory' of such models. Note: GARCH and EWMA models (with a decay factor of 0.97 or greater) perform well at the 99% confidence level due to the in-built memory of these models.

- VAR estimation is easier for portfolios than for individual assets due to the averaging of volatility changes across all the assets in a portfolio.

NOTES

1. For mathematicians: the numbers (1,1) after GARCH refer to the order of the equation with respect to previous day's information. (1,1) means that the model is only using the previous day's price change and estimate of volatility in estimating today's volatility. Clearly this model can be extended to include older historic data, however, there is little evidence that this results in a general improvement of estimation accuracy for VAR models.

2. Note that 16,110 is actually $(90 \times 180) - 90$. The correlations are repeated either side of the diagonal, so we only need calculate them once; i.e. the correlation of A to B, is the same as the correlation of B to A. We also know that the diagonal of a correlation matrix is always 1, so we do not have to calculate this either.

3. The same tests for 95% and 99% confidence were repeated using log changes instead of percentage changes. Using the assumption that the natural log of price changes are normally distributed made no difference to the results. The results were slightly better for some assets and slightly worse for others.

5
Implementing value at risk

INTRODUCTION

The previous three chapters have described the various methods of calculating VAR and the parameters that go into the calculation, i.e. volatility and correlations. The final parts of the jigsaw are the asset positions. The main problem with asset positions is that there are normally an awful lot of them. Consider a bond portfolio where each bond is traded as a separate asset. If each bond were taken to be a separate asset in a VAR calculation you would quickly run into problems calculating VAR.

The main problem would not be the computation effort, however, if it were, more computing power could be thrown at the problem. Computing power is so cheap these days that this problem could be solved without massively increasing the VAR implementation budget. The real problem would be the time and effort required to create and maintain the volatilities and inter-correlations between every single tradable asset.

In practice, implementing VAR is a trade off between reducing the number of assets – or risk factors (see below) – to manageable proportions and the inaccuracies introduced by grouping risk factors (assets) together. This chapter describes the approaches used to reducing the number of assets and the typical problems to avoid in this process. To take a slightly wider perspective, the determination of how to treat the various instruments and products present in your portfolio is part of the overall process of deciding how to implement VAR in your organisation.

IMPLEMENTING VAR – THE DECISION PROCESS

Chapters 2 and 3 described the three main methods of calculating VAR. The main differences, advantages and disadvantages of each method were also identified. Understanding these differences is a crucial part of the decision-making process on how to implement VAR.

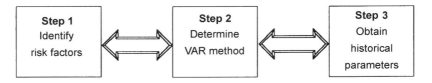

Figure 5.1

The VAR implementation decision process is illustrated in Figure 5.1. Although there is a general flow of logic through steps 1 to 3 there is also an element of iteration. As discussed in previous chapters, the type of VAR model to be used is dependent on the types of risk present, now and in the future, in the portfolio and the availability of historical price series or estimates of volatilities and correlations. For example, although one might prefer the historical simulation approach for calculating VAR, if the portfolio contains options for which it is impossible to obtain, or create, a historical series for the implied volatilities, then it may not be possible to use this method. Hence, it may be necessary to go back and reconsider the use of Monte Carlo simulation.

It is possible to use the Monte Carlo approach to generate missing historical series for use in historical simulation. Typically though, the problem would be to generate a fake historical series with the right volatility and correlation characteristics given that historical simulation uses relative few historical events.

Similarly, iteration can occur between steps 1 and 2. If a few option positions were identified in a portfolio this would point towards the use of historical simulation or Monte Carlo simulation. Once the increased effort and cost of implementing either of these VAR methods had been considered it may well be that one would want to go back and determine the exact extent of optionality within the portfolio with the intention of taking a view as to whether the optionality can be ignored. In general, even small amounts of optionality should not be ignored as it will often have a disproportionately large effect on the overall VAR number.

IDENTIFYING RISK FACTORS

First things first. Know what types of risk your organisation is exposed to. It is also essential to know the magnitudes of the exposures. In this chapter we largely concentrate on market risk exposures which is the area of risk in which the use of VAR has become standard practice. This chapter deals with the analysis of different types of market risk using risk factors.

What are Risk Factors?

VAR is normally implemented by representing individual assets as risk factors. A single risk factor may be used to represent hundreds or even thousands of individual assets. Each individual asset must be 'mapped' onto one or more risk factors. The process of mapping assets onto risk factors is described in the sections below dealing with the main classes of assets. The definition of a risk factor is:

A parameter whose value changes in the financial markets and whose change in value will cause a change in the portfolio value.

A risk factor may be a directly observable market price, such as the price of gold, or a foreign exchange rate. Alternatively, a risk factor may not be directly observable. An example of such risk factors are zero coupon yields. Many implementations of VAR (see section on interest rates below) use zero coupon yield curves. In the US and French markets, zero coupon curves are directly observable and tradable, however, in most markets zero coupon yields have to be derived from par yields, futures and swaps.

The concept of risk factors is not new to VAR. Traders and risk managers have always used sensitivities (such as the value of a basis point move) to manage positions and risk. A sensitivity quantifies the portfolio's exposure to an underlying risk factor. The concept of risk factors is well illustrated by considering the classic risk analysis of yield curves. A yield curve's movements are described in terms of three risk factors:

1. Parallel shift in the yield curve.
2. Twist (e.g. steepening/flattening yield curve).
3. Bow (humping or dipping in the middle part of the curve).

Of the three risk factors, the parallel shift is by far and away the most important, accounting for 70–80% of yield curve movements. This explains why the sensitivity measure, PVBP (present value of a basis point parallel shift), is the main measure of risk still used by many interest rate trading businesses as the risk factor underlying the PVBP sensitivity is a parallel movement in the yield curve.

Using Sensitivities to Calculate VAR

Sensitivities are often used as the key mechanism, along with risk factors, for implementing VAR. A sensitivity quantifies the exposure of a portfolio to a given risk factor, i.e. a PVBP of £1,000 means that the value of the portfolio will change by £1,000 for a one basis point parallel shift in the yield curve. Remembering the simple equation to calculate VAR for a single position:

$$VAR = P.V$$

Table 5.1   Equivalent VAR calculations for a bond

	$10m, 10 year bond. Price volatility: 0.84%; PVBP: $7,000 Volatility in basis points: 12	VAR
Position-based calculation	VAR $=$ 10m $\times$ 0.84/100	$84,000
Sensitivity-based calculation	VAR $=$ 7,000 $\times$ 12	$84,000

For a single asset, VAR is simply the position multiplied by the volatility of that position. We can now see that VAR can be calculated by substituting the position with the sensitivity of the position to one or more risk factors. The volatility must then be expressed in the same terms as the sensitivity. Table 5.1 illustrates two equivalent VAR calculations for a bond.

One of the immediate attractions of the use of sensitivities is that they are readily available in almost all trading operations. As mentioned above, traders have traditionally managed (and still do) their positions using sensitivity measures of risk and exposure. The ready availability of sensitivities can lead to a rapid implementation of VAR if the sensitivities correspond to the risk factors identified for the portfolio.

Cash Flows versus Sensitivities

One of the most common ways VAR is implemented is via the use of cash flows. In this approach, assets are decomposed into cash flows and then the cash flows are mapped onto pre-defined risk factors. This approach assumes that any position can be decomposed into cash flows. A cash flow may represent an interest rate risk, a foreign currency exposure, or perhaps an equity or commodity position.

The best description of one cash flow-based VAR implementation approach is given by J P Morgan in their *RiskMetrics*^{TM} *Technical Document* (Guldimann, 1995). It should be noted that this approach works well for linear instruments but is not applicable to options (as per the whole of RiskMetrics^{TM}). The application of this approach to linear instruments is described in the sections below on the VAR treatment of various instrument types.

What is really needed is an approach to decomposing any instrument including options into risk factors. Sensitivities allow us to do this. The decomposition of options into the sensitivities known as 'the Greeks' was described in Chapters 2 and 3. Chapter 2 described the risk factors underlying the Greeks. The Greeks can be used to allow an infinite number of individual options to be represented by a handful of risk factors, in fact the more options in a portfolio the better it will be represented by the Greeks.[1] The problems shown in Chapter 3 for options which are close to expiry and at-the-money are likely to be minimised in a large diversified portfolio of options.

The use of sensitivities also avoids the discussion of exactly how to represent an awkward product as a collection of cash flows. Cash flows work well for standard products but an accurate representation rapidly becomes difficult as the product becomes more non-standard. For example the decomposition of standard swaps into cash flows is straightforward; the fixed side cash flows are known and the floating side cash flows can be generated using a forward curve. This becomes impossible for non-standard swaps such as 'set in arrears' swaps. The use of sensitivities avoids this type of problem altogether.

Sensitivities to underlying risk factors can be calculated for most instruments. All instruments must have a valuation model (otherwise they cannot be traded and the position cannot be managed) ranging from a simple derivation of present value to exotic option models. The valuation model for all instruments, no matter how complex, can be used to calculate the valuation impact of changing one of the valuation parameters. The valuation parameters are specific examples of risk factors. The change in value of the instrument, for a given change in a particular risk factor, is the sensitivity of the instrument to that risk factor. Sensitivities simply quantify the portfolio exposure to risk factors. This approach cannot be used for exotic options such as barriers, or digitals, which have discontinuous price functions (i.e. sudden change in price or behaviour under specific circumstances).

When using the sensitivity approach it is important to ensure that the sensitivities are accurate as they directly affect the resultant VAR. This is particularly true for options where the sensitivity can change significantly dependent on whether the option is at-the-money. Therefore, it is important to ensure that the option valuation models used to generate sensitivities are consistent with the approach to pricing that is used in the markets. Mis-specified or mis-calibrated valuation models can give rise to significant 'model risk'. Model risk is the risk that exposure and risk figures (including VAR) are incorrect/inaccurate. Model risk can also lead to ineffective hedging and unexpected losses.

In conclusion, the use of sensitivities allows risk exposures for linear and option-based instruments to be combined, whereas cash flows are only applicable to linear instruments. Sensitivities, although often readily available, cannot be taken at face value. It is essential to ensure the valuation models that produced them are consistent with market pricing practice.

Identifying Risk Factors in a Portfolio

The correct identification of risk factors is absolutely critical to obtaining a good estimate of VAR. There is no magic recipe for choosing risk factors correctly. To a certain extent, identifying risk factors is a matter of trial and error. Each portfolio must be examined critically to determine the main sources of risk. Such an examination may well be aided by the use of volatilities and correlations. In some cases it will be obvious which are the main risk factors. Identifying risk factors consists of two main steps:

1. *Identify all risk factors*   Most of this chapter is dedicated to describing the main categories of risk factors to be found and discusses how to represent different types of instrument and markets as risk factors efficiently.
2. *Determine their relative importance*   Determination of the relative importance of risk factors is largely an examination of the relative magnitudes of exposures to risk factors. The following example will illustrate this process.

Consider a portfolio which is mainly made up of positions in foreign currencies but also has some bonds, its composition is given in Table 5.2.

The bonds constitute nearly 20% by nominal position size of the portfolio and therefore may have a significant impact on the overall risk of the portfolio. Of course, in VAR terms, the relative volatilities also matter. Given that the bonds have a significantly lower volatility than the currencies in this portfolio, the VAR effect of the bonds is much less than indicated by their proportion of the portfolio. In fact the VAR of this portfolio with the bonds is $467,707, and $467,039 without the bonds. This is a difference of 0.14%, i.e. virtually no difference at all!

It might be concluded that the bonds could be ignored; this would be a safe conclusion if:

- The proportion of bonds never grew to be significant (beyond about 30% with the same volatilities).

- The ratio of the volatilities between the currencies and the bonds did not change significantly (with the bonds making up 20% of the portfolio, bond volatilities would need to be multiplied nearly ten-fold to contribute 10% of the overall VAR).

Given the above, barring a significant change in the proportion of bond trading or a fairly fundamental change in the price change behaviour of these assets, it would be safe to ignore the bonds. In practice, they would be included for completeness.

Table 5.2 Relative importance of risk factors

Description	Position ($m)	Volatility (%)
Mexican Peso currency	5	7
Japanese Yen currency	5	1.5
Rand currency	10	3
Bonds – US$	5	0.5

However, they would not be modelled with much precision. The bonds could be represented as a single bond with a volatility arrived at by averaging the volatilities of the individual bond positions. In addition, it would not be appropriate to spend a lot of effort in maintaining a historical price change series for the bond position, whereas it would be critical to get an accurate measure of volatility for the Rand currency.

This example demonstrates the process of identifying and ranking risk factors in general. The remaining sections of this chapter describe how the main asset classes are decomposed into risk factors. The interest rate section also deals with alternative approaches to mapping cash flows and sensitivities to risk factors.

INTEREST RATE ASSETS

The value of interest rate based assets, without optionality, is essentially the present value of all future cash flows. The present value of a single cash flow is given by:

$$PV = CF.e^{-r.T}$$

where: $CF =$ value of cash flow
  $PV =$ present value of cash flow
   $r =$ the interest rate being used to discount the cash flow
   $T =$ the time to the value date of the future cash flow, i.e. the date on which you expect to receive the future cash flow.
  $e^{-rT} =$ a general equation for discounting future values. e is the natural logarithm and its use implies a continuously compounded rate of interest. Zero coupon curves are normally constructed with continuously compounding rates and are used to value instruments that can be broken down into cash flows. The interest rate for any maturity given by a zero coupon curve is the continuously compounded rate of interest that is consistent with market prices.

From the above it can be seen that the value of interest rate based assets is sensitive to changes in the interest rates associated with the dates of future cash flow. Unfortunately, interest rates for future dates are not identical. Interest rates or yields are a function of the following:

- *The maturity of the deposit or cash flow*   Yields have a 'term structure', i.e. the yield offered on a deposit will differ according to the maturity of the deposit. The term structure of yields is normally called the 'yield curve'. In general, yield curves are upwards sloping, i.e. the longer the maturity of the deposit the greater is the offered yield.

The yield curve has other interesting properties. In general, yield volatility decreases with maturity and the correlations between yields at two adjacent maturities increases with maturity. This gives a clue as to how interest rate assets should be treated when calculating VAR.

- *The credit risk of the deposit taker also affects the yield offered*   The lower the credit rating (the higher the risk of bankruptcy), the higher the yield that must be offered to compensate an investor. Assets with different credit risk have different volatilities and the correlations between bonds with different credit ratings although high, are materially lower than unity. Thus Eurobond prices have some independence of movement from government bonds. This is known as credit spread risk or just spread risk.

- *Liquidity is another factor that affects yield levels and yield volatilities*   Although some market observers consider liquidity at least as important as credit in determining yield levels and volatilities, liquidity is typically not treated separately from credit risk and the term structure of yields.

Credit Risk and Interest Rate Assets

Interest rate risk factors are normally chosen to take account of, firstly, the term structure and then, if required, credit risk. In the portfolio described in the section on identifying risk factors, bonds constituted a small and relatively unimportant portion of the portfolio. In this case it would not matter if the two bonds were lumped together regardless of the fact that one is a Eurobond with credit risk and the other is a government bond, notionally, without credit risk. Merely taking the net bond position would only take account of the interest rate risk but would ignore the spread risk between Euro and government bonds.

Consider a portfolio consisting of two bonds, $100m long of a five-year Eurobond with a price volatility of 0.5806 and short $80m of a government bond with a volatility of 0.5534; the correlation between the two bonds is 0.96192. Table 5.3 shows the VAR for the portfolio treating the portfolio first as a net open position of $20m of the Eurobond and then taking account of both of the bond positions. The difference between the two VAR figures is the credit spread risk.

Table 5.3   VAR for simple bond portfolio

Portfolio treatment	VAR ($'000s)
Simple net open position	116
Two separate bonds	196

Basis Risk

In practice, all significant bond trading operations would model the spread risk. Spread risk is a type of basis risk. Basis risk occurs between any pair of interest rate instruments which are priced off different 'bases'. These bases are typically embodied in yield curves which are specific to an instrument class. For example, the swap yield curve although highly correlated with the government curve does have some independence of movement; the swap curve is considered to reflect the credit risk associated with an average bank, i.e. typically a credit rating of double A (AA) (as at time of going to press). Another significant basis risk is that between swaps and three-month interest rate futures. Interest rate futures have a life of their own – especially around the rollover date from one contract to the next. Therefore, when implementing VAR for interest rate portfolios it is critical to identify all the basis risks present in the portfolio and to determine their relative importance, i.e. the VAR impact of each basis risk. Each basis risk to be modelled will require a set of instrument specific risk factors.

Interest Rate Risk Factors

A typical interest rate portfolio will contain hundreds of instruments, all of which will have price, or value volatilities and all of which will be correlated to each other. In theory at least we should measure all their volatilities and correlations. Clearly it is not practical to measure volatilities and correlations between maturities for every instrument at every maturity down a yield curve. Also, there would be no risk parameters for new instruments added to the portfolio. In practice the structure and behaviour of yield curves are studied to see where the volatility and correlation behaviour changes down the curve. Such studies have shown that a yield curve can be represented by relatively few maturity points, as shown in Table 5.4.

Table 5.4 gives an example set of maturities that could be used. It is not uncommon to use different maturity points for different currencies; even within one currency, curves for different instruments may have different maturity points.

In particular, for large bond trading operations, at least one separate curve will be used for non-government bonds to capture the credit spread risk. Sophisticated bond trading operations may not treat all non-government bonds as a single asset class. Instead, non-government bonds may be split into separate asset classes based on credit rating. Therefore curves, volatilities and correlations will be created for several different groupings of credit rating. Individual bonds are then mapped to the curve corresponding to the credit rating of the bond. The potential problem with this approach, as with all attempts at subdivision of risk factors, is the creation and maintenance of a large number of volatilities and correlations. There may be insufficient data available to calculate meaningful volatilities and correlations.

Table 5.4   Yield curve risk factors

Representative maturities
Overnight
1 week
1 month
3 months
6 months
1 year
2 years
3 years
4 years
5 years
7 years
10 years
20 years

The maturity points to be used are determined not only by the behavioural characteristics of the curve but also by the availability of quality data to determine volatilities and correlations. Quality data is best obtained from large highly-liquid markets such as the swap and futures markets.

In addition, the maturity points will be chosen with regard to the maturity of the organisation's portfolio. If the maturity of the portfolio is largely at the long end, then there is little reason to have a large number of short maturity points, whereas, more points should be used at the long end.

The maturity points (often referred to as 'vertices' or 'pillars') are in fact the risk factors to be used for a particular yield curve. As can be seen from the discussion above it is easy to end up with a large number of risk factors for interest rate portfolios. If significant basis and credit spread risk positions are being run it may be necessary to have several yield curves per currency, each with a dozen maturity points. It is essential to back test your VAR model using different risk factors to determine the necessity for the risk factors being considered.

So far so good. We have now reduced a yield curve from having one risk factor per day to having only 12 or so risk factors per instrument type. The trouble is that the maturity of most individual assets will not fall on one of the risk factors specified. Therefore, we must now 'map' the assets onto the specified risk factors or find some other way of determining the exposure to each risk factor. The two main approaches used are described below:

1. The cash flow mapping method.

2. The sensitivity-based approach.

Cash Flow Mapping

As noted before, the cash flow mapping approach assumes that all instruments can be represented as cash flows – this is not true for options and for other complex instruments. Cash flows which fall between the maturity points chosen as risk factors must be 'mapped' to the two maturity points on either side of the cash flow. This is shown in Figure 5.2.

It is the market value of the cash flow that is mapped, rather than the actual amount of the cash flow. The market value is, of course, the present value of the cash flow, discounted using the yield curve used to value the instrument. The objective in the mapping process is to ensure that the VAR is the same for the single cash flow as it is when split into two, i.e. VAR equivalency is maintained.

Unfortunately, if exactly the same answer is required before and after mapping, it is not possible to simply apportion the market value to the two reference vertices depending on the distance between the two. The equation below, from Chapter 2, was used to find the variance of a portfolio of two assets, A and B:

$$\sigma_P^2 = a^2.\sigma_A^2 + b^2.\sigma_B^2 + 2a.b.\rho_{AB}.\sigma_A.\sigma_B$$

If σ_P is the price (market value) volatility of the single cash flow, σ_A and σ_B are the price volatilities of the vertices on either side of the cash flow and ρ_{AB} is the correlation between the two vertices, then this equation can be used to ensure that market risk equivalency is maintained. The quantities a and b (the quantities of assets A and B) need to be replaced with the proportion, x, of the cash flow to be mapped to each vertex:

$$\sigma_P^2 = x.\sigma_A^2 + (1 - x).\sigma_B^2 + 2x.(1 - x).\rho_{AB}.\sigma_A.\sigma_B$$

This equation takes the form of a quadratic:

$$a.x^2 + b.x + c = 0$$

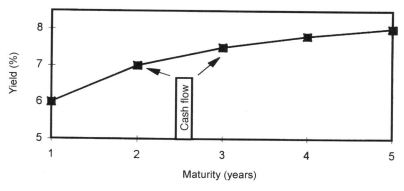

Figure 5.2 Mapping cash flows to vertices

which can be solved for x:

$$x = \frac{-b \pm \sqrt{b^2 - 4a.c}}{2a}$$

where: $a = \sigma_A^2 + \sigma_B^2 - 2.\rho_{AB}.\sigma_A.\sigma_B$
         $b = 2.\rho_{AB}.\sigma_A.\sigma_B - 2.\sigma_B^2$
         $c = \sigma_B^2 - \sigma_P^2$

The price volatility, σ_P, of the cash flow can be arrived at by linear interpolation of the price volatilities of the vertices on either side of the cash flow, using the following equation:

$$\sigma_P = y.\sigma_{P1} + (1 - y).\sigma_{P2}$$

where: $y =$ the fraction of distance between two vertices. If vertices 1 and 2 have maturities of two and four years and the cash flow to be mapped has a maturity of two and a half years then $y = 0.25$, i.e. $(2.5 - 2)/(4 - 2)$.

σ_{P1} and $\sigma_{P2} =$ price volatilities of vertices 1 and 2.

It should also be noted that there are two possible roots to the above quadratic. The rule is to use the root which is between 0 and 1.

Sensitivity-based Approach

The sensitivity-based approach to VAR works with a portfolio's sensitivities to changes in the value of risk factors. For interest rate assets, the yield at each vertex is a risk factor and shifted independently, as shown in Figure 5.3, to determine the sensitivity of the portfolio to a change in the yield at the vertex.

Figure 5.3 shows how the sensitivity to a small shift in rates (typically a one basis point shift) is calculated. The idea is to determine the portfolio value sensitivity to a change in yield at each vertex. Traders use this information to assess the amount of curve risk they are running. This analysis is also known as a delta ladder. The yield at each vertex is raised and then dropped again, progressing down the curve. Table 5.5 gives an example of a delta ladder report for a portfolio. This report shows the impact of yields changing independently at each of the chosen vertices.

Figure 5.3 shows shifts at two adjacent vertices; these two shifts are made separately, one after the other. Figure 5.3 shows that yields are raised, typically in a straight line, between zero and one basis point from the vertices on either side of the vertex being shifted. Rates at all other vertices are left unchanged.

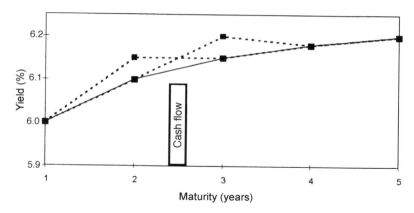

Figure 5.3   Calculating delta ladder sensitivities

The sensitivity value for the two-year point will include the value change of all positions whose value is partly or wholly dependent on yields between one and three years. For example, a two-year bond would clearly be affected, so would a five-year swap, as it will have cash flows that fall within the one to three-year maturity range. A five-year bond would not be affected as its value is only sensitive to changes in the five-year par yield. The amount the yield will be shifted will depend on exactly where between the one and three-year vertices the cash flow or position falls.

Figure 5.3 shows that a cash flow between two vertices will affect the sensitivity value at the vertices on either side. In effect the sensitivity of the cash flow is mapped to the vertices on either side of the cash flow using linear interpolation.

Table 5.5   Delta ladder sensitivity report

Maturities	Sensitivity PVBP ($)
Overnight	1,000
1 week	5,645
1 month	−7,376
3 months	−12,045
6 months	2,368
1 year	15,284
2 years	7,345
3 years	7,565
4 years	7,878
5 years	7,999
7 years	8,102
10 years	70,225
20 years	0

Table 5.6 Market risk data for 2, 3 and 4-year maturities

Maturity (years)	Price volatility (%)	Yield volatility (%)	Yield (%)
2	0.2146	1.69	6.96
3	0.3487	1.75	7.31
4	0.4747	1.73	7.56

Whilst this method will ensure constant sensitivity it does not ensure constant VAR as with the cash flow mapping method described above.

The difference between the two approaches will depend on the correlations between the vertices and how steep the volatility term structure is. If the correlations are close to one and the volatility term structure is not too steep the methods will give very similar results.

Using as an example a single cash flow at three years, Table 5.6 shows the actual price volatilities, yield volatilities and yields needed to compute VAR for the cash flow in various ways. The correlation between the second and fourth years is 0.9698. Of course as we actually have the price volatility at the three-year point there is no need to map the cash flow, however, it serves to illustrate the difference between the calculated VAR when calculated directly compared to the cash flow and sensitivity-based approaches.

Table 5.7 summarises the results of the three methods of calculating VAR for a single cash flow that have been discussed. The first method – the original cash flow – is taken to be the 'correct' VAR for the cash flow. Note that the quadratic method does not give exactly the same answer as that directly calculated for the cash flow. The answer is different because the price volatilities are not perfectly proportional to maturity (i.e. the volatility is not a straight line). Table 5.7 indicates that the error introduced through use of a mapping technique is likely to be small. This will be true except in rare circumstances, i.e. low correlation between vertices and a steep volatility curve.

As a general point, far more error is likely to be introduced into a VAR model through the use of inappropriate valuations or cash flow models than the minor errors generated through the different approaches to mapping sensitivities or cash flows.

Table 5.7 VAR mapping estimations

Method	VAR	Difference
Original cash flow	282.2	–
Mapped cash flow – quadratic mapping	280.9	−0.4%
Mapped sensitivity – delta ladder	280.4	−0.7%

As already stated, when using the sensitivity-based approach, it is essential to ensure that the valuation model used to generate the sensitivity is consistent with market practice. If using a cash flow-based approach, be sure that your instruments can be effectively modelled using cash flows and that the modelling is correct. This should be done by comparing results against a sensitivity-based VAR model of the instrument. The remainder of this chapter describes the cash flow and sensitivity-based treatment of various instrument types grouped together by asset class.

INTEREST RATE INSTRUMENT TREATMENT

The cash flow-based approach is most applicable to simple interest rate instruments. Given the very wide range of interest rate instruments in use in the financial markets, only a subset is addressed here. It is intended that the reader will be able to understand the general approach to modelling instruments from the description below. All interest rate instruments can be modelled using the sensitivity-based approach as long as an appropriate valuation model is available.

Loans and Deposits

Loans and deposits are the simplest of the interest rate instruments and can be modelled successfully as cash flows, or as sensitivities. The value of a loan or deposit is simply the present value of all future cash flows using a zero curve; this allows for the simple representation as cash flows. The present value of the cash flows or the sensitivities associated with loans and deposits can be determined and mapped to risk factor vertices.

Swaps

Swaps can be modelled in various ways. Swaps are often thought of as a combination of fixed rate and floating rate bonds and can be modelled as such by decomposing the two bonds into cash flows and mapping the present value of the cash flows to vertices.

In practice, however, swaps are not valued in the same way as bonds. The value of a swap is the present value of all the cash flows associated with it. Swaps normally use zero coupon curves as the valuation curve. The fixed rate side of a swap is easy to model as the cash flows are known. For the floating rate side, only the next cash flow is known. The best approach to modelling the floating side is to generate the forward floating rate cash flows from the forward curve derived from the zero curve. Once all the cash flows are known they can then be mapped onto the risk factor vertices, as described above.

Bonds

Bonds, too, are often modelled as a series of cash flows and then mapped onto a zero coupon curve. In practice bonds are not valued using a zero curve but, rather, using the yield-to-maturity. The yield-to-maturity is equivalent to the internal rate of return, i.e. it is the interest rate which when used to discount all future cash flows will give a present value equal to the price of the bond. The bond markets work off yield-to-maturity, or 'par', curves. This means that a bond price is only sensitive to a change in yield at the redemption date of the bond.

Therefore, it does not make sense to map a bond's cash flows onto a zero curve. Rather the approach, which more accurately reflects market pricing practice, is to create a par curve for government bonds and map either the sensitivity of the bond, or a cash flow equal to its market value onto the par curve. If a bond is decomposed into cash flows (as implemented by some system vendors) its VAR will display sensitivity to changes in volatilities and correlations down the curve, however in practice, only a change in yield at the maturity of the bond will affect its price.

Bond Futures

Bond futures are contracts in which a known quantity of one of a set of deliverable bonds is delivered to the holder of a long position in the future. The value of a bond futures contract is primarily dependent on the value of the bond to be delivered at any point in time, known as the cheapest-to-deliver bond (CTD). A straightforward implementation of VAR for bond futures represents the future as an equivalent amount of the cheapest-to-deliver bond and is given by the following equation:

$$\text{Equivalent CTD position} = \text{nominal value of futures positions} \times \text{price factor} \times \text{market value of the CTD bond}$$

The price factor (also called the conversion factor) is given for each deliverable bond by the exchange. The equivalent position should also include accrued interest at the time of delivery. It should also be noted that a bond futures contract is effectively a forward purchase of the CTD bond. Therefore, the cash flow corresponding to the purchase of the CTD bond should be included in the VAR modelling of this product. As a bond future is a forward purchase of the CTD, any coupon payments between now and delivery date of the contract should be excluded.

Basis trading involves taking equal and opposite positions in bonds and bond futures. There is a basis risk between the two which should be modelled if bond future basis trading is a significant business activity. Bond future basis risk is probably best modelled by taking the bond and the future together and calling it a basis position with its own volatility. For example, a basis position of $100m long of the CTD bond combined with a short position of $100m short the future can be modelled as a $100m position in the bond-future-basis.

One of the features of bond futures trading is that the CTD bond will change as yields move up or down. Therefore a sensitivity-based approach to modelling bond futures could model the change in CTD for a yield shift equivalent to the yield volatility. This will give a value change in the bond future equal to the VAR of the bond future.

A full understanding of the pricing of bond futures is a lengthy subject in itself and is beyond the scope of this book. For an introduction to the subject see Hull (1993, p. 88) and for a more comprehensive treatment see Burghardt *et al.* (1994).

Forward Rate Agreements (FRAs)

FRAs are interest rate contracts that lock in the future value of the interest rate for a specified period in the future. FRAs can be accurately represented as cash flows. If the trader buys a 12 × 15 FRA, i.e. a FRA that locks in the value of three-month interest rates in one year's time and is settled in one year, this can be represented by a forward three-month deposit commencing in one year. Using this approach, FRAs can be represented as cash flows and mapped to the appropriate zero curve. Consider a 12 × 15 FRA for £500,000, i.e. a FRA for the three-month interest rate prevalent in 12 months time (6.82%). This would typically be represented in terms of cash flows as shown in Table 5.8.

The information required to calculate VAR is given in Table 5.9. Working this through using the covariance VAR calculation gives a VAR for the FRA of £202.[2]

Alternatively, we can use the sensitivity-based approach and calculate the

Table 5.8 Representing a 12 × 15 FRA as cash flows

Maturity	Cash flow	Present value
1 year	−£500,000	−£470,000 Mapped to the one year vertex
1 year 3 months	$500,000\left(1 + \left(\dfrac{6.82}{100}\right)\cdot\left(\dfrac{90}{360}\right)\right) = £508,525$	£470,000 Mapped to the 1 and 2-year vertices. The quadratic solution indicates that the proportion of this cash flow that must be mapped to the one year vertex is 0.7214

Table 5.9 Volatility and correlation data for the VAR calculation for 12 × 15 FRA (correlation between 1 and 2-year vertices is 0.862377)

Vertex	Price volatility	Mapped NPV cash flow positions
1 year	0.0752	−130,941 (−470,000 + 470,000 * 0.7214)
2 year	0.2146	130,941 (470,000 * (1−0.7214))

sensitivity of the FRA to a one-basis point shift in yields, using the correct market valuation method. First we need the valuation equation for a FRA, V:

$$V = \left(\left(\frac{P.(F-S)}{100} \right) . \left(\frac{T}{B} \right) \right) . \left(\frac{1}{1 + \left(\frac{F}{100} \right) . \left(\frac{T}{B} \right)} \right)$$

where: $P =$ principal amount of the FRA
$F =$ forward rate for the tenor of the FRA which in this example is the three-month forward rate in one year
$S =$ strike rate which is the three-month forward rate at the time the deal was executed
$T =$ tenor of the FRA, in this case, three months, taken to be 90 days
$B =$ day basis: actual/360 in the United States and for most currencies; actual/actual in the UK

The valuation equation gives the difference in the three months of interest between the three-month forward rate when the deal was struck and three-month LIBOR when the deal is settled which is at the beginning of the calculation period, i.e. in 12 months in this example. As the deal is settled at the beginning of the calculation period, the amount to be settled is discounted back from the end to the beginning of the calculation period.

If we now assume that the strike rate was 6.82%, then we can work out the value change for a one-basis point change in yields by setting the forward yield to 6.83%. Therefore the PVBP of the FRA in this example is £12.12. The PVBP is the value change of the FRA in 12 months time; this needs to be discounted back to today giving a PVBP of the FRA of £11.40.

Now VAR can be calculated for the FRA once we have volatility expressed in terms of basis points. The volatility in basis points is given by:

$$VOL_{BP} = VOL_Y.Y$$

where: $VOL_Y =$ the forward yield volatility
$Y =$ the forward yield.

If the forward three-month yield is 7.17% and the volatility of the forward yield is 2.42%, then volatility in basis points, is $2.42 \times 7.17 = 17.3514$. Thus VAR for the FRA is given by:

$$\text{FRA VAR} = 17.3514 \times 11.4 = £197.81$$

This must be the correct answer as the sensitivity was arrived at using the standard market valuation method (if we shift the forward rate by 17.3514 basis points we get a direct valuation change for the FRA of £197.74). This is very close to the answer that we achieved using cash flows (£202).

Interest Rate Futures

Interest futures are contracts on forward three-month interest rates and are very similar to FRAs. They are margined and therefore the marking-to-market is undertaken daily by the exchange and any change in the value of contract is either received from or paid to the exchange daily. With interest rate futures the sensitivity is also part of the contract definition. For example, for a Sterling contract the nominal size is £500,000 and the value of a basis point change in the forward yield is specified as £12.50.

Given that the sensitivity is a known and fixed quantity it does not seem to make sense to represent an interest rate future as cash flows in a VAR model; the given sensitivity should be used directly. However, if a cash flow-based approach must be used, then an interest rate future can be represented as cash flows in essentially the same way as a FRA. The only difference being that as a future is margined daily, the forward value change of the contract is settled daily without discounting back to today's value. Therefore, the future cash flows need to be adjusted for this lack of discounting. This is done by dividing the FRA cash flows by the discount factor for the value date of each cash flow. If this is done, a sensitivity of close to £12.50 will be achieved.

FOREIGN EXCHANGE

All foreign currency positions must be expressed in terms of the base valuation currency of the organisation, normally the currency of the country in which the organisation is incorporated.

Spot Foreign Exchange Positions

As demonstrated in the treatment of Portfolio 1 in Chapter 2, foreign currency positions are expressed as an equivalent amount of the organisation's base currency. For example, with an exchange rate of 2 DEM (Deutschmark) to the US dollar, a DEM 1 million position would be represented as $500,000 worth of DEM mapped to the DEM currency risk factor.

Forward Foreign Exchange Positions

Forward foreign exchange rates are determined by adding interest to today's spot rate. The interest to be added is the difference between the interest (for the relevant maturity) in the first currency and the interest in the second currency. Thus the forward exchange rate is given by;

$$F = S.e^{(R-r).T}$$

where: F and S = the forward and spot exchange rates respectively
           R and r = the interest rates of the two currencies for the maturity of the forward position.
           T = the time between the spot date and the value date of the forward foreign exchange position
           $e^{r.T}$ = a general formula for working out the forward value of a unit cash amount, at a given time in the future, T, with a given interest rate, r. In the equation above r is replaced by $R - r$, i.e. the difference between the interest rates in the two currencies. R is the interest rate for the base currency of the portfolio, r is the interest rate of the foreign currency.

From the above we can see that forward foreign exchange positions are sensitive to changes in the spot rate and to changes in the interest rates of both currencies. Therefore, forward foreign exchange positions can be successfully treated as cash flows or as sensitivities. The cash flow representation is arrived at by considering a forward foreign exchange position to be a combination of a spot foreign exchange position and an exchange of the principal amount of the forward contract. The example below illustrates the method.

Example: Forward contract to buy 1 million Deutschmark in one year at a forward rate of 2.0401 DEM/US$ (US$-based portfolio). Spot rate is: 2.

Risk factor	Cash flow	Present value ($)	Sensitivity/position
Spot Deutschmark	DEM 1m in one year	481,043	481,043
One-year DEM interest rate	Cash flow of DEM (1m)	481,043	46.119
One-year US$ interest rate	Cash flow of $490,172	(462,750)	−92.384

The present values are arrived at by discounting the cash flows back to today using the DEM one-year rate for the DEM flows and the US$ one-year rate for the US$ flow. The interest rate sensitivities are arrived at by changing the interest rate in the equation for the forward value of an exchange rate given above. In practice both approaches give similar VARs. Note the sensitivity approach still uses the spot Deutschmark position, whilst the other cash flows become sensitivities.

COMMODITIES

Settled commodity positions can be treated in the same way as spot foreign exchange positions. There will be a single risk factor for each different commodity held. Forward commodity contracts are treated in a slightly different way to forward foreign exchange positions. There is an additional factor to consider with commodities, this is the 'convenience yield'. The forward value of a commodity is given by:

$$F = S.e^{(R+C)T}$$

where: $C =$ the convenience yield
         $R =$ the interest rate of the contract
F and $S =$ the forward and spot prices of the commodity, respectively

The convenience yield is often taken to include the cost of storing the commodity as well as expressing future supply and demand. In fact, storage costs only affect commodities, such as gold, which are held for investment purposes. For other consumable commodities, the convenience yield only reflects the market's judgement of future supply and demand for the commodity. Just like interest rates, the convenience yield has a term structure, therefore there is a term structure of volatility for the convenience yield of each commodity.

Strictly speaking a forward commodity position could be split into a physical position, plus positions in the convenience yield and the relevant interest rate. In practice this is rarely done in VAR implementations. Instead, the interest rate and convenience yield are considered together; both are embodied in the forward prices of commodities. For the calculation of VAR this is an adequate representation and follows market pricing convention. However, for stress testing, when stressing interest rates, the impact on future commodity prices should be modelled in terms of interest rates and convenience yields separately. Stress tests should be undertaken on the value impact of changing the convenience yield and the relevant interest rate. The example on page 124 shows how a forward contract to purchase a commodity is normally represented.

Example: Three-month forward contract to purchase 1 million ounces of gold for $350m.

Risk Factor	Position
3 month gold	The present value of $350m of gold, discounted using the combined US$ and convenience yield rate.

The present value of the dollar equivalent of the gold position would then be multiplied by the volatility of three-month gold prices, to find the position's VAR.

EQUITIES

The appropriate treatment of equities will depend on the number of stocks in the portfolio. Equity portfolios can contain hundreds of stocks, each with individual volatilities and correlations if treated as individual stocks. We wish to reduce the number of risk factors to a minimum without seriously compromising the resultant VAR estimate. If there are a large number of stocks then it is possible to represent individual stocks as positions in the associated stock index. If there are only a few stocks, then each stock must be modelled individually.

An equity's return (percentage price change) can be described in terms of the performance of the relevant index and the performance of the individual company. This can be expressed mathematically:

$$R_A = \beta_A.R_i + E_A + \epsilon_A$$

where: R_A = return of stock A
β_A = beta of stock A. The beta of the stock is the extent the stock's price will change in relation to the index. For example, a beta of 1.5 indicates that the stock's price is more volatile than the index, i.e. a 1% change in the index will result in a 1.5% change in the stock's price, on average.
R_i = return of the index
E_A = expected return for stock A – less the expected return of the index. For equities there is an expected positive daily price change which, again, is partly down to the index and partly down to the individual stock. E_A is that part of the expected return that is only down to the stock A.
ϵ_A = the random return associated with stock A

In a similar manner, the volatility of an individual stock can also be decomposed in terms of the volatility of the index and of the individual stock:

$$\sigma_A^2 = \beta_A^2.\sigma_i^2 + \sigma_\epsilon^2$$

where: σ_A^2 = variance of stock A
σ_i^2 = variance of the index
σ_ϵ^2 = variance of stock A due to the company – known as specific risk

When a sufficient number of stocks are present in a portfolio, the specific risk can be considered to be diversified away. J P Morgan (Laubsch, 1996) show that the number of stocks required to give effective diversification in the US market is approximately 25, though this will depend on the weighting of the stocks being fairly even and there being no concentrations to specific industry sectors. It should also be noted that the number of stocks required to achieve a reasonable level of diversification will not be the same for all equity markets.

Therefore, if a US equity portfolio contains less than 25 stocks it should probably be represented as individual stocks. However, this does depend on the importance of equities to the organisation's overall portfolio. If equities account only for a small proportion of the overall portfolio, say less than 15%, then it is probably safe to represent the equities in terms of an equivalent index position, i.e. the small proportion of equities in the portfolio will have a small impact on the VAR of the portfolio. This also assumes that the equity part of the portfolio is reasonably diversified, i.e. upwards of 20 individual stocks.

Assuming there are sufficient stocks present in the portfolio, then specific risk can be ignored and the stocks can all be represented as equivalent positions in the index using the following equation:

$$\text{VAR}_P = \sigma_i \sum_{j=1}^{n} \beta_j.P_j$$

where: VAR_P = VAR of the equity portfolio
σ_i = volatility of the relevant equity index (calculated for required confidence level)
β_j = beta of stock J
P_j = market value of stock J in the base currency of the portfolio

This approach reduces equity positions to a single risk factor for each equity market, i.e. the relevant equity index. To calculate VAR for an equity portfolio with positions in more than one market, correlations between the markets must be taken into account. For portfolios with significant concentrations to particular industrial sectors, further accuracy can be gained by using industrial sector indices instead of the index of the whole market.

As an example of the calculation of VAR for an equity portfolio in a single equity market, consider a portfolio made up of stocks A, B and C. The portfolio is shown in Table 5.10.

Table 5.10 Equity portfolio

Stock	Position ($)	Beta
A	30	1
B	50	0.8
C	20	1.5

Using the equation above we can calculate the VAR of the portfolio, the one day 95% confidence volatility of the index is given as 2.2%:

$$VAR_P = 0.022 \times (30 \times 1 + 50 \times 0.8 + 20 \times 1.5)$$

$$VAR_P = \$3.19$$

Forward Equity Positions

Individual equities pay a dividend which can be thought of as a dividend yield, d. Stock indices can be thought of in the same way. Therefore, the future value of a stock or stock index is given by:

$$F = S.e^{(R-D)T}$$

Forward equity contracts are converted into equivalent positions in stock indices as described above. From the equation above, the sensitivity to a change in the interest rate, dividend yield and current index value can be determined. Alternatively, a forward stock index position can convert into cash flows as shown in the example below:

Example: Contract to purchase £1m of the FTSE index in 3 months

Risk factors	Cash flows	Present values
Spot FTSE index value	£1m position in FTSE	£1m discounted back using three-month UK rates
Three-month UK interest rates	−£1m three-month cash flow	−£1m discounted back using three-month UK rates
Three-month FTSE dividend yields	£1m position in dividend yield	£1m discounted back using three-month UK rates

Both the sensitivity and cash flow approach will yield similar results.

SUMMARY

This chapter has illustrated the two main methods of representing instruments in VAR models: as cash flows or as sensitivities and how to map the cash flows or sensitivities onto risk factors. Sensitivities are generally to be preferred over cash flow representation as sensitivities can be calculated directly from the valuation method prevalent in the market and will therefore accurately follow market valuation practice. The cash flow methodology is only applicable to relatively simple instruments and is definitely not applicable to options.

Previous chapters have presented and discussed different ways of implementing options in VAR models. There are a large number of choices to be made along the way to implementing VAR. This is a type of model risk, i.e. the risk that the VAR model does not accurately reflect changes in the market values of instruments. The choices presented above can give rise to significantly different calculated VARs. Marshal and Siegel (1996) asked a number of system vendors who have all implemented J P Morgan's RiskMetrics^{TM} to calculate VAR for a carefully defined portfolio containing a variety of interest rate and foreign exchange-based instruments. The results were fascinating; they found significant variations in the VAR numbers produced. All vendors were given exactly the same volatilities, correlations and portfolio information.

For example, VAR numbers for interest rate instruments had a standard deviation of 55% and the VAR for the whole portfolio had a standard deviation of 25%! The differences were mainly attributed to the different ways in which instruments had been decomposed and implemented in the VAR model. They found that, the more complex the instrument, the greater the variation in the VAR numbers produced. Or, to put it another way, the greater the instrument complexity, the greater the model risk.

This study reinforces the point that great care must be taken in modelling instruments and the need to ensure that the implementation of any specific instrument does actually reflect the way in which the instrument is priced in the market. As a final point, it is worth reiterating the need to undertake hypothetical back tests by instrument type to ensure the VAR model works correctly.

NOTES

1. Note that analytic option sensitivities should not be used. Deriving sensitivities from actual changes in underlying parameters allows them to be combined with sensitivities for options for which no analytic sensitivities exist.

2. $[-130,941 * 0.752 \quad 130,941 * 0.2146]*$

$$\begin{bmatrix} 1 & 0.8624 \\ 0.8624 & 1 \end{bmatrix} * \begin{bmatrix} -130,941 * 0.0752 \\ 130,941 * 0.2146 \end{bmatrix}$$

6
Stress testing

INTRODUCTION

So far this book has concentrated on VAR as a measure of risk. VAR measures risk, expressed as a potential loss, in so called 'normal' markets, i.e. when price changes experienced form a normal distribution. As discussed in Chapter 4, all financial assets are subject to very large price changes that fall outside the normal distribution. Such price changes are known as outliers and are called the fat tails of the price change distribution. This is because in a standard normal distribution only the minutest proportion of price changes would lie at these extremes. Figure 6.1 shows the outliers for gold over a period of five years. As discussed in Chapter 4 there are far more outliers than could be expected in a normal distribution.

It is possible for any bank with a significant trading operation to suffer a loss which, if not an immediate cause of bankruptcy, would cause a severe financial and market embarrassment. In cases where banks have lost significant amounts of money they have often managed to recover purely from a financial point of view. However, the damage to their reputation is likely to affect their share price for

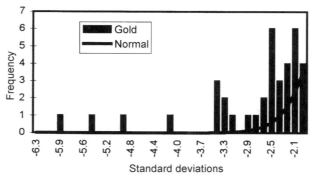

Figure 6.1 Gold distribution – tail

several years and may cause the rating agencies to down-grade the bank which may have a severe impact on the bank's trading business.

Risk management must provide a way of identifying and quantifying the effects of extreme price changes on a bank's portfolio. VAR is insufficient as it only identifies and quantifies changes that can be expected relatively regularly (95% confidence – one day in 20). The methods used to identify and quantify the effect of extreme price changes is a class of methods known as stress testing. This chapter describes and discusses the main methods of stress testing.

One of the main objectives of risk management is to protect against bankruptcy. Risk management cannot guarantee bankruptcy will never happen but it must identify the market events that would cause a severe financial embarrassment. The bank's management can then compare the loss implied by an event against the promised and experienced return from the business unit.

Stress testing must identify extreme events that would cause a significant loss. Management must then decide whether it is acceptable to run the risk of such a loss at a particular point in time. The probability of such an event on an average day will typically be very low. Therefore, the judgement as to whether it is an acceptable risk will be subjective and will rely on management's interpretation of current economic conditions. This is an important point, particularly as risk management has become based more and more on statistical estimation. Good risk management is still and always will be based on good risk managers first and foremost, rather than statistical estimates.

Stress testing should be part of a bank's daily risk management process rather than an occasional investigation. To ensure full integration in the bank's risk management process, stress testing should be used to define limits that represent the bank's extreme appetite for loss. The use of stress testing and its integration into the bank's risk management framework is discussed in the next chapter.

SCENARIO ANALYSIS

When banks first started stress testing it was often referred to as scenario analysis. Scenario analysis seeks to investigate the effect, i.e. portfolio value change of a particular event in the financial markets. Scenarios were typically taken from past, or potential future, economic/natural phenomena, such as war in the Middle East. This might have a dramatic impact on many financial markets:

- Oil price up 50% which causes
- a drop in the US dollar of 20% which, in turn, leads to
- a rise in US interest rates of 1%.

These primary moves would have significant knock-on effects to most of the world's financial markets. Other political phenomena include the unexpected death of heads of state, sudden collapse of government and unexpected economic figures. In all cases it is the unexpected or sudden nature of the news that causes an extreme price move. Financial market prices very quickly take account of news and rumour. Sudden natural disasters can also cause extreme price moves, for example, the Japanese earthquake in 1995. A failed harvest is unlikely to cause an extreme price move, as there would have been plenty of prior warning, unless the final figures are much worse than the markets were expecting.

Stress Testing with Historical Simulation

Another way of scenario testing is to recreate actual past events. The historical simulation method of calculating VAR lends itself particularly well to this type of stress testing. Historical simulation demands a price history for the calculation of VAR. Even if a fairly short period of history is used in the calculation of VAR there is no reason why a much longer history of prices should not be kept for future scenario analysis.

Scenario testing with historical simulation simply involves identifying a past day on which there would have been a large change in the value of today's portfolio, using price changes from that day. Note that a large change in the portfolio value is sought rather than large changes in individual assets. Taking Portfolio 1 as used in the chapters on calculating VAR, i.e. $3m sterling, $2m gold and $1m Rand, Figure 6.2 shows 100 days of value changes for this portfolio.

It is easy to see the day on which the worst loss would have occurred. The size of the loss is in itself an interesting result; −$135,000 compared to a VAR using historical simulation of $43,000. Historical simulation allows easy identification of the percentage changes in each asset on that day (see Table 6.1). This is also useful information as a bank would be able to discuss these results in the context of its trading strategy or intended market positioning.

Historical simulation makes it very easy to identify all losses greater than a given value or percentage and to describe the asset price changes that caused these losses. This enables a profile to be built up of the assets that have extreme price movements at the same time. Identifying the number of extreme price moves for

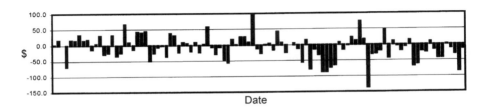

Figure 6.2   Portfolio value change

Table 6.1 Asset price changes

Asset	Change (%)
Sterling	−2.5
Gold	−5.6
Rand	−0.2
Total (weighted)	−2.3

any given asset is straightforward. Historical simulation enables you to go a step further and identify which assets typically move together in times of market stress. Table 6.2 shows the price changes that caused the biggest ten losses in the five years of history used.

It can be seen from Table 6.2 that the two currencies in the portfolio seem to move together in times of market stress. This is suggesting that in times of economic stress the price changes for the currencies have a higher correlation than they do normally. If this was shown to be the case with a larger number of big portfolio value changes then it is extremely important information and should be used when constructing specific scenario tests on a portfolio.

In fact for Portfolio 1, when all changes in the portfolio value of more than 1% were examined, it was found that approximately 60% of them arose as a result of large price moves (greater than 0.5%) in both of the currencies. This is particularly interesting as it was shown earlier in this book that the correlation between Rand and Sterling is close to zero. It would appear then, that in times of market stress, that the correlation between Sterling and Rand increases significantly – to above 0.5 for large portfolio value changes.

Table 6.2 Top ten portfolio losses

Percentage change Gold	Rand	Sterling	Change in portfolio value
−1.41	−13.31	−0.05	−162,956
−0.17	−5.62	−2.53	−135,453
−3.30	−1.77	−0.67	−103,728
0.06	−3.72	−1.77	−89,260
−0.29	−0.71	−2.54	−89,167
−0.33	−3.12	−1.66	−87,448
0.88	−0.79	−3.23	−87,222
0.03	−2.62	−1.98	−85,157
−0.60	−2.14	−1.72	−85,009
−0.60	1.44	−2.68	−77,970

Assessing the Effect of a Bear Market

Another form of scenario testing that can be performed with historical simulation is to measure the effect on a portfolio of a sequence of downward price moves, no one price move among which would cause any concern. This is similar to the maximum drawdown in fund management, i.e. maximum amount of loss that can be suffered during a successive number of days. The benefit of using historical simulation is that it enables a specific real-life scenario to be tested against the current portfolio. Figure 6.3 shows how a particular period of time can be selected and used to perform a scenario test. The portfolio value would have reduced by $517,000 over the period shown; far greater than the largest daily move during the whole five years of history being examined.

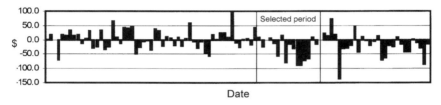

Figure 6.3   Portfolio value change

A bank must be able to survive an extended period of losses as well as extreme market moves over one day. Clearly, it is easier to manage a period of losses than it is to manage a sudden one-day move, as there will be some opportunity to change the structure of the portfolio or even to liquidate the position. Although in theory it is possible to neutralise most positions in a relatively short period of time this is not always the case. Liquidity can become a real issue in times of market stress. In 1994 there was a sudden down turn in the bond markets. The first reversal was followed by a period of two weeks in which liquidity in Eurobonds was much reduced. During that two week period it was extremely difficult to liquidate Eurobond positions. Eurobond positions could be hedged with government bonds but that still left banks exposed to widening of the spreads between government and Eurobonds. This example illustrates why examining the impact of a prolonged period of market stress is a worthwhile part of any stress testing regime.

STRESSING VAR – COVARIANCE AND MONTE CARLO SIMULATION METHODS

The adoption of VAR as a new standard for measuring risk has given rise to a new class of scenario tests. Scenario tests can be undertaken with any of the three main VAR calculation methods described in this book; the use of historical simulation for scenario testing was discussed in the preceding section. With the covariance and Monte Carlo simulation methods the basic VAR inputs can be stressed to produce a new hypothetical VAR. Scenario testing using either covariance or Monte Carlo simulation is essentially the same as volatilities, and correlations are the key inputs for both the VAR methods.

Before describing stress testing using covariance it is worth considering what the results of such tests will mean. At the beginning of this chapter stress testing was defined as the quantification of the potential loss on a portfolio due to extreme moves in the price of assets making up the portfolio.

It was also suggested that stress tests should be used to ascertain whether the bank's portfolio represents a level of risk that is within the bank's extreme appetite for risk. VAR is also used to help define a bank's risk appetite. As most bank's measure VAR with 95% confidence and with a one-day holding period, then VAR limits can be set that represent the bank's operating risk appetite, i.e. the level of risk that the bank is prepared to run on a daily basis. In fact this is a good rationale for using a confidence level of 95% and a one-day holding period.

Scenario and stress testing have been implicitly defined so far as investigating the portfolio impact of a sudden change in market prices. Stress testing covariance VAR is not testing the impact of sudden market moves on a portfolio as correlations and volatilities are measured over a period of time, rather than a single day. The stressing of covariance input is asking how the bank's operating, or day-to-day, level of risk would change if volatilities or correlations changed. This is a fundamentally different result than is given by scenario testing.

Nonetheless it is a valid question to ask whether the bank would be happy with the day-to-day level of risk implied by the VAR produced by different volatilities and correlations. At the time of writing, it appeared that the world's financial markets were moving into a period of lower volatility. History suggests that prices as well as volatility levels are cyclical and will therefore change at some unknown point in the future due to global macro-economic factors. Such a change is not sudden and clear-cut but takes time to develop and become more than merely a short term period of high (or low) volatility. Given that changes in volatilities and correlations are not instantaneous,[1] they do not pose the same threat to a trading institution as a one-day extreme price move. Longer-term changes to volatilities and correlations will show up over time in daily VAR numbers rather than suddenly arriving one day out of the blue.

Stressing Volatility and the Holding Period

In Chapter 2 (covariance), the holding period was introduced as the time horizon over which volatility is measured. The holding period is normally chosen to be one day, thus giving a VAR that represents the day-to-day level of risk. As volatility is proportional to the square root of time, then stressing the holding period is effectively the same as stressing volatility. Chapter 2 also pointed out that the cost of liquidating a portfolio over the holding period is not the same as VAR. Therefore, there is no need to consider stressing the holding period separately from stressing volatility.

When stressing volatility in a VAR calculation it is important to be clear as to what is being changed with respect to the real world. Often, when volatility is stressed in a VAR calculation it is intended to imitate the effect of a sudden extreme movement in prices. If this is the intention, then it is better to apply the price move implied by the stressed volatility directly to the portfolio and measure its effect. Consideration of the derivation of volatility illustrates why using VAR calculations to simulate the effect of extreme price moves is inappropriate.

Volatilities are a statistical measure of the range in which price changes are expected to fall. Chapter 4 described the main methods of calculating volatility. The various methods show that volatility can reflect almost any number of observations – from a few days to several years. For VAR calculated using a stressed volatility to be comparable to the bank's normal VAR implies that volatility changed to the stressed level over the time horizon used in the volatility calculation method. This is normally a long period of time when compared to sudden market shocks. Even using the exponentially weighted volatility calculation used in RiskMetrics^{TM}, in which recent observations have a disproportionately higher weighting, yesterday's observation only has a weight of 6%. Therefore, we should conclude that the change in VAR given by stressing volatilities in a VAR calculation is answering the question 'What would my day-to-day level of risk be if volatilities change to X?'.

Stressing Correlations

Similar arguments apply to correlations as to volatilities. Stressing correlations is equivalent to undertaking a price move stress test directly on a portfolio. Consider a portfolio of Eurobonds hedged with government bonds. Under normal market conditions these two assets are highly correlated with correlations typically lying between 0.8 and 0.95. A VAR stress test might involve stressing the correlation between these two asset classes by setting the correlations to zero. Note that the requirement for a consistent set of correlations still apply. Therefore, any correlation matrix perturbed for the purposes of stress testing should be checked to ensure it still has positive eigenvalues. See the Appendix to Chapter 3 for more detail of this requirement. Again, the question that must be asked is 'What is meant by stressing correlations?'. A more direct way of undertaking this stress test is to stress, or change, the price of one of the assets whilst holding the price of the second asset constant.

In conclusion, applying scenarios to VAR calculations will give some useful insights and an interesting perspective on where the sources of risk are in a portfolio and equally, where the sources of diversification, or risk reduction are in a portfolio. Notwithstanding this, stressing a VAR calculation by altering volatilities and correlations is not the most effective or efficient way of performing stress tests.

Stressing volatilities and correlations in a VAR calculation will establish what the underlying risk in a portfolio would become if volatilities and correlations were to change to the levels input. Bank management can then be asked whether they would be happy with regular potential losses of the level given by the new VAR.

THE PROBLEM WITH SCENARIO ANALYSIS

The main problem with scenario testing, however it is performed, is that it only reveals a very small part of the whole picture of potential market disturbances. As shown below, in the discussion on systematic testing, there are an extremely large number of possible scenarios. Scenario analysis will not identify all the scenarios which would cause significant losses.

A second problem with scenario analysis is the next crisis will be different. Particular market stress scenarios rarely, if ever, repeat themselves in the same way. Over a period of time there will be several significant market shocks for any individual asset. Each of the one-day moves for an individual asset will look similar. What is unlikely to be the same is the way in which the price shock for one asset combines with price shocks for other assets. A quick examination of Table 3.2 on page 38 shows this to be true.

'All right so next time will be different. We will use our economists to predict the next market stress scenario for us.' Wrong! Although this may be an interesting exercise it is unlikely to identify how price shocks will combine in the next market stress scenario. This is simply because the world's financial system is extremely complex and trying to predict what will happen next is a bit like trying to predict the weather. The only model complex enough to guarantee a forecast is the weather system itself. An examination of fund management performance shows that human beings are very bad at predicting market trends, let alone sudden moves. Very few fund managers beat the stock indices on a consistent basis and if they do, then only by a small percentage.

What is needed is a more thorough way of examining all credible price shock combinations.

Are Simulation Techniques Appropriate?

One way of generating a very large number of market outcomes is to use simulation techniques, such as the Monte Carlo technique. Simulation techniques produce a random set of price outcomes *based on the market characteristics assumed.* One of the key market characteristics usually assumed is that price changes are normally distributed. Simulation models will only produce as many extreme price moves as dictated by the assumed distribution.[2] For stress testing we are interested in price moves of greater than three standard deviations as well as market moves covered by a normal distribution.

SYSTEMATIC STRESS TESTING

What is needed is to systematically (or deterministically) impose a large number of different combinations of asset price shocks on a portfolio to produce a series of different stress test outcomes. Table 6.3 shows a matrix of different stress tests for an interest rate portfolio that includes options.

Table 6.3 is an example of a matrix of systematic stress tests. The columns represent different parallel shifts in the yield curve and the rows represent different multiples of volatility. The first thing to note is that the worst case loss does not occur at the extremes of the price moves applied. In fact, had only extreme moves been used then the worst case loss would have been missed altogether. In this case, the worst case loss occurs with small moves in rates because the book is gamma positive, i.e. if there is a significant move up or down in rates the portfolio will make money. Explanation of option risk characteristics is outside the scope of this book, the point of showing the stress test on page 137 is to show that not only must price moves be tested with different combinations of assets but that a range of price changes must be used as well.

Table 6.3 shows a stress test on a complete portfolio where price changes are applied to all products in the portfolio at the same time. It should be noted that this implied a correlation of one between all assets. During times of market stress assets often become far more correlated, so assuming a correlation of one may make sense. Thought should be given to what correlations should be implied in the stress tests performed.

Table 6.3 is only one of a number of combinations of price moves that must be tested. Table 6.3 consists of a total of 69 different price shocks. In theory, to get the total number of stress test combinations, the number of different price shocks must be applied to each asset in turn and to all combinations of assets. If the price shocks shown in Table 6.3 were applied to a portfolio of 10 assets, there would be a possible 690 stress tests. With a typical bank's portfolio the number of possible stress tests would render comprehensive stress testing impractical. In practice a little thought can reduce the number of stress tests required.

Identifying Stress Tests Needed

The approach to determining which stress tests to perform is best described by considering a simple portfolio. Consider a portfolio of two assets, a five-year Eurobond hedged with a 10-year government bond. The portfolio is hedged to

Table 6.3 Stress test matrix for an interest rate portfolio

(£'000s)

| Volatility multipliers | | | | | Parallel interest rate shifts (%) | | | | | |
	−2	−1	−0.5	−0.1	Null	0.1	0.5	1	2	4
× 0.6	1.145	435	34	−119	−102	−102	−188	−220	37	−130
× 0.8	1.148	447	78	−60	−48	−52	−145	−200	−10	−165
× 0.9	1.150	456	100	−33	−24	−29	−125	−189	−12	−164
× 1	1.153	466	122	−8	0	−6	−103	−173	2	−151
× 1.1	1.157	478	144	18	25	18	−77	−151	32	−126
× 1.2	1.162	490	167	46	52	45	−46	−119	80	−90
× 1.4	1.174	522	222	113	118	114	37	−25	223	21

be delta neutral or, in bond terminology, has a modified duration of zero. In other words the value of the portfolio will not change if the yield curve moves up (or down) in parallel by small amounts. If the stress test matrix shown in Table 6.3 were performed on the portfolio the results would be zero (there would be some small losses shown due to the different convexity of the bonds). Although it is a valid set of stress tests, it does not pick up all the risks present in the portfolio.

The portfolio is of course not risk free though it is delta neutral. In particular, this portfolio is subject to spread risk, i.e. the risk that the prices of Euro and government bonds do not move in line with each other. The other risk that the portfolio is subject to is curve risk, i.e. the risk that yield curve moves are not parallel. Stress tests must be designed that capture these risks. Curve risk can be captured by applying curve tilts to the portfolio rather than the parallel moves used in Table 6.3. Spread risk can be captured by applying price shocks to one class of assets only; in this case price shocks could be applied to the Eurobonds only.

This example serves to illustrate the approach to identifying the stress tests that need to be performed. A bank's portfolio must be examined to identify the different types of risk that the portfolio is subject to. This is similar to the identification of risk factors that was described in Chapter 5 (Implementing VAR). Stress tests should test the portfolio against price shocks for all the risk types identified.

There are typically fewer types of risk than there are risk factors in a portfolio. When implementing VAR the yield curve will be split into a number of different maturities or risk factors. This is not necessary for stress testing; a portfolio can be tested against parallel yield curve shifts and curve tilts. Stress tests should also be tailored to the products present in the portfolio. A portfolio without options does not need as many separate yield curve shocks as shown in Table 6.3 as such a portfolio will behave in a largely linear way. From this discussion it can be seen that the actual number of stress tests that need to be performed, whilst still significant, is much smaller in number than the theoretical number of combinations.

Which Price Shocks Should be Used?

The other question that needs to be answered is what price shocks to use – and how big should the price shocks be?

A basic approach will entail undertaking research for each risk factor to be stressed to identify the largest ever move and also the largest move in the last ten years. Judgement must then be used to choose price shocks from the results of the research. The size of the price shocks used may be adjusted over time. At the time of writing the world appeared to be in a low volatility environment. In such an environment it may make sense to use slightly smaller price shocks. The price shocks used will not change often but should be reviewed once a year or as dictated by market behaviour.

A more sophisticated approach would involve the use of extreme value theory (EVT). EVT has been used extensively in the insurance and engineering industries to predict the likelihood of extreme events. The use of EVT is now becoming more prevalent in the financial world and specifically in the field of stress testing. EVT involves fitting density functions to historical price series. The density functions can incorporate a variety of shapes and weights of fat tails. EVT produces statistical estimates of the probability of extreme events based on past experience. The density functions used assume that normal daily price changes are consistent with occasional extreme price shocks.[3] There are two approaches to designing stress tests with EVT:

1. Find the magnitude of price change that will only be exceeded, on average, once during a specified period of time. The period of time is a subjective decision and must be determined by the risk manager; typical periods to be considered may be 10, 20 or 50 years. If 20 years were chosen the price change identified that would not be exceeded on average more than once in 20 years is called the '20-year return level'. Of course this analysis could be done with a normal distribution but would then completely ignore the fat-tailed nature of financial asset price change series.
2. The second approach is merely the inverse of the first and is perhaps more appropriate. Given that a bank will have identified its risk appetite (see Chapter 7) in terms of the maximum loss it is prepared to suffer then EVT can be used to determine the likelihood of such an event. If the probability is considered to be too great (i.e. would occur more often than the bank is prepared for) then the risk appetite must be revisited.

CONCLUSION

Due to the extreme price shocks experienced in the world's financial markets, VAR is not an adequate measure of risk by itself; stress testing should be used to complement VAR. The primary objective of stress testing is to identify the scenarios which would cause a significant loss along with the probability of such scenarios.

Stress testing must be undertaken in a systematic way. *Ad hoc* scenario tests may produce interesting results but are unlikely to identify the worst case loss a bank could suffer. Care must be taken to identify the stress tests required by examining the types of risk the bank's portfolio contains. Stress tests should be run daily as a bank's portfolio can change significantly over a 24-hour period.

Stress testing facilitates a better control over unacceptable losses than VAR. Therefore stress testing should be a central part of the risk control framework and not just an *ad hoc* procedure. Chapter 7 describes how stress testing should be built into a risk control limit framework.

NOTES

1. See Chapter 4. All measures of volatility are an average of a number of price changes – exactly how many will depend on the volatility model being used.
2. There is no reason why a normal distribution has to be assumed, but in practice this is often the case.
3. A good introduction to EVT is given by Embrechts *et al.* (1998). For a more comprehensive coverage the reader is directed to Embrechts *et al.* (1997).

7

Managing risk with VAR

INTRODUCTION

The objective of risk management is to protect an institution against unacceptable losses. The responsibility for providing this protection was traditionally in the hands of the trading functions themselves. In other words, traders were self regulated. As the financial markets became de-regulated (see Chapter 9), the amount of risk a trading operation could take sky-rocketed. At the same time the potential rewards available from taking risks, to both financial institutions and to individual traders, also became astronomical. The potential gain to individuals became so large that the self-regulation of traders became an untenable proposition. Not that it should have been needed, but Barings was the final nail in the coffin of trading self regulation.

As a result, independent risk management functions are now a regulatory requirement in most G10 countries. The creation of independent risk management has created a new profession, that of the risk manager. Many traders complain that risk management is mis-named, that risk managers are in fact risk controllers, it is they, the traders, who manage the risk of traded positions on the trading floor every day. True, traders do manage the risk of their positions, risk managers just ensure that the risks associated with various trading positions stay within certain limits. But who decides the magnitude of the limits? The risk manager manages the bank's risk in the sense that he must determine what limits should be set. It is the risk manager who must find a way to quantify the institution's risk appetite and then set up an infrastructure to ensure that risk is kept within the agreed bounds.

This chapter describes the process of determining an institution's risk appetite and the type of infrastructure, in terms of risk limits required to control risk. The focus in this chapter is on market risk, however the same process also applies to credit risk.

ESTABLISHING A RISK MANAGEMENT FRAMEWORK

A bank's risk appetite is ultimately the amount of money it is willing to lose. Of course this needs qualification, which we will come to. In general, banks and fund managers are trying to balance risk and return. For banks this must be applied at the business unit level, for example, for a specific trading unit. Of course a bank's management wish the trading unit to increase its return, or profit, but not at any cost. There is a limit to the amount of risk the bank will accept. Determining a bank's risk appetite requires a top down approach. Setting limits, on the other hand, mainly involves an analysis of the business unit's trading intentions. This said, limits must be set in the overall context of the bank's risk appetite.

Determining Risk Appetite

If we start with the premise that a bank's risk appetite is expressed as a monetary amount, let us assume $10m, then a natural question follows. Are you prepared to lose $10m every day, once per month, or how often? The regularity with which a loss of a given magnitude can be tolerated is the key qualification of risk appetite. Figure 7.1 shows how a bank's risk appetite can be defined. Several different losses are identified, along with the frequency with which each loss can be tolerated.

The amount a bank is prepared to lose on a daily basis is defined as the daily 95% confidence VAR. This size of loss is likely to be experienced fairly frequently. The daily VAR limit should be set after consideration of the bank's or trading unit's profit target. There would be little point in having a daily VAR limit that is larger than the annual profit target, otherwise there would be a reasonable probability that the annual profit would be lost during the year.

The second loss on the chart is the 99% monthly VAR. This figure indicates to management the amount that may be lost during a bad month. Again the monthly loss should be set with the annual revenue target in mind.

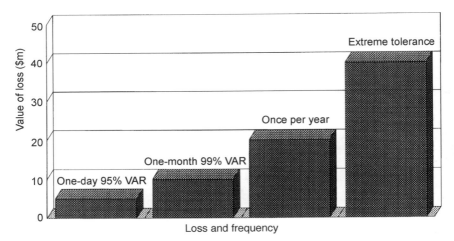

Figure 7.1   Defining risk appetite

The third figure is the amount the bank is prepared to lose on an infrequent basis, for example once per year. This amount should be set after consideration of the available or allocated capital. This magnitude of loss would arise from an extreme event in the financial markets and will therefore not be predicted by VAR. The extreme event will be estimated by either an analysis of historic price changes or by extreme value theory (EVT). EVT can be used to estimate the probability of extreme events (see Chapter 6). Available capital must more than cover this figure.

Stress tests should be used to identify scenarios that would give rise to losses of this magnitude or more. Once the scenarios have been identified, management's subjective judgement must be used in conjunction with EVT to judge the likelihood of such an event in prevailing market conditions. Those with vested interests should not be involved in this process. The judgement will be subjective, as the probabilities of extreme events are not meaningful over the short horizon associated with trading decisions. In other words the occurrence of extreme price shocks is so rare that a consideration of the probability of an extreme event would lead managers to ignore such events. EVT should be used in conjunction with management's subjective judgement of the likelihood of such an event, given present or predicted economic circumstance.

The loss labelled 'extreme tolerance' does not have a frequency associated with it as it is the maximum the bank is prepared to lose – ever. Again stress tests should be used to identify scenarios and position sizes that would give rise to a loss of this magnitude. Although it is not possible, this is attempting to identify the loss that would arise from the worst imaginable shift in market prices. EVT should then be used to estimate the probability of such an event.

Having identified the bank's risk appetite, the risk manager can now proceed to set limits which protect the bank against losses greater than the bank's risk appetite. From this discussion on risk appetite, it is clear that exposure to risk must be limited. There are various ways that this can be done. This chapter describes the use of VAR and stress test limits to control exposure to market risk. As can be seen from this discussion, both VAR and stress test limits are required to ensure a bank's risk appetite is not breached.

Setting Limits

Limits cannot be set in a vacuum, therefore it makes sense to establish the bank's risk appetite before setting specific limits. A limit structure needs to meet the following objectives:

- To control the risks taken by the trading unit.
- Not to constrain trading beyond the overall constraint of the bank's risk appetite.

Therefore limit setting is a balancing act. It is essential to sit down with traders and trading management to understand the type of trading they intend to undertake. Such a discussion will have been successful if the risk manager walks away with an understanding of the types of positions the traders intend to create and how they hope to make money. These discussions will allow the risk manager to identify the types of risk that will be taken. A limit infrastructure can then be created that will control all material risks identified.

It is fairly easy to devise a limit framework that will constrain trading and will therefore prejudice the trading unit in the achievement of its goals, i.e. it may fail to meet its revenue target. For example, consider a bond trading business that makes money from customer flows (i.e. bid/offer spread) and new issues. If a risk manager were concerned about the basis risk between bonds and bond futures, he may introduce too small a limit on the total book size (i.e. total value of bonds held). This would have the effect of constraining the business from issuing more than a given volume of bonds and would thus impact the revenue stream. In practice the risk manager's chance of introducing a constrictive limit is small. Traders and trading management will generally shout loudly if they feel overly constrained.

One of the things a risk manager must understand from trading management is the size of limits the business requires to conduct its business efficiently. The risk manager will then need to compare the requested limits against the bank's risk appetite and also against the projected return. If the projected return is not large enough to justify the limits requested, then questions need to be asked about the validity of entering into this business activity (see Chapter 8 for a discussion of required return).

VAR LIMITS

The wonderful thing about VAR limits is that the same limit structure can be used across all products. This is one of the major attractions of VAR for senior management. Once they have mastered the meaning of VAR it becomes easy to compare the VAR limits being used by different trading activities to see which trading activity is taking the most risk.

The acceptance of VAR on the trading floor is often much more difficult. Traders will use measures of exposure to risk which reflect the way their products are traded. Spot foreign exchange dealers will refer to positions in currencies versus the US dollar (regardless of the base currency of the bank) and 'cross' positions against the German Deutschmark. Swap traders will talk about futures strips, i.e. exposure to changes in interest rates, at different maturities down the yield curve, converted into the number of futures needed to hedge the risk.

For most traders, VAR is not initially an intuitive measure of risk. This gives rise to problems when trying to implement VAR as a bank-wide risk measure. There are various approaches to overcoming this problem:

- *Implement VAR at a trading unit level* VAR limits can be used purely at the trading unit level to control the amount of market risk that any trading unit can take in a consistent manner across a number of trading units. This approach leaves trading management free to set limits in terms traders are familiar with, within the trading unit. The disadvantage of this approach is that the trading manager must become an expert at translating between VAR and the traders' limits. This approach can be seen as a first step towards comprehensive use of VAR limits.

- *Implement VAR limits for traders* If VAR is to be used to set risk limits at a lower level then it is essential that traders are given the systems to enable them to calculate it. Too often, VAR is imposed on traders who have little understanding of how it is calculated. VAR is calculated for their positions overnight by a 'black box' computer. The trader has no way of verifying the calculations and no feel for the VAR of his position. This is a recipe for disaster; if traders are to use VAR limits then they must be trained and given a system into which they can enter their positions and see the effect on their VAR during the day. All of this is possible with today's technology. A good approach to implementing VAR is to introduce it alongside existing traditional limits until the traders are comfortable with using VAR.

Assuming VAR limits are implemented at the level of each trading desk, it should be clear to the reader by now that diversification will mean that the VAR limit for a trading unit will be lower than the sum of the desk level VAR limits. There is no problem with this. Traditional limits are often implemented in the same way with overall limits being smaller than the sum of the parts.

VAR Limits and Increasing Volatility

One question that is often asked is, 'What should be done when there is a passive breach of a VAR limit?'. A passive breach of a VAR limit is what happens when volatility increases but the trader's position remains unchanged. The increase in volatility increases the VAR on the trader's book and he breaks his limit. The simple answer is that passive breaches should be treated in the same way as other limit breaches. VAR is an amount of risk, higher volatility means higher risk, therefore risk should be reduced so that the VAR limit is not breached. Chapter 4 showed us that volatility clusters in time, i.e. a large price change is likely to be followed by another large price change. Therefore an increase in volatility due to a large price change on day one does increase the risk on the same position for day two.

If a trader is rewarded on the return on risk capital that he generates, then he would wish to reduce exposure as volatility increased unless he had a strong directional view of the markets. This is because one of the constituent parts of risk capital is VAR. See Chapter 8 for a further discussion of risk-adjusted performance measurement.

Controlling Concentration Risk

If you consider an interest rate trading operation, a risk manager would normally be concerned to control several different types of interest rate risk, including:

- Outright interest rate exposure – sensitivity of the portfolio to a parallel shift in the yield curve.
- Curve risk – sensitivity of the portfolio to a twist in the yield curve.
- Basis risk – sensitivity of the portfolio to a shift in the yield curve of one of the major product groups, independently from other products in the portfolio.

Traditionally, separate limits would be used to control these three risks and as a result it would be clear which type of risk was dominant in the portfolio. A single VAR limit could replace the three separate limits. This has advantages and disadvantages.

There are advantages of flexibility for the trader. The risk manager no longer appears to care which type of risk the trader takes as long as he is within his VAR limit. Therefore, the trader can take more curve rather than outright risk as his view or position requirements dictate.

This approach is too simplistic and would leave the risk manager and the bank unacceptably exposed. If implemented as indicated above, one could imagine a situation in which the chief executive asks the risk manager to brief him as to the types and concentrations of risk that the bank is exposed to. The risk manager would only be able to answer that today's VAR is x and that all trading units are within their limits. This is not particularly useful if the economists are predicting a parallel rise in the yield curve in Germany and the risk manager has no idea what part of the total VAR exposure relates to Germany.

It would be normal to set VAR limits that control the extent to which concentrations of a particular type of risk are allowed. This can be done on a diversified or undiversified basis. On an undiversified basis, the VAR of German outright interest rate risk would be calculated as if it were a standalone portfolio. On a diversified basis, the VAR of the whole portfolio would be calculated, first with and then without the German interest rate risk factors included.

Risk limits are normally set based on an undiversified calculation of VAR for specific types of risk. This is because a trading unit can only manage its own exposure and generally does not consider and has no control over the diversification benefits of its portfolio for the bank as a whole. Another way of identifying exposure to specific sectors is via comprehensive stress testing.

STRESS TEST LIMITS

A bank must limit the amount it is prepared to lose due to extreme market moves, this is best achieved by stress test limits. As VAR only controls day-to-day risk, stress test limits are required in addition to VAR limits. Having determined the bank's risk appetite, stress test limits can then be established. Stress test limits are entirely separate from VAR limits and can be used in a variety of ways. However they are used, it is essential to ensure that stress test limits are consistent with the bank's VAR risk management limits, i.e. the stress test limits should not be out of proportion with the VAR limits. In terms of what size loss should stress test limits be set at, if a single stress test limit is used, it makes sense to set it at a size which is equivalent to the 'once per year' tolerance (refer to risk appetite, Figure 7.1). It is easier for trading and senior management to have a meaningful discussion about a loss which is not so large or infrequent as to be beyond the experience of the management team.

Stress test limits are especially useful for certain classes of products, particularly for options. Traditional limits for options were based around the Greeks: delta, gamma, vega, rho and theta. A single matrix of stress tests can replace the first three Greeks. The advantage of stress tests over the Greeks is that stress tests quantify the loss on a portfolio in a given market scenario. The Greeks, particularly, gamma, can provide misleading figures. When options are at-the-money and close to expiry gamma can become almost infinitely large. This has nothing to do with potential losses and everything to do with the option pricing function. Figure 7.2 gives an example of stress limits for an interest rate option portfolio. It shows three stress test limits which increase in magnitude with the size of the shift in interest rates and the change in volatility. Using stress tests like this, trading management can see that losses due to various specific market shifts are limited to a given figure. Using the Greeks, the loss caused by specific market shifts is not specified (except for the tiny shifts used by the Greeks).

Stress test limits can be used as are standard VAR, or other, risk limits, i.e. when a stress test identifies that a portfolio could give rise to a loss specified by the stress test limit, then exposure cannot be increased and must be decreased if the limit is

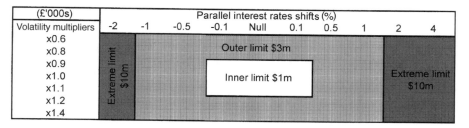

(£'000s)	Parallel interest rates shifts (%)									
Volatility multipliers	-2	-1	-0.5	-0.1	Null	0.1	0.5	1	2	4
x0.6										
x0.8				Outer limit $3m						
x0.9	Extreme limit $10m								Extreme limit $10m	
x1.0				Inner limit $1m						
x1.1										
x1.2										
x1.4										

Figure 7.2

exceeded. This approach establishes stress test limits, along with standard risk limits, as absolute constraints on positions and exposures that can be created.

Another approach is to set stress test limits but use them as 'trigger points' for discussion. Such limits would have to be well within the bank's absolute tolerance of loss. When a stress test indicates that the bank's portfolio could give rise to a specified loss, then the circumstances that would cause such a loss are distributed to senior management along with details of the position or portfolio. An informed discussion can then take place as to whether the bank is happy to run with such a risk. Given the rare nature of such losses, the judgement will have to be subjective and will be based on the experience of the people making the decision.

SUMMARY

The clear objective of an independent risk management function is to protect an institution against unacceptable losses. With this as an objective, it is clear that VAR limits are insufficient by themselves. VAR covers only day-to-day or relatively frequent moves in market prices. Stress test limits provide a better control over risk and are an essential part of any risk management infrastructure as long as they are comprehensive in terms of the scenarios tested and are performed daily.

A limit framework must be established by both a top down and bottom up approach. Top down limits must be set in the context of the bank's risk appetite. The risk appetite describes the maximum size of loss the institution is prepared to suffer with a given regularity. Bottom up limits must control the many different types of risk being taken by a trading operation within the bank's risk appetite, whilst at the same time not constraining the business. The only real constraint should be to ensure that the business makes a return that is commensurate with the risk it is taking. This is elaborated on in the next chapter.

8
Risk adjusted performance measurement

INTRODUCTION

Consider a bank with two business units, A and B; both units wish to expand and are asking the board to commit more capital to them. However, the bank's capital is close to being fully utilised. The bank must make a strategic decision as to which business it should encourage and, therefore, how it will allocate the available capital between them. The board has been presented with the following earnings information for the prior year:

- Business unit A earned £10m.

- Business unit B earned £12m.

Which one has performed better? Perhaps an initial reaction would be to say that business unit B has performed better. In fact, solely with information on earnings, the superior performance cannot be ascertained.

Banking is about managing risk and return, therefore, the risk must be quantified before the superior performance can be ascertained. Table 8.1 gives the average annualised VAR of both business units over the previous year. This allows a simple measurement of market risk versus return to be calculated. From Table 8.1, it is clear that unit A has achieved a much higher ratio of return to risk than unit B; therefore, more capital should be allocated to business unit A than to B.

Table 8.1 Simple calculation of risk versus return

Business unit	Revenue ($m)	VAR	Revenue/VAR
A	10	50	20%
B	12	120	10%

The calculation in Table 8.1 is a crude measure of risk adjusted performance measurement (RAPM). As will be shown in this chapter, we still do not have sufficient information to make a rational allocation of capital between the two business units:

- What about other types of risk, e.g. credit, operational?
- How have the business units performed in the past?

Nonetheless we can already make a better decision than we could when we only had revenue information.

The purpose of this chapter is to put VAR into the context of managing a bank's capital and making strategic decisions. This chapter shows that VAR is one of the key building blocks required for modern bank management.

DEFINING CAPITAL

From the way in which the term 'capital' is banded about one would think that its definition is crystal clear. In fact, there are many definitions, depending on the context in which it is being used. Therefore, we must now describe the main definitions and particularly the definition of capital with respect to RAPM. Externally to a bank one thinks of capital as equity (shares). There is also a regulatory measure of capital; regulatory capital is the amount of equity and long-term debt (see Chapter 9 for a more complete definition) that a bank's regulators believe each bank should provide in order to ensure the stability of the world's financial system, i.e. keep bank defaults to an acceptable number. Regulatory capital should, therefore, be sufficient for the bank to survive extreme market shocks.

For the purposes of RAPM and capital allocation we need to use a measure of capital that will cover the estimated day-to-day level of risk (or variation in daily revenue) in a business. We will call this capital measure 'risk capital'. Note that the definition of risk capital is careful to exclude rare events such as extreme moves in market prices and other financial shocks that may befall a bank. From the preceding chapters it should be clear that VAR is a measure of the day-to-day riskiness of a trading business. Thus, for the measurement of RAPM and capital allocation, VAR can be equated to the risk capital for market risk. Clearly there are other financial risks that a bank is exposed to. The most obvious of these is credit risk; a method of calculating the risk capital for credit risk is outlined in a later section of this chapter. Another type of financial risk is operational risk which can be loosely defined as financial loss resulting from operational errors and, or, poor operational control. At the time of writing the quantification of operational risk and its inclusion in an overall measure of risk capital is becoming increasingly prevalent in the industry but as yet no consensus exists.

For most banks, risk capital will form a relatively small fraction of the bank's total capital. Business units must be supported by more capital than the amount calculated as risk capital. In reality, a bank must have sufficient capital to ensure it could continue as a business in the event of a severe loss resulting from any of the following:

- An extreme move in market prices.

- A significant loss resulting from the default of one or more of a bank's trading partners (counterparties) or borrowers.

- Fraud.

- Loss of reputation, leading to loss of business and possible regulatory sanctions.

The amount of capital required to survive the above can be thought of as 'economic capital'. Its quantification is far more subjective than the measurement of risk capital, though Chapter 6 (stress testing), describes an approach to the quantification of economic capital required to survive extreme moves in market prices.

SHAREHOLDER VALUE ANALYSIS – A STRATEGIC DECISION MAKING TOOL

Probably the dominant philosophy for making strategic decisions within corporations at present is shareholder value analysis (SVA) (Rappaport, 1986; Copeland *et al.*, 1994). The objective of SVA is to improve the total return (dividends plus capital growth) given to shareholders. This means that companies should assess all potential strategic moves in terms of whether they improve the return to shareholders.

Simply put, SVA says that the value of a company is equal to the present value of its expected future 'free' cash flows (plus cash). Free cash flow is the surplus or shortfall of cash generated in each financial period, i.e. annual profit. In banking, free cash flows are measured as the bank's future net profits after tax, adjusted for depreciation and changes in regulatory capital (Matten, 1996).

The choice of discount rate used to calculate the present value of free cash flows for each business unit is critical. The cash flows must be discounted with a discount rate that is related to the riskiness of the business. Put another way, the discount factor is the required return on an investment of a given amount of capital,[1] where the required return is dependent on the risk associated with the investment. Thus, the measurement of return on capital (or RAPM) is linked to SVA via the required return (discount factor) used for each business unit.

This approach can have far-reaching ramifications. Consider a business unit which is profitable but which has historically suffered from large swings in its earnings. The high earnings volatility will require a higher rate of return. If the business unit is not making the required return on capital, then it will be destroying shareholder value as the discount rate used will be greater than the return it is generating. Of course many things can affect a business unit's performance and SVA is only one tool to help management make strategic decisions. Nonetheless, SVA would suggest that such a business unit's performance be carefully reviewed and the business discontinued if no way can be found to improve its return on capital.

SVA also implies that banks with excess capital should either find activities in which to invest, or, return the capital to shareholders, either via special dividends or share buy-backs. Evidence of the increasingly common use of SVA can be seen by the number of banks which have undertaken share buy-backs in recent years.

DETERMINING THE REQUIRED RETURN ON CAPITAL

One model which links risk and return is the capital asset pricing model (CAPM). CAPM states that the required return on an investment is proportional to the risk, or uncertainty, associated with that return. This can be expressed for any stock as:

$$R_s = R_f + \beta(R_m - R_f) + \epsilon \tag{8.1}$$

where: R_s = required return on a stock or equity

R_f = risk free rate of return, or risk free interest rate. Typically the interest rate given by a government bond.

β = beta is a factor for each individual stock which describes how its price moves in relation to the market. A stock with a beta of one will move exactly in line with the market. A stock with a beta of two will respond aggressively to changes in the value of the market, i.e. for a 1% change in the value of the index, the price of a stock with a beta of two will change by 2%.

R_m = the historical return associated with the stock market. Therefore $(R_m - R_f)$ is the excess return of the market over the risk free rate, or the risk premium that an investor in the market demands over the risk free rate to compensate him for investing in the risky stock market.

ϵ = error term, that can be ignored for our purposes here.

Banks can use this equation to determine the total return they must generate for shareholders. At any point in time a bank can determine its beta – the risk free rate is also known – typically taken as the forecast government yield over the planning horizon. This leaves the risk premium of the stock market – a subject on which there are many published studies. As a rule of thumb, the average risk premium can be taken as 5% in the USA and UK and 4% for European stock markets other than the UK.

In CAPM, risk is defined as the volatility of earnings; this is another way of defining risk capital. The return given by equation 8.1 is the bank's cost of capital and is the minimum return a bank must produce to satisfy investors. Clearly, a bank must aim to beat the return implied by the equation or it will not be adding value to its shareholders. Thus CAPM can be used to determine the target rate of return on capital for a bank as a whole.

When looking at business units within a bank we need to be able to apply the CAPM in the same way as we have for the bank as a whole. As individual business units are not publicly traded it is not possible to measure their beta directly. However, we can measure the volatility of revenues. Therefore, what is needed is a relationship between revenue volatility and beta. Chris Matten (1996) provides persuasive evidence of a relationship between beta and the volatility of revenue from which the required return can be calculated. The relationship was established by examining the correlation between revenue volatility and the observed betas for a large number of banks; Matten found that there was a correlation of 0.92 between them. The regression analysis performed yielded the following equation between revenue volatility and beta:

$$\beta = 10.82 V_R + 0.14 \qquad (8.2)^2$$

where: V_R = the revenue volatility expressed as a percentage

The first two columns of Table 8.2 reproduce Matten's analysis of revenue volatility and the beta calculated using the above equation. The third column gives examples of required returns.

This analysis is enormously useful when considering the required return for either a bank as a whole or for individual business units within a bank. If there is one point to take away from this section, it is that the appropriate required return on capital (or discount factor) is dependent on the volatility of the business unit's revenue. It does not make sense to use the same discount factor across all the

Table 8.2   Required return vs revenue volatility

Revenue volatility (%)	Beta	Example required return (%)
4	0.57	8.9
6	0.79	9.9
8	1.01	11.0
10	1.22	12.1
12	1.44	13.2
14	1.65	14.3
16	1.87	15.4
18	2.09	16.4
20	2.30	17.5

Note: The example required return was calculated assuming a risk free rate of 6% and an historical premium of 5%. The betas were calculated from equation 8.2 and the returns from equation 8.1.

Table 8.3   Assessment of business units

Bank/ business unit	Required return (%)		Present value ($m)		Projected revenues ($m)		
	Bank wide	Business unit	Bank wide	Business unit	Year 1	Year 2	Year 3
Asset management	14	10	25.3	27.2	10	11	12
Trading	14	16	27.7	26.7	11	12	13
Bank total	14	na	53.0	na	21	23	25

business units of a bank, all with different revenue volatilities. If the same discount factor is used, it will lead to higher-risk activities being preferred to lower-risk activities. This is because higher-risk activities are likely to generate a higher average revenue, even though their revenue volatility will also be higher.

Consider a bank which has two business units, for example, an asset management business and a trading business. Table 8.3 shows the effect of using a bank-wide discount factor versus a discount factor corresponding to the revenue volatility of the business unit. The middle columns show that, using the bank-wide discount factor, the trading business would be preferred to the asset management business. This would not be a rational decision, as in fact, the trading business is not generating sufficient additional revenue, relative to the asset management business, to justify its higher revenue volatility. If the appropriate discount factors are used, the asset management business would be preferred to the trading business.

At the start of the chapter, risk capital was defined as the day-to-day level of risk with VAR being a measure of day-to-day market risk. By now it should be clear that revenue volatility is closely allied to risk. This makes sense as all realised financial losses will be included in a business's revenue stream. Therefore, by definition, revenue volatility is an expression of the amount of risk a business has taken. Therefore, there are two possible measures of risk capital:

1. *Revenue (or earnings) volatility – earnings-at-risk*   Earnings-at-risk (EAR) looks at realised losses. Realised losses will, at least, partially reflect the amount of risk the bank has taken. It is, of course, possible to take risks which are not realised; such risks will be missed by the EAR approach.
2. *Asset volatility*   Asset volatility-based approaches seek to quantify the amount of risk a bank is running now rather than how much risk it ran in the past. Asset-based approaches quantify potential losses and are therefore not dependent on a risk being realised for it to be taken into account. Asset volatility-based approaches are essentially forward looking, whereas revenue volatility-based approaches are fundamentally retrospective.

The rest of this chapter examines these two approaches to capital measurement and their use in RAPM and capital allocation.

EARNINGS VOLATILITY-BASED PERFORMANCE MEASURES

The concept of risk capital is that the bank must be prepared and able to survive ups and downs in its performance, or more specifically, its revenue stream. The job of risk capital is to quantify the magnitude of the business' potential losses. Revenue volatility, clearly, will reflect the risk a bank takes, assuming that the current risk profile of the bank is fairly represented by past losses. Using the EAR approach, return on capital is measured as:

$$\text{Return on capital} = \frac{\text{Return}}{\text{EAR}}$$

Return is simply the business unit's income, net of both direct and indirect costs. EAR is the annualised average revenue volatility. This will normally be calculated from daily or monthly revenue figures. For example, if the daily revenue volatility is $10m for a particular business unit then it can be scaled up to give an annual figure by using the square root of time rule (see Chapter 4). Assuming 260 days in a year, we can scale up the daily revenue volatility as follows:

$$\text{Annual revenue volatility} = 10\sqrt{260} = \$160m$$

Performance measures based on volatility of earnings, or earnings-at-risk, were around long before the relatively recent popularity of VAR-based measures. One classic performance measure that utilises the volatility of earnings is the Sharpe ratio. The Sharpe ratio has been used in making investment decisions since the end of the 1960s.

Sharpe Ratio

The Sharpe ratio is useful for evaluating the performance of a single portfolio and assessing the relative performance of a group of portfolios. The Sharpe ratio is the ratio of the excess return that the portfolio achieves (above the risk free rate), to the volatility of the portfolio return. As discussed above, volatility is a measure of risk, therefore the Sharpe ratio is a measure of risk versus return. The Sharpe ratio is given by:

$$S_R = \frac{\overline{r_P} - \overline{r_f}}{\sigma_P}$$

where: S_R = Sharpe ratio

r_P = return on the portfolio – the bar indicates that average return should be used

r_f = risk free rate – again the average risk free rate over the measurement period should be used (unless it was constant over the measurement period)

σ_P = volatility of the portfolio return

The portfolio return should be measured net of cost. After all, if a business unit requires a more expensive infrastructure, then it must generate sufficient additional revenue to cover its extra costs. The parent organisation is only interested in a business unit's net contribution to the business.

When we look, in the next section, at asset volatility-based measures of return on capital, we will see that there they are quite similar to the Sharpe ratio with capital being a measure of unexpected losses, i.e. volatility. In fact return on capital (ROC) measures are derivations of the Sharpe ratio.

One of the potential problems with the Sharpe ratio is that it requires the capital invested to be known, so that the portfolio return can be measured. This is straightforward for an investment portfolio where it is clear how much money has been invested. For a trading operation we are left with the problem of identifying how much capital a trading operation is using.

The following sections on ROC will discuss measures of capital for trading operations; however, one potentially easy solution is to use the trading unit's regulatory capital. If this measure of capital is used, then calculating the Sharpe ratio becomes easy as net revenues will definitely be calculated by a trading operation.

The Sharpe ratio can be used to evaluate historical performance over some given period, for example, the previous year or the last five years. In trading rooms the measure is often calculated regularly (monthly is probably the shortest period that makes sense) and used to identify trends in both risk and return. Such an analysis can be used to answer questions such as:

- Is a business unit consistently taking more risk?
- Are the returns going up in line with the risks being taken?

If regulatory capital is considered to be too arbitrary a measure of capital or is not available for individual business units, then a more basic approach to assessing risk versus return can be used. Using the example above of a bank with two business units, we can graph risk (revenue volatility) and return (average daily revenue) for the two business units (see Figure 8.1). Figure 8.1 shows that the investment management business unit is producing a steady, if unexciting, average revenue, whilst the trading business is generating a higher average revenue but with much higher volatility.[3] However, Figure 8.1 cannot be used to determine which business is performing better. For example, is the trading business generating sufficient additional return to justify its higher revenue volatility? This graph cannot help you answer this question.

The beauty and simplicity of this approach is that both risk and return can be seen graphically; this allows an intuitive grasp of how different business units are positioned with respect to risk and return. The arrow on the diagram shows the direction in which one would like the performance of business units to move. The main use of this technique is not as a comparative measure (unlike the Sharpe ratio which does allow

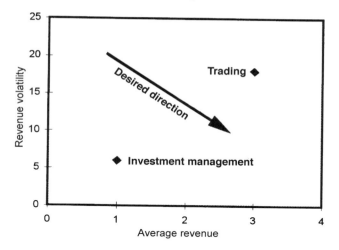

Figure 8.1 Risk versus return

business units to be compared) as it is not possible to say from the graph whether you would prefer to buy the trading or investment management business, but as an indication of whether each business unit is moving in the right direction.

RETURN ON CAPITAL – VAR-BASED APPROACH

Modern measures of risk adjusted performance measure return on risk capital. In general, risk capital in these models measures the volatility of asset values. VAR measures the volatility of asset value due to changes in the asset prices. VAR does not measure asset value volatility due to the counterparty defaulting. VAR measures the day-to-day or normal level of risk associated with a portfolio of assets. The concept of risk capital must be extended to cover other types of risk, as discussed below, if the definition of risk capital is to be successful at capturing the true risk an institution is running. There are several models or names for risk adjusted return on capital in use in the industry. They all share the common characteristic of trying to measure return on a risk-adjusted basis. A generic model is given by the following:

$$\text{Risk adjusted return on capital (RAROC)} = \frac{\text{Net revenue} - \text{Expected credit loss}}{\text{Risk capital}}$$

and

$$\text{Risk capital} = \text{VAR} + \text{Unexpected credit loss} + \text{Operational value at risk}$$

It is worth noting at the outset that RAROC may produce a high number which may appear to have little to do with the required returns identified for the bank as a whole. A later section discusses how to link the required return on equity capital with the return on risk capital. We must now define each of the terms in the RAROC equation.

Net Revenue

This is the most straightforward of the terms in the RAROC equation. Net revenue should be net of all costs, both direct and indirect. In some banks there is lengthy discussion about the precise definition of net revenue. In the final analysis it does not really matter, as long as the same approach is applied across all business units.

Expected Credit Loss

The quantification of credit risk is a large subject area in its own right and would need a dedicated book to do it justice.[4] This section should be taken as a brief and at times simplistic introduction to the subject.

The name – Expected Credit Loss[5] – gives a clue as to why it appears above the line in the RAROC equation. There is no doubt that companies will default. One can debate the precise percentage, but the fact that a number of companies will default is not in question. If we expect a certain percentage of defaults, then we should take account of this in the way we price transactions and in the way in which we measure the revenues generated by any business that creates credit exposure. As defaults are expected, the cost of defaults is surely then just another cost of doing business. As such, it should be deducted from revenues. This is exactly what RAROC does. Turning now to the quantification of expected credit loss, it is a function of:

- *The underlying exposure or future market value of the position*   Credit loss is dependent on there being something to lose. If a counterparty defaults today, the amount that can be lost is defined by the value of the position today. For products whose value can vary with time, the credit exposure is taken from the range of potential future values which a position could have through its life (see the example of a swap below).

- *The expected default rate*   The probability of default over a given period of time.

- *The expected recovery rate*   The percentage of liabilities of the company that it is expected can be recovered after liquidation of the counterparty.

Expected credit loss is given by the following equation:

$$C_E = (1 - R_E).\frac{\displaystyle\sum_{P=1}^{P=M} E_P.D_P}{M} \qquad (8.3)$$

where: C_E = expected credit loss

E_P = expected exposure of the transaction at period P. Period P could be any period of time, such as a month. In practice, however, time is normally divided into years for expected credit loss calculations. This is partly for convenience but more particularly because accurate default rates are difficult to obtain even for periods of a year.

D_P = expected default rate at period P; i.e. percentage of companies that are expected to default in period P.

R_E = expected recovery rate

M = number of periods in the expected credit loss calculation. M is normally taken as the number of years equal to the tenor of the transaction (e.g. for a seven-year swap, $M = 7$)

Very few banks have invested in the collection of company default information to allow an internal analysis of default and recovery rates. Most banks use default rates and recovery rates from either Moody's or Standard and Poor's (S&P). Table 8.4 shows cumulative default rates for various credit ratings.

Thus, the expected credit loss on a $10m five-year loan to a counterparty with a credit rating of 'A' is $0.0084 \times 10,000,000 = \$84,000$, assuming a recovery rate of 0% and that the value of the loan is constant. Assuming a recovery rate of 40%, would reduce the expected credit loss to $50,400. The recovery rate will depend mainly on the ranking of the debt. If it is senior or secured debt then the recovery rate will be relatively high. Table 8.5 shows an example set of recovery rates.

Table 8.4 Standard and Poor's cumulative default rates (%), 1981–93

	Year									
Rating	1	2	3	4	5	6	7	8	9	10
AAA	0.00	0.00	0.00	0.00	0.00	0.15	0.33	0.78	1.06	1.39
AA	0.00	0.03	0.18	0.40	0.64	0.97	1.30	1.64	1.90	2.12
A	0.06	0.17	0.30	0.53	0.84	1.13	1.47	1.80	2.20	2.71
BBB	0.28	0.70	1.11	1.86	2.54	3.22	3.83	4.48	5.13	5.68
BB	1.27	3.89	6.72	9.55	12.12	14.89	16.67	18.33	19.97	21.49
B	5.70	11.71	16.94	20.53	23.20	25.05	26.75	28.35	30.03	31.98
CCC	19.67	27.31	31.82	36.61	41.14	43.02	43.66	44.70	45.95	47.52

Table 8.5 Moody's average recovery rates (1970–95)

Ranking of debt	Recovery rate (%)
Senior secured	53.1
Senior unsecured	45.9
Senior subordinated	37.0
Subordinated	29.6
Junior subordinated	16.4
Preferred stock	6.0

Source: Moody's Investors Service, Corporate Bond Defaults and Default Rates 1938–1995, January 1996. Rates are based on reported market prices for defaulted bonds one month after the default.

The above example assumed that the exposure remained constant over the life of the loan; this is a reasonable assumption for commercial lending which generally works on accruals-based accounting. Even so, it should be noted that the expected credit loss would need to be adjusted over time to take account of the remaining time to maturity. Therefore, in one year the expected credit loss would reduce to $53,000 (assuming a recovery rate of zero) as the appropriate default rate to use would then be the four-year rate. This assumes that the counterparty still has the same credit rating. In practice, the expected credit loss should also be adjusted to take account of any change in the credit rating.

For trading instruments a different approach must be used. The credit exposure for instruments which are marked to market will vary daily. This means that we need to quantify future potential exposures. Future exposure is dependent on the volatility of the underlying market variables which determine the value of an instrument.

Expected Credit Loss – A Swap

An interest rate swap consists of a set of fixed, and therefore known, cash flows and a set of opposite but unknown floating rate cash flows (the first floating cash flow is, of course, known). The future value of a swap is dependent on future interest rates from two perspectives:

1. Future interest rates will determine the magnitude of the as yet unknown floating cash flows. The floating cash flows can be estimated from a forward interest rate curve. A forward curve is the market's best estimate of the future value of six-month interest rates today (six months is taken as an example, any other period could be used). In practice, however, forward curves have been found to have very poor predictive qualities. Future six-month interest rates will in fact depend on the path taken by interest rates between now and each floating rate fixing date.

2. Since the value of a swap is simply the present value of all future cash flows, the future value of a swap will depend on the future level of the zero coupon curve used to discount the cash flows.

Probably the most popular technique used to calculate the future value of swaps and other derivatives is the Monte Carlo simulation which generates a large number of future interest rate paths. Such a Monte Carlo simulation is given parameters within which to operate, just as the Monte Carlo simulations described in Chapter 3. The main difference being that this simulation must model future paths of interest rates and not just the value of the interest rate tomorrow, as with VAR simulations. When modelling future paths it is important to include features such as mean reversion. Apart from mean reversion the simulation will probably (though not necessarily) assume that rate changes are normally distributed and will use the same volatility estimate as would be used with a VAR simulation. It is outside the scope of this book fully to describe future-value simulations. However, a rough approximation can be put together with a spreadsheet by using volatility to determine potential future floating rates and discount rates.

Take, for example, a 10-year, $10m, interest rate swap with a credit rating of BBB where we are receiving fixed at 7% and paying floating initially also at 7%. To simplify the example, assume that both the fixed and floating side pay annually and that the yield curve is flat and is also 7%. From these details, a little thought will show that the initial value of the swap is zero as all the fixed and floating cash flows are $700,000 and they are all discounted at the same rate.

Fixed side
Consider the first fixed cash flow in one year's time; we can approximate the effect interest rate volatility might have on the present value of this cash flow. At time zero, the discount factor for the first cash flow will be:

$$\text{One year discount factor} = \frac{1}{1 + 0.07} = 0.9346$$

Therefore the present value of the first cash flow is $700,000 \times 0.9346 = \$654,200$.

At the end of the first year, the discount rate is likely to have changed. Our best guess of its value must be given by the volatility of the change in interest rates. Assume that the one-day volatility, with 95% confidence, is 10 basis points. Ignoring mean reversion and assuming that rate changes are normally distributed, we can scale up the one day volatility, by the square root of time:

$$\text{One year volatility} = 10\sqrt{260} = 160 \text{ basis points, or } 1.6\%.$$

Therefore, as an approximation, we can assume that interest rates will be 7% $\pm$ 1.6% with 95% confidence that rates will not be outside this range. Therefore, in one year's time, the one-year discount factor will be in a range given by:

$$\frac{1}{1+0.054} = 0.9488 \text{ to } \frac{1}{1+0.086} = 0.9208$$

Therefore, the present value of a fixed cash flow in one year will be somewhere in the range: $664,100 to $644,600. This process can be extended for all the discount factors up to the maturity of the swap and for all the fixed cash flows. When working out the potential future value of the swap we must step forward each year and add up the present values of all the remaining cash flows.

Floating side
We can apply a similar process to the floating side. Each year the floating rate will be fixed at the prevailing interest rate. Again, our best guess of the prevailing level of one year interest rates is the interest rate volatility. The initial floating rate was 7%; from the above discussion, it can be seen that in a year's time the floating rate will lie in the range 5.4% to 8.6%. Therefore, the second floating rate cash flow will be between $540,000 to $860,000. The present value of the floating cash flows will be derived using the same discount factors as for the fixed rate cash flows.

The value of the swap is the sum of the present values of all remaining cash flows on both the fixed and floating sides. Figure 8.2 shows the potential future value of the swap used as an example here. The shape is well known to credit risk managers and the potential future value peaks at approximately one-third of the way through the life of the swap. Figure 8.2 was produced using the simple approach described above. In practice, most banks who model credit risk use a Monte Carlo simulation to generate the potential value shape shown in Figure 8.2. The description of this method is beyond the scope of this book. Those readers who wish to delve further into sophisticated credit modelling should see Rowe (1996).

Having generated the future potential value, we are now in a position to calculate the expected credit loss. One of the first things to note about Figure 8.2 is that it is

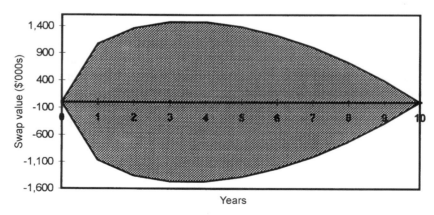

Figure 8.2 Swap – potential future value

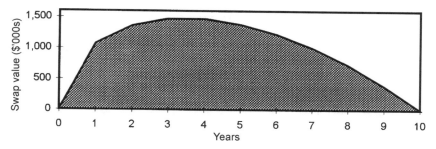

Figure 8.3 Swap – potential credit exposure

symmetrical about a mean value of zero, i.e. there is an equal probability of the swap having a positive or negative value at any point during its life. We cannot have credit exposure to the swap counterparty if the swap has a negative value, i.e. it would cost our bank money to close-out the swap. In this situation the counterparty has a credit exposure to us. Therefore, we can ignore the negative half of the potential future swap values. Figure 8.3 shows the potential future credit exposure of a swap.

We can now use equation 8.3 to determine the expected credit loss for the swap in Figure 8.3. Table 8.6 shows the expected credit exposure, default rate and resultant expected credit loss for each year of the swap.

Note that as cumulative default rates are used, the default rate applied to the potential future value for each year is conditional on the default not having occurred yet. Therefore, the default rate for each year, from year two on, must be multiplied by the probability that a default has not yet happened, i.e. by (1−the previous year's cumulative probability). If we assume that the recovery rate is a

Table 8.6 Calculation of expected credit loss for a swap

Year	Potential future value of swap ($)	Default rates (%)	Expected credit loss ($)
0	0	0	0
1	1,068,986	0.28	2,993
2	1,359,347	0.70	9,489
3	1,470,066	1.10	16,204
4	1,468,381	1.84	27,009
5	1,381,808	2.49	34,445
6	1,224,470	3.14	38,425
7	1,004,246	3.71	37,224
8	725,539	4.31	31,259
9	390,559	4.90	19,138
10	0	5.39	0
		Total	$216,187

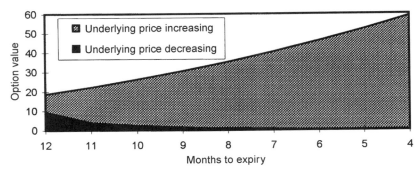

Figure 8.4 Potential future value of option

lowly 20%, then, using equation 8.3, the expected credit loss is:

$$\text{Expected credit loss} = \frac{(1-0.2).\dfrac{216,187}{10}}{2} = \$8,647$$

Note: The whole sum is divided by two, to reflect the fact that there is only a 50% chance of the swap having positive future values. Only positive swap values create a credit exposure, i.e. half the possible outcomes.

Of course not all instruments display the same symmetrical future value profiles as swaps. Figure 8.4 shows the future value for a call option purchased at-the-money.

Figure 8.4 shows that there is a small value on day one of the option (equal to the option premium), which increases steadily if the price of the underlying increases and decreases to zero, but never goes below zero, if the price of the underlying decreases. This makes sense, as the maximum you can lose if you purchase an option is the premium; the future credit exposure must reflect this.

It is worth restating the RAROC equation at this point:

$$\text{Risk adjusted return on capital (RAROC)} = \frac{\text{Net revenue} - \text{Expected credit loss}}{\text{Risk capital}}$$

and

$$\text{Risk capital} = \text{VAR} + \text{Unexpected credit loss} + \text{Operational value at risk}$$

We have now described how the numerator of the RAROC equation is arrived at. The denominator is 'risk capital'. How risk capital is arrived at is described in the following sections.

Risk Capital

Risk capital is the day-to-day level of risk assumed by a bank in the course of its various activities, i.e. the maximum amount of money that the bank may lose on a regular basis with a given level of confidence (one day in twenty for 95% confidence). Risk capital should be all inclusive and therefore has a wider definition than just market risk, i.e. VAR, where other sources or types of risk must be included. Risk capital is generally assumed to consist of the three elements given in the above equation. The following sections describe each of the elements of risk capital.

VAR for RAROC

There is no fundamental difference between the VAR used in RAROC and the VAR described so far in this book as a measure of market risk. The only difference is the time horizon; RAROC is focused on annual returns, rather than the potential loss over a one-day holding period.

It is not possible to calculate directly VAR for a one-year holding period, because of the amount of data required (a minimum of 30 years) and also because the very old historical data used would not represent the current behaviour of the financial markets. Therefore, we must measure VAR using some shorter holding period and scale it up to give VAR for the period of a year.

We could scale up the VAR calculated for a one-day holding period. If we assume there are 260 working days in a year then we could arrive at an annual VAR figure by multiplying by 16 (square root of 260). However this is not an ideal solution because of mean reversion. Particularly for interest rates and price spreads, annual volatility is unlikely to be 16 times greater than the one-day volatility; the multiple required will be significantly lower than this. Probably the best solution in practice is to calculate VAR directly for a one-month time horizon and then scale up to VAR for a one-year holding period (multiply by 3.46 – square root of 12). VAR calculated with a one-month holding period will include a degree of mean reversion.

One potential problem with calculating VAR for RAROC is that VAR, used as a risk measure, changes daily, sometimes by a substantial amount. The changes are of course due to changes in volatility and correlations. When measuring RAROC a stable measure of capital is required. This can be achieved by either taking an average of daily VAR or by using more stable measures of volatility and correlation. In Chapter 4, it was stressed that VAR should be calculated using measures of volatility and correlation which are responsive to changes in behaviour of the underlying assets. Such models of volatility and correlation use a short observation period, typically no more than 100 days. For RAROC, volatility and correlation could be calculated using a longer observation period, such as two years. This would give far more stable measures of volatility and correlation.

Unexpected Credit Loss

Expected credit loss assumes that companies default in the numbers predicted by default rates. Expected credit loss also relies on recoveries being made from defaulted companies as per the assumed recovery rates. Default and recovery rates will only represent real life if the bank has a very large and even spread of companies as counterparties. In fact, a bank would have to have the same spread of counterparties as used by the rating agencies when compiling their default rates.

Some banks change the default rates and recovery rates they use to better reflect the mix and concentration to counterparties present in their portfolio (for example, concentrations to specific industry sectors, or to company types, e.g. mid-size technology corporates). Default and recovery rates can also be adjusted to reflect the current point in the economic cycle. Such adjustments may help to ensure that the expected credit loss, or credit reserve, more fairly reflects the credit losses that the bank will suffer; however, this still leaves fluctuations in default and recovery rates over time. In any one year, default experience may vary considerably from both the previous year and from the longer-term average of default rates. Note that the default rates given in Table 8.4 are averages over a period of 12 years.

Unexpected credit loss must account for the risk that more money is lost through defaults than is given by the expected credit loss figure. The majority of this book has been dedicated to describing the distributions of changes in market values. In practice default rates and recovery rates also vary with time; default and recovery rates have distributions, though they are not normally distributed. Therefore, the unexpected credit loss can be arrived at by combining the three distributions and taking the worst case loss with a given level of confidence. The mathematical description of the default and recovery rate distributions and their combination with the distribution of future position values is complex and beyond the scope of this book. The following example is an approximation, demonstrating the principles of the calculation. First, let us define unexpected credit loss:

Unexpected credit loss = Maximum credit loss − Expected credit loss

We will continue with the example based on a swap. We must first adjust the default and recovery rates used in the expected credit loss calculation for their volatility. Let us assume that the 95% confidence level volatility of default rates and the recovery rate are 100% and 30% respectively.[6] Figure 8.5 shows the loss for each year, generated by multiplying the potential future value of the swap by the 95% confidence default probabilities. As can be seen, the maximum loss occurs later in the life of the swap than the maximum future value because default probabilities increase rapidly with maturity.

The maximum loss shown in Figure 8.5 is $77,000; this must now be multiplied by the 95% confidence level recovery rate. The original recovery rate was 20% and it was assumed that the 95% confidence volatility of the recovery rate was 30%. Therefore the 95% confidence recovery rate is 14% (20 − 20 × 0.3). Assuming a 14% recovery rate gives a figure for the maximum credit loss of $66,000 ((1 − 0.14) × 77,000).

Just as the expected credit loss needed to be divided by two to reflect the fact that there is only a 50% chance of the swap having positive future values, so the

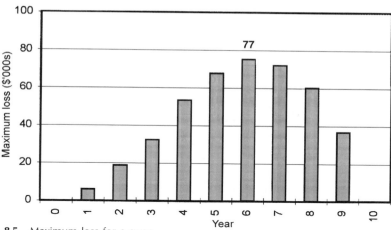

Figure 8.5   Maximum loss for a swap

maximum credit loss must also be divided by two. This gives a final figure for the maximum credit loss of $33,000.

The unexpected credit loss is equal to maximum credit loss – expected credit loss, which gives a figure for the unexpected credit loss of $24,000 (33,000 – 9,000). This figure for the unexpected credit loss must be added to the VAR of the position, to which must be added the figure for operational loss.

Operational Risk

Operational risk is perhaps the greatest source of risk financial institutions face. Most of the recent major banking disasters and losses have been due first and foremost to operational risk. As such it is important that operational risk is included in risk capital. The problem is not its inclusion, but its quantification.

Quantifying operational risks is not easy to do in a manner which has meaning to operational managers. With both market and credit risk there are externally available analyses (price volatilities, default rates, etc.) which enable us to quantify market and credit risk. This is not the case with operational risk at the present time. Each bank must come up with its own quantification methodology. Generally speaking, the methodologies used fall into one of two camps:

1. *Analytical*   In this approach, strong assumptions are made about the frequency and magnitude of losses. These are then put into some form of statistical model and an operational risk figure is produced. One of the major problems with this type of approach (especially in the absence of any *de facto* industry standard) is that the bank's management are unlikely to believe or easily accept the operational risk figure produced. A common complaint is of the application of pseudo-science. If this approach is taken, it is essential to fully involve the

management responsible for achieving the required return on capital. In reality, the so-called analytical approach is just as subjective as the following approach due to the assumptions made in the model.

2. *Subjective*   In the subjective approach, an independent area of the bank (typically the internal audit function) assesses the operational control weaknesses of each business activity and assigns them a grade or score. A capital cost (agreed with management) is then applied to each area, based on headcount or some other criterion, dependent on the score achieved.

As an example, consider two business units within a bank. The first business unit has been in operation for several years and is a mature business. This business unit has an exemplary operational set-up and continues to invest in high-quality staff, training and new systems, etc. This business unit is given an operational risk grade of 'A'.

The second business unit is a new business activity which is growing very fast. The operational areas are struggling to keep up with the pace of growth of the business and suffer from a lack of investment. This business unit is given a grade of 'D'.

An operational risk grade of 'A' might equate to a capital charge of $1,000 per person, whereas a grade of 'D' may equate to a capital charge of $10,000 per person. Clearly, there is a strong incentive for the second business unit to improve the quality of its operations. It will be required to achieve its target return on capital on a much higher capital usage. It should be noted that this subjective allocation of risk capital for operational risk has more to do with internal bank objectives than an analytical quantification of business risk.

The whole area of the treatment of operational risk is developing fast, spurred on by regulators realising that the main risks in many banks are not the market or credit risk but the operational risks. When giving model approval, regulators now spend far more time scrutinising bank's operational controls than anything else.

At this point we are now in a position to calculate RAROC and have shown how VAR fits in to an overall business management framework for banks. RAROC is an excellent tool for measuring the performance of any business unit within a bank. However, before concluding this chapter, it is important to consider the relationship between risk capital and the bank's actual capital base.

CAPITAL ALLOCATION

Now that the risk capital of each business unit has been calculated, we can move on to consider how capital is allocated to individual business units within a bank. This involves relating risk capital to the bank's actual capital. In this section, a bank's actual capital will be taken to be its equity capital. The following discussion of capital allocation will refer to risk capital and show how actual capital can be allocated to business units based on the usage of risk capital. The methods discussed are applicable both to risk capital calculated as revenue volatility (earnings at risk – EAR) and risk capital calculated for the RAROC measure.

RAROC and EAR allow the measurement of return on risk capital not the bank's actual capital. Therefore, we need to link the bank's actual capital to risk capital. We need some way of allocating the bank's actual capital to individual business units. The capital allocation method differs depending on which of the following is being considered:

- *Internal performance measurement* The objective of internal performance measurement is to identify the performance of each of a bank's different business activities. Absolute performance must be examined to see whether the business unit is producing a return commensurate with its revenue volatility. Relative performance is important management information, facilitating informed strategic decisions and performance tuning of individual activities.

- *External performance measurement* The objective of external performance measurement is to ensure that the bank, as a whole, is producing the return required by its investors. To do this, return on capital must be calculated for the whole bank and for each individual business activity. Each business activity can be examined to see whether it is producing the required return on its share of the bank's capital.

Internal Performance Measurement

Each individual business unit must achieve a return on the actual capital allocated to it that is commensurate with the business unit's volatility of earnings. But how much actual capital does a business unit use? In most banks, the sum of the risk capital for all business units is a relatively small fraction of the bank's actual capital. How should the actual capital be allocated to individual business units?

For individual business unit performance measurement, actual capital is usually assumed to be used by business units on a pro-rata basis with respect to each unit's risk capital. For example, consider ABC Bank with three business units as shown in Table 8.7.

Table 8.7 ABC Bank: risk capital by business unit (actual equity capital $1000m)

Business unit	Risk capital ($m)
A	51
B	46
C	124
	Total risk capital $221m

Table 8.8   ABC Bank: capital allocation for internal performance measurement (actual equity capital $1000m)

Business unit	Risk capital ($m)	Pro rata % of risk capital	Actual capital allocated ($m)
A	51	23.0	230
B	46	20.9	209
C	124	56.1	561

As is often the case, the risk capital is considerably less than the actual capital base of the bank. As stated in an earlier section, this needs to be the case as risk capital only covers day-to-day risks. Risk capital will not necessarily cover extreme market events which a bank must be able to survive. Thus, actual capital can be allocated to business units on a pro-rata basis as shown in Table 8.8.

External Performance Measurement

Due to diversification, the revenue volatility of a bank with several business units will be lower than the sum of the revenue volatilities of each of the business units. This is the same portfolio effect we have been modelling through most of this book. The risk capital required for a bank is, therefore, less than the sum of the risk capital amounts for all business units. When considering external performance, capital should be allocated on a diversified basis.

On a diversified basis, the total capital allocated should equal the risk capital of the bank as a whole. This can be achieved by multiplying the risk capital of each business unit by the correlation between its revenue volatility and the revenue volatility of the whole bank. Thus, revenue volatility must be used for diversified capital allocation. Consider ABC Bank used in the example above. Table 8.9 shows the risk capital of each business unit, the correlation of each business unit and the actual capital allocated to each business unit.

With respect to external expectations, a bank's management needs to compare the risk adjusted return generated by each business unit against the return required by investors for the revenue volatility displayed by the bank. In the case of external performance measurement, the return on capital used must be the return on the diversified risk capital. As was stated in an earlier section, if a business unit is not generating (as a minimum) the level of return required by investors, then it is destroying shareholder value. Therefore, the fact that a business unit makes a substantial profit is not necessarily an indication of satisfactory performance. Failure to increase shareholder value should be reflected in bonus pool allocation

Table 8.9 ABC Bank: capital allocation for external performance measurement

	A	Business unit B	C	Whole bank ($m)
Risk capital ($m)	51	46	124	152
Correlation	0.5735	0.2432	0.9053	–
Diversified risk capital ($m)	29	11	112	152
Diversified percentage	19.1	7.4	73.5	
Actual capital allocation ($m)	191	74	735	1,000

and will eventually lead to questions being asked about whether the bank should continue in that area of business.

This section has shown how a bank can use VAR in the return-on-capital measure – RAROC – to help it ensure that all its different business activities are adding to shareholder value and helping the bank achieve its required return on capital.

REWARDING TRADERS ON RISK ADJUSTED PERFORMANCE

At the present time, most traders are rewarded solely on the revenue they generate. The trader is given a clear incentive to make money, which is what the bank wants. We have, however, noted that banking is about managing risk and return. The problem with the current method of rewarding traders is that it only focuses on one side of this equation – return.

Put yourself in the place of a trader. If you make a lot of money you are going to get a bonus large enough to buy a good size family house. If you make only a little money you will receive a small bonus – large enough to stop you moving to another bank. If you make a loss you will probably not be sacked and will still receive your salary. Therefore, the return formula is stacked heavily in your favour. From the bank's perspective the reward formula is not symmetrical. If the trader makes money he receives a significant proportion of the money he has made. If he loses money the bank must bear the full loss, i.e. the trader does not share in the loss he has made.

The result of this is that the trader has a natural tendency to take more risk. Taking more risk will increase the volatility of his revenue but he is protected from the down side by the asymmetric reward system.

The thrust of this chapter suggests that performance of business units and of traders should be assessed on a risk adjusted basis using a method such as RAROC. This view is gaining momentum in banks and regulators are strongly in favour. However, at the time of writing very few banks have successfully managed to introduce a reward system for traders based on the return on risk capital that they have generated. This is largely due to competitive pressures. If a bank tries to introduce such a system, the traders will simply leave and go to work for a bank where their bonus is purely dependent on the revenue they generate. As with many outmoded work methods, what looks like an unassailable fortress will eventually be breached when sufficient pressure for change builds up.

When it arrives, the move to reward traders on RAROC will benefit the whole banking industry and will lead to lower volatility of earnings. In the longer term, one of the benefits of the resultant steadier revenue stream will be higher credit ratings for banks and a reduction in the return required by shareholders.

SUMMARY

When implementing VAR, it is essential to understand how it can be used and how it fits in to a general performance management framework. This chapter has introduced the reader to the concepts of managing capital and measuring risk adjusted performance.

Being clear as to what is meant by the word 'capital' is important. This chapter has introduced the concept of risk capital as the day-to-day level of risk in a bank. The amount of capital a bank must hold economically (economic capital) must be determined by the need to survive severe market shocks or a concentration of credit defaults. In the final analysis, risk capital must be linked to a bank's actual equity capital if the relevant return on capital is to be measured for a business unit. Actual capital is often allocated on a pro-rata basis with respect to the risk capital calculated for the business unit.

The return on capital required from a business unit is determined by its volatility of earnings which also determines the return demanded by the market for the bank as a whole. As the volatility of earnings is closely linked to risk, the return on capital required from a business unit will depend on the amount of risk it takes. The required return will be different for each business unit within the bank.

A business unit which does not produce a return commensurate with the risk it takes is likely to be destroying shareholder value. Therefore, understanding and measuring risk and return is essential and is at the centre of managing a banking business. Understanding and measuring VAR is in turn central to the understanding and measurement of a bank's risk.

NOTES

1. In this context the capital referred to is equity.
2. It should be noted that this equation is not universally applicable as it represents an analysis of a certain set of banks over a certain period. The

relationship between beta and revenue volatility may change over time. For details of the analysis performed refer to Matten (1996, pp. 99–100).

3. The volatility of revenue can be taken as any number of standard deviations. Using the same level of confidence as is used in VAR may make sense for consistency. However, the most important thing is that volatility is implemented consistently across business units.

4. For a good introduction to credit risk see Rowe (1996).

5. Expected credit loss is synonymous with the 'credit reserve' in accounting language.

6. Volatility of default and recovery rates can be obtained from Moody's, or Standard & Poor's.

9
Regulators and risk management

INTRODUCTION

Regulation of the banking industry has increased significantly over the last few years and it is still developing. These developments have provided a spur to the efforts put into risk management by the banking industry. As such it is essential to understand why regulation has increased, what regulators are trying to achieve and what is the current state of play of banking regulation. This chapter addresses all three of these issues.

First, however, to set the scene. Prior to the 1980s banking regulation had been largely concerned with credit and liquidity risk. Exchange controls, national banking cartels and accounting practice had kept market risk in the banking industry to a minimum. In most countries with the exception of the USA and Switzerland, exchange controls prevented domestic institutions from holding foreign investments and foreign currency positions. Banking cartels in many countries effectively divided up the various finance activities between them with mutual agreements not to step on each other's patches. This resulted in the finance markets acting as a series of individual national islands with no real international integration.

As the national banking cartels collapsed and exchange controls were repealed at the end of the 1970s, so the largest banks reached out to become truly international. The ensuing internationalisation had a profound effect on the banking industry, increasing banks' exposure to markets on a global basis and away from a purely national focus.

Prior to the mid 1980s the prevalent accounting practice within banking was to account for all security positions on an accruals basis. This accounting practice meant that day-to-day changes in bond prices, for example, were not reflected in banks' profit and loss statements. Accrual accounting was implicitly supported by the central banks who needed banks to buy government debt. Central banks could not ask banks to buy government bonds one day and then expect banks to recognise losses on those positions on the following day. The change in accounting practices in the early 1980s also coincided with national governments using interest rates to control the economy. This in turn led to far greater volatility in the financial markets and, in particular, in the interest rate markets. These market changes led to pressure to adopt mark-to-market (MTM) accounting for all trading activities. As MTM accounting became the standard, so daily changes in the value of banks' portfolios became visible and so did swings in daily trading P&L.

Taken together these changes created an environment in which market risk could become a real issue in the banking industry. Nonetheless, it took several years for market risk to have sufficient magnitude to have the potential to cause damage to the world's financial system. Before this could happen the Third World debt crisis hit.

Central banks and governments had implicitly encouraged banks to lend to the Third World. Commercial lending by banks reduced the requirement for aid from supranational bodies such as the World Bank. By the early 1980s Third World sovereign governments who, it had been assumed, could not go bankrupt, defaulted on their debts. As the crisis gathered pace, regulators realised that the crisis presented a real threat to the world's financial system. Banks were forced to make huge provisions against bad debts which significantly reduced the bank's capital reserves. The regulators initial response was therefore aimed primarily at credit risk. The Basle based Bank for International Settlements (BIS) 1988 Accord was aimed at establishing a common international standard for the regulation of credit risk. By the time the 1988 Accord was in place the BIS knew that they urgently needed to move onto market risk.

In the 1990s regulators have begun to move more quickly and are now focusing on the regulation of market risk. The development of the regulatory framework for market risk is not yet complete. It is likely that it will go through several iterations before the methods for regulating market risk are agreed and implemented, not least because several sets of regulators (often within a country) are involved. This mirrors developments within the industry itself. The management of market risk is still being debated within and between financial institutions, with value at risk being at the centre of this discussion.

REGULATORY OBJECTIVES

Before specific regulations are discussed the motivation behind banking regulation is outlined as a set of regulatory objectives. The main regulatory objectives driving banking regulation are discussed below.

Stability of the Financial System

The overriding concern and objective of banking regulators around the world is to maintain the stability of the financial system, firstly in their own country but also across the industrialised world.

In order to ensure the stability of the financial system in their own countries regulators must endeavour to ensure that the financial system does not collapse. The primary mechanism for this in the past has been to act as the 'lender of last resort'. Acting as the lender of last resort means that if a bank collapses, or finds itself in a position which threatens its survival, that the central bank will step in, provide liquidity and ensure that it survives. In the UK the Bank of England stepped in to prevent the collapse of Johnson Matthey, buying the institution for the nominal sum of £1 and underwriting its losses. Some years later, with a significantly changed business profile, the Bank of England sold Johnson Matthey back into the market place.

The necessity for central banks to act as the lender of last resort needs to be explained. The theory is that the collapse of one large bank could bring down other banks in a kind of domino effect, although it only requires a little thought to see that any bank in a financial system is connected with so many other banks that the effect would be more like a chain reaction, radiating out in 360°, with the destruction accelerating outwards from the starting point. For this to work in practice it would require banks involved with the collapsing bank to have very large payments or sums owing to them. This was partly dealt with by the Large Exposures Regulations in the 1988 Basle Accord (see page 183). The potential for this problem is also dealt with as part of the overall credit risk management within any bank. The possibility of a systemic failure of the financial system remains a concern of the global financial regulators.

The financial markets have undergone considerable globalisation over the last 10 years. At first sight this may appear to have made the problem of a systemic failure of the financial markets more complex and very much an international issue. In practice, most studies on the subject have concluded that the globalisation of financial markets, linked with institutions' diversification of business has in fact reduced the likelihood of a systemic failure. Nonetheless, the main economic countries are keen to ensure that the banking regulations in place in each country are adequate to prevent systemic failure within each domestic financial market and therefore internationally.

Thankfully, there is not a large body of 'case law' relating to the situations in which central banks will act as the lender of last resort. The recent collapse of Barings shows that the Bank of England will not support 'small' banks whose collapse does not threaten the financial system. This tends to suggest that the Bank of England will not step in unless either a very large bank is in trouble, which could conceivably cause, if not systemic failure, then at least significant damage to the financial system, or perhaps in the case when a critical part of the financial system was threatened, for example, a futures exchange or a clearing house.

Security of Financial Market Institutions

A separate but closely-related objective is to ensure the financial security of the institutions that make up the financial system as going concerns. This is motivated by both economic and political considerations. The objective can be restated as ensuring that banks are secure places to put your money, i.e. that they are unlikely to go bust.

The financial markets ensure that money is redistributed from those people or organisations that have a surplus to those who need to borrow it. This remains true even after the 'disintermediation' between banks and lenders caused by the much increased use of debt issuance as a cheaper way for corporates to borrow money. To perform this 'middle-man' role banks need to be financially secure.

An effective and efficient financial market is essential for a successful economy. Therefore, central banks and their governments have a vested interest in ensuring that banks do not go bankrupt on a regular basis.

For the biggest financial centres there is an additional motivation for ensuring the stability of the financial institutions forming the financial markets. For these centres there are substantial economic benefits from maintaining and encouraging the continuance of the domestic financial centre also as a world financial centre. The regulators have a balancing act to perform between providing an adequate regulatory environment and over-regulating so that regulation adversely affects the efficiency of the industry and drives market participants away to other financial centres.

The collapse of Barings was an object lesson to regulators that it is impossible for them to prevent banks failing. Barings was a considerable embarrassment for the Bank of England; regulators had been performing closer and closer checks on banks and their internal management. This did not enable the Bank of England to predict or prevent the collapse of Barings. Post Barings the Bank of England has announced that it is going to significantly increase the size of its bank monitoring and supervision teams. The history of the accountancy industry, one of whose jobs is to protect shareholders against fraud and financial malpractice, suggests that it is unlikely that any size of regulatory organisation can prevent banks collapsing.

Harmonisation

Regulatory frameworks are increasingly set internationally, notably by the BIS. However, regulations are actually implemented by national governments and are administered by national regulatory bodies.

Harmonisation is a collective international objective to ensure that there is a common regulatory framework in all countries with a significant role in the world's financial markets. The BIS regulations are law in the G10 countries. The sub-objectives of harmonisation are to establish an international level playing field for the finance industry and also to reduce international systemic risk.

In theory at least, the 1988 Basle Accord established common levels of capital requirement across the world. This process was extended in Europe where the Capital Adequacy Directive (CAD) was established in 1996. In practice, however, implementation of CAD is down to individual countries. The result in Europe is that the playing field, although no longer resembling the ploughed field of old, is still far from flat, with each government, or central bank, putting their own interpretation on the CAD directive.

RATING AGENCIES
Who are they?

The main rating agencies are Moody's and Standard & Poor's. There are various other regulators such as IBCA, but it is the view of the two American agencies that most people respect above the others. Banks pay to have a rating agency apply a rating to them; this can be a fairly expensive process. Rating agencies publish the credit ratings of banks and other companies. The ratings provide guidance as to the likelihood of default. Ranging from the Triple A rating, that means that there is a negligible probability of default, down to Triple B, which is the lowest 'investment' grade rating. Rating agencies are saying that any company shares or bonds issued by a company with a rating lower that BBB should be considered only as a speculative investment, i.e. that there is a reasonably high probability of default. Table 9.1 shows default probabilities over a 10-year period for different credit ratings (Standard & Poor's).

Rating Agencies as Industry Standard Setters

In the 1990s the rating agencies have exerted a strong influence over the banking industry. This is because the credit rating given to a bank by a rating agency is a critical factor in determining both the type and volume of business it can undertake. The liquidity in the financial markets is created and maintained by interbank trading. By far the greatest volume of trades are transacted between 'market professionals', i.e. mainly banks and securities houses.

Table 9.1 Default probabilities

Credit rating	10-year default probability (%)
AAA	1.4
AA	2.1
A	2.7
BBB	5.7
BB	21.5
B	32.0
CCC	47.5

Source: Standard & Poor's

Banks all have internal credit limits that limit the total maximum exposure they can have to other players in the market. These limits are partly dependent on a bank's own internal analysis of the credit worthiness of other banks but are also heavily dependent on the credit ratings of other banks published by the rating agencies. A lower credit rating will mean that a bank will be given smaller overall credit exposure limits by other banks. In addition, the type of transaction that the market is prepared to undertake with a bank will also change. In particular the permitted maximum maturity of OTC transactions will be reduced in line with reductions in the credit grade. This is because there is a higher probability of a bank going bust over a period of five years than there is over a period of one year. OTC transactions, such as swaps, are not freely tradable securities that could be disposed of at any time. In addition to this it is known that the top three credit ratings (AAA, AA and A) deteriorate over time. The main rating agencies publish credit rating transition matrices that show the transition from and to different credit ratings.

The effect of this can be to severely constrain the business a bank can undertake. This is true of all banks but is especially true of smaller institutions. The market operates under the assumption that larger banks operate with the safety net of the lender of last resort from the central banks, though this differs from one country to another. As a result, the largest banks in some domestic markets are partially protected from the effects of a credit rating downgrading.

In contrast, small independent English merchant banks have found, post Barings, that many banks have reduced their credit limits and maximum permitted maturities to them. In some cases this has severely limited their ability to act as market makers in certain products. This in turn is forcing these banks to refocus their trading activities.

As can be seen from the above discussion, it is critical to be able to convince the rating agencies of the certitude of your viability as a going concern. This is clearly dependent on a large number of factors that are beyond the scope of this book. Suffice it to say that two of the key factors which rating agencies look at are the capital ratios and a bank's ability to manage risk.

It is perhaps for this reason that since 1990 the majority of banks have built up capital in excess of that required by the Basle 1988 Accord. As capital is expensive to raise and maintain (in the form of return on equity) banks must have very good reasons for wishing to maintain capital in excess of that required by regulators. Most banks believe that high capital ratios will help persuade rating agencies to improve their credit rating. There is certainly a reasonable correlation between low capital ratios and low credit ratings. Sufficient time has not yet passed to establish a positive correlation between banks establishing higher capital ratios and higher credit ratings being granted by rating agencies. Most market players, however, assume that this will be shown to be the case in due course.

A second key factor considered by rating agencies is a bank's ability to manage risk. A number of banks have set up so called 'Triple A' companies (also referred to as derivative product companies). These are wholly-owned subsidiaries of large banks that are heavily capitalised. The vehicles are set up solely on the basis that a

Triple A credit rating will allow them to undertake OTC transactions that they would not be able to transact through the parent bank.

Before the rating agencies will grant a Triple A rating, they insist on seeing and understanding how the company intends to calculate and manage risk. This process of review of internal procedures is similar to the model approval process adopted by the Bank of England when it considers the appropriate capital ratios that should apply to an individual bank (see the discussion on internal models on pages 193–4).

The rating agencies are particularly concerned to ensure that the prospective Triple A vehicle has systems that can predict the expected credit loss on a portfolio at any point through to the maximum maturity that the vehicle intends to trade. This normally involves a Monte Carlo simulation of market and default scenarios over the life of the longest intended instrument. The risk management reviews by rating agencies have had the effect of raising the barriers to entry of this type of business.

It can be seen that rating agencies are in a position to exert a strong influence over industry practice. Credit ratings are a key (perhaps the most important) consideration for banks when deciding how much capital to have. In addition, rating agencies are now actively involved in reviewing and therefore setting standards for the calculation and management of risk.

RECENT REGULATORY HISTORY

The mid 1980s saw banks carrying balance sheets swollen by lending to developing countries as well as to domestic markets. Banks, which are highly-geared businesses by definition, had balance sheets with higher gearing than had ever been seen before. This did not matter as long as only a small proportion of loans defaulted; banks could increase their return on equity by continually expanding the balance sheet. The flaw in this business strategy was exposed by the developing world debt crisis.

American commercial banks started to make huge provisions against bad debts and reported losses, many for the first time in their histories. Governments and central banks became seriously worried about the possibility of a systemic failure in the financial system.

Prior to the Basle Accord, banking supervision was based on supervisory judgement by individual regulatory authorities. Naturally, this judgement differed from one authority to another and from one bank to another. The 1988 Basle Accord changed the basis of banking regulation. This process of change continues.

BIS and the Basle Supervisory Committee

The process of change started when the Cooke committee was established under the umbrella of the BIS to propose common international regulatory capital standards for banks. Subsequently, the Cooke committee has become the Basle Supervisory Committee (BSC). The BSC has central bank and supervisory representatives from the G10 countries[1] and Luxembourg. Although the Basle recommendations and the 1988 Accord are often referred to as the 'BIS proposals or regulation', the committee is not actually part of the BIS; the BIS is merely a convenient home for this international committee. The G10 governments implement BSC Accords as national law by common agreement.

The 1988 Basle Accord

The 1988 Basle Accord was a decisive step in creating a level international playing field for banking. The Basle Accord established clear minimum capital requirements for all banks. In so doing the G10 countries also took a decisive step along the road to ensuring that systemic risk was constrained. Global systemic risk is reduced if individual national regulators follow a standard supervisory policy that effectively reduces the risk of insolvency of individual banks. The 1988 Accord was not sufficient by itself but dealt with what was perceived to be the greatest source of financial risk – the risk of a bank's counterparties defaulting – credit risk. Indeed, when one considers the tens of billions that were allocated by banks around the world as reserves against bad debts, one can see that the Basle committee hit the nail on the head.

The 1988 Basle Accord imposed minimum amounts of capital to be held against exposure to a bank's counterparties. The exposure to counterparties is expressed in terms of a measure called 'weighted risk assets'. The 1988 Basle Accord specified that a bank's capital must, as a minimum, be equal to 8% of the bank's weighted risk assets. The 1988 Accord also specified certain constraints to the extent of a bank's business. These constraints are described below.

Capital

'Capital' as defined by the 1988 Accord (Basle Supervisory Committee 1988) specifies two components of capital, as described below:

1. *Tier 1*   Tier 1 capital includes equity and disclosed reserves. Tier 1 capital is also known as 'core' capital.
2. *Tier 2*   Tier 2 capital (sometimes known as supplementary capital) includes undisclosed reserves, subordinated debt with a maturity longer than five years, perpetual debt securities and unrealised gains on investments.

In terms of the capital that is allowed to count against weighted risk assets, Tier 2 capital must not be bigger than Tier 1 capital.

Weighted Risk Assets

Exposure to counterparties is measured in terms of weighted risk assets. Weighted risk assets are calculated by multiplying assets by a percentage that is dependent on the type of asset and counterparty. Table 9.2 shows the weightings that are applied to various assets.

In addition to the above, a credit equivalence must be calculated for off-balance sheet instruments (derivatives). Two methods are available as outlined below. Both methods are structured to calculate a credit exposure equal to the maximum likely value of the trade during its life. When calculating a bank's exposure only positive credit equivalents are considered, i.e. those derivative transactions for which a counterparty would owe the bank money in the event of the counterparty defaulting.

Original exposure method

Under the original exposure method, the notional amount of the contract is multiplied by a percentage that is dependent on the original maturity of the trade.

Table 9.2   Risk asset classification

Asset type	Weighting
• OECD government debt	
• Cash held	0%
• Gold bullion held	
• Cash to be received	
• Claims on OECD banks	20%
• US government agency securities	
• Agency CMOs	
• Municipal general obligation bonds	
• Municipal revenue bonds	50%
• Corporate bonds	
• LDC debt	100%
• Claims on non-OECD banks above 1 year to maturity	
• Equity	
• Real estate	
• Plant and equipment	
• Mortgage strips and residuals	

Current exposure method

In this method, an 'add-on' is added to the current market value of the transaction. The add-on is calculated by taking a percentage of the notional principle. In this method the percentage is dependent on the *remaining* time to maturity. The current value of all contracts with a positive value is known as the 'gross replacement value'.

Example

Take an interbank interest rate swap with a notional principle of £10m and with a residual maturity of two years. Before the appropriate risk asset weighting can be applied the credit equivalent amount of the swap must be calculated. Using the current exposure approach, the credit equivalent is equal to the current value plus a maturity dependent add-on. For this example let us assume the current value of the swap is £2m. As the residual remaining time to maturity is two years, the add-on is calculated by multiplying the notional principle by 0.5%; therefore, the add-on = £10,000,000 × 0.005 = £50,000. Therefore, the total credit equivalent of the swap = 2,000,000 + 50,000 = £2,050,000.

Table 9.3 gives an example of calculating the capital charge on a portfolio of three assets. The table shows how the credit equivalent of a derivative is incorporated into the overall calculation of weighted risk assets.

Table 9.3 Calculation of weighted risk assets

Asset	Credit equivalent	Asset risk weighting	Weighted risk assets (£m)
Loan £10m	10,000,000	100%	10
Government debt £10m	10,000,000	0%	—
Swap £10m (as above)	2,050,000	20%	0.41
		Total weighted risk assets	£10.41m

Large Exposures

At the same time as establishing minimum capital requirements for banks, the Basle Accord set certain restrictions on credit risk positions that banks could take. These restrictions are known as the Large Exposure Regulations. Large exposures are defined as any exposures that are equal to or greater than 10% of a bank's capital. The total of these exposures must not exceed 800% of capital. In addition to this, the maximum exposure allowed is equal to 25% of a bank's capital.

These restrictions clearly help banks avoid bankruptcy due to the failure of a counterparty. This in turn has the knock-on effect of reducing the possibility of a systemic failure in the banking industry.

Netting

The original 1988 Accord was amended in 1993 and again in 1995 to allow for the netting of counterparty exposures. Netting refers to the offsetting of positive and negative exposures, i.e. positive and negative MTM values. This is only possible when there is a legally binding contract signed by the bank and its counterparty; these are known as bilateral netting agreements and usually form part of the 'master' agreement covering the majority of vanilla trading between the two companies. Banks typically have netting agreements in place between themselves and their main counterparties; however, to be recognised by the regulators for the purpose of reducing the regulatory capital requirement there must be established legal precedent in the countries of both counterparties.

In the absence of a netting agreement each transaction between a bank and its counterparty is treated separately. A typical trading relationship would involve a large number of transactions, for some of which the bank will owe the counterparty money (i.e. the bank's MTM is negative) or vice versa. In the event of a counterparty default, its liquidators would claim from the bank for all transactions with a positive value, i.e. transactions for which the counterparty's MTM is positive.

Example

Consider the case where a bank has two swaps outstanding with a counterparty, for one of which the counterparty owes the bank £10m (i.e. the counterparty had transacted a swap with the bank, which now has a positive current value for the bank of £10m), the second in which the bank owes the counterparty £8m.

In the event of the counterparty defaulting and without a netting agreement in place the bank would receive a small proportion (for the purposes of this example we will assume the bank recovers 10% of debts due to it) of the £10m that the counterparty owes the bank for the first swap. Meanwhile, the liquidators of the counterparty would be entitled to collect the £8m due to the counterparty on the second swap. Thus, the bank would pay the £8m due and would receive $0.1 \times £10m = £1,000,000$. Therefore, the bank would pay out a total of £7,000,000.

Had a legally enforceable netting agreement been in place, the bank could register as a creditor for the *net* value of the transactions between the counterparties, i.e. $£10m - £8m = £2m$. The bank would then eventually receive $£2m \times 0.1 = £200,000$ (assuming 10% recovery).

The BSC revised the original Accord to allow for netting subject to certain criteria being met. The revision allows banks to calculate the weighted risk assets based on the total net replacement value instead of the gross replacement value.

Criticism of the 1988 Accord

At the time of writing the industry is still trying to develop a single measure of risk that accurately covers all risks that a bank is exposed to. As the industry still has not arrived at a solution to this problem, if indeed a solution exists, it is not surprising that banks felt that the 1988 Accord had several failings in terms of measuring and capturing a bank's risks. The main criticisms were as follows:

- *Ignorance of credit quality* Many banks have large exposures to corporate counterparties. All such exposures are given a 100% weighting regardless of the credit quality of the corporate. This provides a disincentive for banks to manage the credit quality of their books. Higher returns may be on offer from poorer quality counterparties. As there is not a higher regulatory charge for lower credit quality assets, the 1988 Accord would encourage banks to seek out the higher returns. In practice commercial decisions are rarely based purely on regulatory criteria.

- *No diversification effects* The risk reducing effects of diversifying a portfolio are completely ignored by the 1988 Accord. A bank could substantially reduce its overall level of risk by ensuring that its credit exposures are diversified across industries and countries. Again the 1988 Accord provides no incentive for a bank to consider this.

- *No protection against market risk* The 1988 Accord did not require banks to set aside any capital to cover potential losses from market risk. The BSC was well aware of this shortcoming and saw the 1988 Accord as the first step in establishing a more comprehensive regulatory capital framework. The market risk hole has now been thoroughly plugged. The remainder of this chapter describes the regulatory framework that has been put in place for market risk.

Market Risk Capital Regulation

In January 1996, the Basle Supervisory Committee issued a Market Risk Amendment to the 1988 Accord, specifying a minimum capital requirement to cover market risk. The 1996 Amendment is now part of the international regulatory framework for banks. This section describes the various proposals and counter proposals that led up to the issue of the 1996 Market Risk Amendment. The development of the 1996 Market Risk Amendment is also a story of the convergence of regulatory risk management proposals with banks' internal risk management practices.

The 1993 Basle Market Risk Proposal

The Market Risk Amendment to the 1988 Accord was first issued by the BSC for discussion in 1993. The proposal presented a framework for the regulatory control of market risk, again utilising the concept of a minimum capital requirement. The 1993 proposal put forward for discussion a method for calculating the capital required to cover market risk. The method is often known as the Standard Model. The Standard

Model is a 'building block' approach, this means that the capital requirements for various components of market risk are calculated and then summed to give the overall capital requirement or charge, in a similar way to the calculation of weighted risk assets in the original 1988 Accord. In the Standard Model no allowance is made for observed correlations either within or across the four risk categories.

The 1993 proposal split market risk into four different categories:

1. Interest rate risk
2. Foreign exchange rate risk
3. Equity risk
4. Commodity risk

The capital charge for each category of risk is calculated and the results are then aggregated to give the total market risk charge.

Tier 3 capital
To compensate for being asked to provide capital to cover market risks as well as credit risks, as per the 1988 Accord, the BSC defined another tier of eligible capital. Tier 3 capital can only be used to support the market risk capital charge and will be limited to 250% of a bank's Tier 1 capital. Tier 3 capital can consist only of short-term subordinated debt with an original maturity of greater than two years.

Banking versus trading
The 1993 proposal also asks banks to divide their activities into banking (e.g. commercial lending) and trading. Positions in those books nominated as 'banking' do not attract a market risk capital charge but continue to attract a credit risk charge as per the 1988 Accord. This is true for all market risk categories, except for foreign exchange. Foreign exchange positions incur a capital charge whether they are in the banking or trading books.

It is not the purpose of this book to describe in detail what are long and complex methods for calculating the market risk capital charge. The reader can find a full description of the methods in the BIS January 1996 Market Risk Amendment. The following describes the main characteristics of the Standard Model.

Interest rate risk
Under the Standard Model, interest rate exposures attract both specific and market risk capital charges. The specific risk reflects the changes in market value due to perceived changes in credit quality. The specific risk capital charge replaces the credit risk capital charge of the 1988 Accord.

The market risk charge is arrived at by calculating net exposures within pre-defined time bands. The exposures in each time band are multiplied by a risk weight that is intended to approximate to a crude volatility term structure. The risk weight is 100 basis points at the short end and 60 basis points at the long end.

The interest rate risk charge is calculated separately for each currency and then summed. There is no recognition of diversification across currencies.

Foreign exchange rate risk

Foreign exchange positions arising from interest rate trading, equity trading and from FX positions (including the present value of forward positions) are given an 8% capital charge. This percentage is charged on the larger of the net long cash and forward position or net short cash and forward position for each currency.

Equity risk

Equity positions attract both a specific and market risk capital charge. Both charges are calculated for each country then summed with no allowance for diversification across countries. The market risk charge is 8% of the overall net position by country. The specific risk charge is 8% of the sum of the absolute values of the long and short positions. The charge may be reduced to 4% if the regulator judges the portfolio to be liquid and well diversified. The charge is reduced still further to 2% for index positions.

Commodity risk

The commodity risk capital charge is 15% of the net position in each commodity, though there is some variation for certain commodity types.

Derivatives

Derivatives are treated as equivalent positions in the underlying instrument. This is also applied to options where a delta equivalent position is used. For options there is an additional capital charge for volatility and gamma effects, known as the 'carve out' approach.

1993 G30 Recommendations

The industry's reaction to the Standard Model proposed by the BSC was predictably one of disappointment. Since the 1988 Accord the science of risk measurement had advanced considerably and VAR had come into use by the leading international banks. The industry wanted any future market risk regulatory framework to use risk measurement methods that were based on the actual behaviour of the financial markets, rather than a somewhat arbitrary building block approach.

The Group of Thirty (G30) is an assembly of representatives from leading banks around the world. The G30 acts as an industry research body and discussion forum for industry issues. In July 1993, the G30 completed and published a report on the derivatives market (Group of Thirty, 1993). The purpose of the study was to understand and document the management of derivatives businesses. The resultant report documented industry practice and also gave 20 recommendations for best practice in the derivatives industry, largely focused on risk management. Recommendation 4 stated that the most appropriate measure of market risk in the derivatives industry was value at risk.

This added to the pressure on the BSC to recognise VAR in its proposed market risk regulatory framework. However, it was clear to the regulators that the use of VAR was restricted to a relatively small number of the world's leading banks, most notably the top American banks. The regulatory community could see no point in incorporating VAR into a regulatory framework if the majority of banks were not in a position to use the technique. The publication of J P Morgan's RiskMetrics^{TM} changed that.

J P Morgan's RiskMetrics^{TM}

In the Autumn of 1994 J P Morgan published its 'RiskMetrics^{TM}' VAR methodology. RiskMetrics^{TM} is a covariance approach to calculating VAR, see Chapter 2 for a full discussion of covariance. J P Morgan published an overview and a more detailed technical description of the statistics behind covariance and J P Morgan's version of it (Guldimann, 1995). Covariance is the easiest form of VAR calculation to implement and the publication of RiskMetrics^{TM} made it freely available to all banks.

J P Morgan also facilitated free access to the volatility and correlation data sets needed to calculate VAR using RiskMetrics^{TM}. Production of these statistical inputs to any VAR calculation is a non-trivial exercise, beyond which it also requires the elapse of an extended period of time, unless one happens to have historical price series lying around for all assets in the portfolio. Now that the methodology and the required statistics had been made freely available there was no longer any reason for the regulators to hold back from incorporating VAR into any proposed market risk framework. J P Morgan even went to the length of providing a list of system suppliers that could calculate VAR using RiskMetrics^{TM}.

1995 BSC Internal Models Proposal

After intense pressure from the industry, headed by the G30 report and the publication of RiskMetrics^{TM}, the BSC decided that it would allow the use of proprietary value at risk models for the calculation of the market risk capital charge. This was a significant step forward. Prior to this, regulatory requirements and internal 'risk' calculations had been diverging at an increasing rate. The banking industry had been researching ever more accurate ways of modelling the true behaviour of financial markets and therefore the real level of risk, whereas regulators had pursued simplistic building block approaches to the calculation of regulatory capital. The 1995 BSC proposal, for the first time, represented a significant convergence between banking regulation and internal risk management practice.

1996 Market Risk Amendment to the 1988 Accord

In January 1996, the BSC produced a final statement of requirement for banks to provide capital against potential losses arising from movements in market prices. The 1996 Amendment was largely unchanged from the 1995 proposal. One important change, for the internal models options, was to recognise correlation effects not only within but also across risk categories.

The BSC realised that it would not be practical to specify a standard value at risk model. Instead the BSC decided to impose certain quantitative requirements on the calculation of VAR. The quantitative restrictions have two effects: firstly they ensure that the resultant capital charge provides a sufficient buffer against potential losses due to changes in market prices, secondly it ensures a level playing field – satisfying the objective for international harmonisation. In addition to the quantitative restrictions the BSC also imposed certain qualitative requirements on those banks that wish to use an internal model. The qualitative requirements, described below, endeavour to ensure that VAR is fully integrated into the bank's internal daily risk management practices. In addition the internal model must be approved by the relevant supervisory authority.

Quantitative VAR calculation requirements
Most banks calculate VAR with a time horizon of 24 hours. This is mainly because their positions will change significantly during 24 hours. The definition of VAR requires a level of confidence to be chosen – most banks use a 95% confidence level. Banks using these assumptions accept that VAR measures potential losses that could be experienced on a fairly regular basis (95% confidence implies that a loss greater than the VAR number may be experienced one day in 20). The quantitative requirements imposed by the BSC will produce a number far greater than most bank's daily operational VAR numbers. This can be explained by remembering that the BSC is not so much concerned with day-to-day risk management as with establishing capital adequacy requirements which must be able to cope with extreme price moves and with prolonged price trends in markets. The following quantitative requirements have been specified by the BSC:

- a one-tailed 99% confidence interval

- a 10-day holding period

- an observation period of at least one year, to be updated at least quarterly

- a multiplication factor, taken to be three unless a bank's risk management capabilities indicate a higher (or lower) figure. See below for further discussion of the multiplication factor.

The bank's capital charge is calculated as the greater of today's VAR number or the average of the last sixty days' VAR numbers multiplied by a multiplication factor (of hopefully no more than three). This can be expressed as the following equation:

$$C = \text{Max}\left(F.\frac{1}{60}\sum_{d}^{60}\text{VAR}_d,\ \text{VAR}_{t-1}\right)$$

where: C = market risk capital charge
         F = multiplication factor
   $\sum \text{VAR}_d$ = VAR for one of previous 60 days
    VAR_{t-1} = VAR for the previous day

Multiplication factor
For any bank VAR is the output of a statistical model. VAR models attempt to model and capture the behaviour of the financial markets. The BSC argue (and very reasonably) that it is impossible to perfectly model the financial markets. There are a number of well-known problems with modelling the financial markets which the multiplication factor is designed to cover:

- cumulative losses, perhaps caused by a prolonged bear market, or bad trading

- non-normality in price change behaviour, fat tails and skewed distributions (see discussion in Chapter 4)

- potentially poor predictive capability of historic data

- intra-day trading

- inaccuracies introduced by simplifying assumptions

- event risk, i.e. exceptional market movements

VAR typically covers potential losses in a 'normal' or continuous market. As described elsewhere in this book there are far more extreme price moves in the financial markets than one would expect. The 1987 equity crash was a 20 standard deviation price move. Clearly banks need sufficient capital to withstand event risks and not just the daily VAR number. If for this reason alone the multiplication factor seems to be well grounded in sound risk management practice and necessity. Taken together, the quantitative requirements and the multiplication factor mean that the BIS VAR number is 13.4 times that produced by a standard covariance model using a 95% confidence level and a one-day holding period.

Qualitative risk management requirements
If the 1988 Accord was a move to replace subjective supervision with clearly defined regulations, then the 1996 Amendment was another decisive step in this direction. For the first time there is a clear statement of what regulators expect from banks' internal risk management functions. In order to be able to use an internal VAR model for calculating regulatory capital, the 1996 Amendment stipulates that the model must be approved by the relevant regulator. Model approval is as much

concerned with the control structure and internal risk management practices as it is with the details of the mathematical VAR model. The qualitative standards set by the BSC include the following:

- independent risk management function.

- regular back testing – this is a major part of the internal models proposal (see below for a description of these requirements).

- board of directors and senior management involved in risk management.

- the Internal Model VAR approach must be used in the bank's internal risk management practice.

- limits must also be set using exposure calculated from the risk model.

- the bank must undertake comprehensive stress testing as part of its internal risk management practice.

- the procedures and policies of the risk management function must be formally documented.

- the risk management function must be regularly inspected by the bank's internal audit function.

Back testing
The Internal Model approach to calculating capital adequacy is a fundamental step away from prescriptive regulation. It relies on a bank to develop and implement a reliable and accurate risk measurement model. If banks are to be allowed to use their own internal models then regulators must provide incentives to encourage or coerce banks to develop models that fairly represent the risks of the markets they trade in. The 1996 Amendment specifies a back testing regime that embodies incentives for banks to develop accurate risk measurement models. The incentive is in the form of an increased multiplication factor if a bank's trading loss figures fall outside the calculated VAR more often than is statistically acceptable.

With the BSC specified confidence level of 99% one would expect, on average, that two daily trading losses would fall outside the calculated VAR numbers during a 200-trading day period. To be certain that a model is working correctly, however, would require a large number of 200-day samples. It may be that the last 200 days saw a number of extreme price movements which would produce more than two exceptions.

The BSC has analysed the possibility of incorrectly deeming a model to be unsatisfactory; this analysis suggests that an acceptable number of exceptions, without meaning that the model is wrong, is four. Any more exceptions than this and the multiplication factor will be increased from the base level of three, except in unusual circumstances, such as a period containing a number of extreme disturbances to the market.

The BSC describes two methods of back testing, as follows:

1. *Trading Outcome*   In this method a *daily* VAR number is compared to the subsequent day's trading P&L. It should be noted that the back testing method specifies a daily VAR number as opposed to the 10-day VAR to be used for calculation of the bank's capital charge. In this method the number of trading P&L numbers which are greater than the calculated VAR are recorded. Actual daily P&L numbers reflect intra-day trading and fee income as well as the change in value of a bank's positions. For this reason the BSC urges banks to develop the capability to undertake hypothetical back testing.

2. *Hypothetical Outcome*   In the hypothetical method the P&L is calculated as if the positions had stayed the same for a 24-hour period and the only source of revenue/loss was from a change in value of the positions when marked to market. The implementation of this method requires banks to keep a record of positions from the previous day and to record value changes for all those positions, regardless of whether the bank still has the positions.

The BSC states that banks should develop the ability to perform both forms of back testing described above. It will be up to national regulators, however, to specify the form of back testing they require. The BSC specifies that back testing must be performed over a 250-day period (i.e. approximately one year). This means that a bank must have been calculating VAR and recording back testing results for at least 250 days before model approval will be granted.

The Pre-Commitment Approach

The Pre-Commitment approach to capital adequacy was put forward separately from the BSC, by the Federal Reserve Board, also in 1995. The Pre-Commitment approach differs substantially from both the BSC Standard Model and the BSC Internal Model approaches. Both the BSC approaches are, to a certain extent, prescriptive about how a bank should calculate a capital charge for market risk. In the Pre-Commitment approach a bank would pre-commit to a maximum trading loss over a designated time frame. This loss would be taken as the capital charge for the bank.

If trading losses exceeded the pre-committed figure, penalties would be imposed and the bank would be subject to closer supervision. The penalty may involve a substantial fine and/or higher future capital charges. The Pre-Commitment approach is a further extension of the incentive-based approach to regulating banks. It is fairly easy to see that there would be a relationship between the amount of capital pre-committed and the fines imposed for exceeding the pre-committed loss. Kupiec and O'Brien (1995) show that a bank's choice of pre-committed capital would be dependent on the proposed level of fines and the bank's estimation of its own risk.

Although not yet adopted as a regulatory measure and not included in the BSC 1996 Amendment, work continues on the Pre-Commitment approach, particularly under the Federal Reserve Board's instruction. Time will tell whether this measure ever comes into force.

Assessment of Recent Approaches to Market Risk Regulation

This section assesses the three main approaches proposed or adopted by regulatory bodies to date, namely:

1. BSC Standard Model as per the 1996 Amendment to the 1988 Accord
2. BSC Internal Model approach as per the 1996 Amendment to the 1988 Accord
3. Federal Reserve Board's Pre-Commitment approach

BSC Standard Model

There are no real advantages to the Standard Model approach. It could be said that it does not necessitate banks developing complex risk management models. This argument is, however, counter productive for the industry. It is in the industry's best interests that it takes advantage of advances in risk quantification techniques.

The disadvantages of the Standard Model can be summarised by saying that it simply does not provide an accurate measure of a bank's risk. The Standard Model does not take account of diversification effects across risk types but is also inaccurate for individual risk types. Take gold, FX and equities, a standard capital charge of 8% is imposed, without reference to actually experienced volatilities. For equities a 100% correlation is assumed within a country.

If a bank is capital constrained then the Standard Model may have the effect of altering portfolio choices. Positions would be chosen that minimise the regulatory capital required. For most banks, at the present time, this is not an issue as the majority are no longer capital constrained as they were at the beginning of the 1990s.

In addition to the above the Standard Model entails a significant cost of compliance.

BSC Internal Model

The Internal Model is a significant improvement on the Standard Model as it allows a far greater alignment of a bank's internal risk management system and the regulatory reporting system. In fact the BSC stipulates that the VAR numbers should be produced from the same system, with just the VAR calculation parameters set differently for the regulatory VAR. The Internal Model approach also allows for the evolution of risk measurement techniques, both in the industry and within a bank.

The 10-day horizon is perhaps the largest draw-back to the Internal Model approach as specified. A 10-day horizon puts an undue amount of emphasis on the composition of the portfolio at a particular point in time. In reality a bank's trading portfolio will change significantly over a 24-hour time frame, let alone a 10-day horizon. The 10-day horizon puts no emphasis of a bank's risk taking strategy, or perhaps more importantly, its risk management ability and control infrastructure.

The Internal Model approach imposes a still significant but lighter compliance cost on a bank. The back testing requirements represent a significant piece of internal infrastructure and cost. Having said this, banks that use VAR as an internal risk measurement tool will be back testing the results to ensure the model is reasonable – regardless of any external regulatory pressure to do this.

The Pre-Commitment approach

The Pre-Commitment approach is significantly different from the other two approaches as it specifies nothing about how a bank should measure or control its risk. Instead it provides incentives, in the form of fines and other penalties, if a bank loses more than the pre-committed amount. As such the Pre-Commitment approach is far less intrusive in a bank's risk management techniques and procedures. This also implies a lower burden on the regulator. Under the Internal Model approach the regulator must employ large teams of staff so that it can assess each bank's models and risk management processes.

The Pre-Commitment approach significantly reduces the compliance burden on banks when compared to either the BSC Standard Model or the Internal Model.

One important point to note is that the Pre-Commitment approach is far more all inclusive than either of the other two approaches discussed here. A bank pre-commits to a maximum cumulative loss figure over a specified horizon. This loss figure would incorporate all potential sources of loss. The other two methods only cover straight credit and market risk losses. The Pre-Commitment approach would also cover losses due to operational failures and other potential sources of loss.

It is said that the Pre-Commitment approach would fail to stop a bank who adopts a 'go for broke' strategy, i.e. the bank could have failed before penalties and closer supervision are brought to bear. At the time of writing the Pre-Commitment approach has not been implemented by any regulatory body and discussion continues as to its potential effectiveness.

EUROPEAN CAPITAL ADEQUACY DIRECTIVE

In 1993 the European Union published its Capital Adequacy Directive (CAD) which became law in January 1996. The CAD is almost identical to the BSC Standard Model and has also been extended to mirror the 1995 Basle proposals for the use of Internal Models. Prior to the CAD, banks had to abide by local regulations relating to the finance industry; this imposed a considerable burden of compliance on European banks operating in another European country. The CAD has replaced all these local regulations with a single piece of legislation. The CAD, unlike the BSC regulations, applies equally to securities houses as it does for banks;

as such the CAD can be seen as a significant step towards harmonisation of the regulatory environment within Europe.

The CAD came about through the European Union's drive to create a single market in goods, services, capital and labour. The CAD creates a level playing field for banks in all countries in Europe, or at least it should have. Some countries, notably Germany, have been tardy in implementing the CAD and have waited until the implementation of the 1996 market risk amendment which now allows the use of VAR for the calculation of market risk capital.

WHICH BSC REGIME SHOULD I USE?

The 1996 Basle Amendment provides each bank with a choice of regulatory regime: either the Standard Model or the Internal VAR Model. For any bank there are two main criteria for choosing which model to use:

1. ease of implementation and compliance
2. most efficient use of capital

Considering the ease of implementation, if an organisation has a good cushion of capital and credit rating then the choice of method to be adopted will depend on the type of internal methods used currently and the regulatory framework to which the organisation is already subject. For those not so well endowed, the capital saving which is likely to arise from use of the BSC Internal Model (VAR) is so great that most organisations will be forced to implement VAR.

If a bank operates in the EU then it will be subject to the CAD. As the BSC Standard Model is very similar to the CAD it will require only a relatively small amount of effort to enable the bank to report capital required as per the BSC Standard Model. Most banks which are subject to the CAD use software packages to calculate the capital required. As soon as the EU has amended the CAD to comply with the BSC Market Risk Amendment, software package suppliers will change their packages to be able to calculate the capital requirement as per the Standard Model.

If on the other hand the bank uses a VAR model for internal risk management purposes then it may be in a position to consider using the BSC Internal Model, i.e. VAR. As discussed above, it will need to be able to produce a 250-day history of VAR versus the actually experienced P&L. The cost of putting VAR in place means that a bank is unlikely to use VAR only for regulatory purposes, unless there is a significant regulatory capital saving. If an organisation already uses VAR then calculating the BSC specified VAR will not be too onerous an overhead and can be done centrally. The Internal Model (BSC VAR) can be implemented centrally without significant changes to the bank's general VAR systems.

The most important criteria is to select the method that gives the most efficient use of capital. A number of studies have been completed which indicate that there are potentially very substantial capital savings to be had from use of the Internal Model, especially for well diversified portfolios. This said, whether the Standard or Internal Model gives the most efficient use of capital is a question that can only be answered for each bank by undertaking trial calculations on the bank's actual portfolio. Crouhy *et al.* (1998) have undertaken trials on CIBC's (Canadian Imperial Bank of Commerce) trading portfolios and have found that use of the Internal Model versus the Standard Model results in a capital saving of between 60% and 85%. No information is given as to the nature of CIBC's overall portfolio, however, given the size of the bank one can reasonably assume that the portfolio is fairly well diversified. Crouhy *et al.* also comment that they have found that well diversified portfolios yield the greatest capital saving through use of an Internal Model. This observation agrees with most comparative studies of the two approaches.

CONCLUSION

Recent years have seen significant changes in the regulatory environment; this regulatory evolution is not about to stop. It is very encouraging to see that the regulatory community has been prepared to embrace modern financial theory and adopt VAR as a valid risk measurement tool. The resultant convergence between regulatory specified and internal risk management practice is a positive force for the industry. As a result of the very favourable capital charge, if nothing else, VAR is now a prerequisite for an effective trading operation.

One aspect of change that is yet to be addressed relates to harmonising regulations across all sectors of the finance industry. At the beginning of the 1980s there was a clear distinction between banks and securities houses. These distinction are now all but invisible when it comes to global trading, where it is nigh on impossible to distinguish between them. A number of trading houses have deregulated as banks to take advantage of the more favourable regulation of securities houses.

This regulatory arbitrage will encourage banking and securities regulatory bodies to work more closely together. The international equivalent of the BSC for the securities industry is IOSCO (the International Organisation of Securities Commissions). At the time of writing IOSCO and the BSC had just agreed to closer cooperation in the development of future regulations. This can only be a positive move for the whole of the finance sector and will hopefully lead to a level playing field for both banks and securities houses.

NOTE

1. The G10 countries consist of: Belgium, Canada, France, Germany, Italy, Japan, Netherlands, Sweden, Switzerland, United Kingdom and the United States.

10

Introduction to the spreadsheets

The disk at the end of the book contains Excel spreadsheet-based examples of all the main VAR calculations described in the book. With the exception of the eigenvalue and eigenvector generator none of the spreadsheets use Visual Basic. In other words, all the calculations are done using standard Excel functions. This approach has been used so that the reader can see easily and exactly what is going on in each spreadsheet. Each spreadsheet has a 'Readme' sheet which describes what the spreadsheet does and how to use it. The spreadsheets contain the same data as the author used when writing the book. Therefore, all the main results presented throughout the book can be recreated using these spreadsheets. The following gives a brief description of each spreadsheet:

Covar1.xls

Accompanies Chapter 2. The spreadsheet demonstrates the covariance method of calculating VAR.

Historic.xls

Accompanies Chapter 3. This spreadsheet illustrates the calculation of VAR for Portfolio 1 using the historical simulation approach.

Eig-calc.xls

Accompanies the Monte Carlo simulation described in Chapter 3. This spreadsheet calculates the eigenvalues and eigenvectors of a correlation matrix. If the correlation matrix is non-sensical it will first be cleaned using the process described in the Appendix to Chapter 3.

Fulmonte.xls

Accompanies Chapter 3. This spreadsheet contains a cut-down version of the Monte Carlo simulation described for Portfolio 1.

Garch.xls

Accompanies Chapter 4. This spreadsheet is one of several spreadsheets used to undertake the empirical investigation described in this chapter. The spreadsheets were all the same except that the volatility model differed in each case. The spreadsheet chosen for inclusion here contains the GARCH volatility model. The GARCH parameters are not generated by the spreadsheet but are included in the spreadsheet. The GARCH parameters were generated by the S+ statistical package which uses a Berndt, Hall, Hall and Hausman maximum likelihood method (see Berndt *et al.*, 1974).

Varres.xls

Accompanies Chapter 4. This spreadsheet contains the full set of results generated during the empirical investigation of volatility models. Space limitations have only allowed summary results to be given in the text.

Implmnt.xls

Accompanies Chapter 5. This spreadsheet illustrates several different ways of calculating VAR for a single cashflow, mapped and unmapped.

Swappot3.xls

Accompanies Chapter 8. This spreadsheet calculates the potential future value of a swap, along with the expected and unexpected credit loss for the swap.

Please note: The spreadsheets on the CD have been created using Microsoft Excel 5.0. You will need Excel 5.0 or a later release in order to access the files.

References and further reading

Abramowitz, M. and Stegun, I. (1972) *Handbook of Mathematical Functions*, Dover Publications: New York.

The Basle Supervisory Committee (1988) *International Convergence of Capital Measurement and Standards*, July, Basle.

Basle Committee of Banking Supervision (1996) *Supervisory Framework for the use of 'Back testing' in Conjunction with the Internal Models Approach to Market Risk Capital Requirements*, January, Basle.

Berndt, E. K., Hall, B. H., Hall, R. E. and Hausman, J. A. (1974) 'Estimation and inference in non-linear structural models', *Annals of Economic and Social Measurement*, 3rd quarter.

Bollerslev, T. (1986) 'Generalised autoregressive conditional heteroskedasticity', *Journal of Econometrics*, vol. 31 (3), pp. 307–28.

Burghardt, G. D., Belton, T. M., Lane, M. and Papa, J. (1994) *The Treasury Bond Basis*, revised edition, Irwin: New York.

Copeland, T., Koller, T. and Murrin, J. (McKinsey & Co.) (1994) *Valuation: Measuring and Managing the Value of Companies*, 2nd edition, John Wiley & Sons: New York.

Crouhy, M., Galai, D. and Mark, R. (1998) 'The new 1998 regulatory framework for capital adequacy: standard approach versus internal models', *Net Exposure*, (www.netexposure.co.uk).

Efron, B. and Tibshirani, R. (1993) *An Introduction to the Bootstrap*, Chapman & Hall: London.

Embrechts, P., Kluppelberg, C. and Mikosch, T. (1997) *Modelling Extremal Events for Insurance and Finance*, Springer-Verlag: Berlin.

Embrechts, P., Resnick, S. and Samorodnitsky, G. (1998) 'Living on the edge', *Risk* magazine, January, pp. 96–100.

Group of Thirty (1993) *Derivatives: Practices and Principles*, G30, July.

Guldimann, T. M. (1995) *Riskmetrics*^{TM} *– Technical Document*, 3rd edition,

Morgan Guaranty Trust Company, Global Research: New York. (Tel: 212 648 6480; e-mail: guldimann_t@jpmorgan.com).

Hendriks, D. (1996) 'Evaluation of value-at-risk models using historical data', *Policy Review*, Federal Reserve Bank of New York, April.

Hull, J. C. (1993) *Options, Futures and Other Derivative Securities*, 2nd edition, Prentice Hall: New Jersey.

Jordan, D. W. and Smith, P. (1994) *Mathematical Techniques: An Introduction for the Engineering, Physical and Mathematical Sciences*, Oxford University Press: Oxford.

Kupiec, P. H. and O'Brien, J. M. (1995) *Recent Developments in Bank Regulation of Market Risks*, in association with the Federal Reserve Board, November.

Laubsch, A. (1996) 'Estimating index tracking error for equity portfolios', *Riskmetrics*™ *Monitor*, 2nd quarter, Morgan Guaranty Trust Company, Risk Management Advisory: New York, pp. 34–41. (Tel: 212 648 8369; e-mail laubsch_alan@jpmorgan.com).

Lawrence, C., Robinson, G. and Stiles, M. (1996) 'Incorporating liquidity into the risk-management framework', *Financial Derivatives and Risk Management*, June.

Markowitz, H. (1952) 'Portfolio selection', *Journal of Finance*, March.

Markowitz, H. (1959) *Portfolio Selection: Efficient Diversification of Investments*, John Wiley & Sons: New York.

Marshal, C. and Siegel, M. (1996) *Value at Risk: Implementing a Risk Measurement Standard*, MIT – Finance Research Center (ref.: FRC no. 316-96R), July.

Masters, B. (1997) *CreditMetrics*™, J P Morgan, New York (e-mail: masters_blythe@jpmorgan.com).

Matten, C. (1996) *Managing Bank Capital*, John Wiley & Sons: Chichester.

Ramberg, J. S., Dudewics, E. J., Tadikamalla, P. R. and Mykyta, E. F. (1979) 'A probability distribution and its uses in fitting data', *Technometrics*, vol. 21 (2), May, pp. 201–14.

Rappaport, A. (1986) *Creating Shareholder Value: The New Standard for Business Performance*, Free Press: New York.

Rowe, D. M. (1996) *Derivative Credit Risk: Advances in Measurement and Management*, Risk Publications: London.

Stein, M. (1987) 'Large sample properties of simulations using Latin hypercube sampling', *Technometrics*, vol. 29 (2), May, pp. 143–51.

Teukolsky, S., Vetterling, W. and Flannery, B. (1994) *Numerical Recipes in C*, 2nd edition, Cambridge University Press: Cambridge.

Zangari, P. (1996) 'A VAR methodology for portfolios that include options', *RiskMetrics*™ *Monitor*, 1st quarter, Morgan Guaranty Trust Company: New York, pp. 4–12. (Tel: 212 648 8641, e-mail: riskmetrics@jpmorgan.com).

Index